EDWARDIAN
DEVON
⟪ 1900–1914 ⟫

EDWARDIAN DEVON

1900–1914

Before the Lights went Out

DAVID PARKER

To Pamela, with love

Front cover image:
Holidaymakers on the beach (possibly at Westward Ho!),
May 1911. (Beaford Arts Old Archive)

Back cover image:
Coach and train at Kingsbridge Station. (Author's collection)

First published 2016

The History Press
The Mill, Brimscombe Port
Stroud, Gloucestershire, GL5 2QG
www.thehistorypress.co.uk

British Library Cataloguing in Publication Data.
A catalogue record for this book is available from the British Library.

ISBN 978 0 7509 6156 1

Typesetting and origination by The History Press
Printed in Malta by Melita Press

CONTENTS

ABOUT THE AUTHOR

Dr David Parker has written several books and many articles for scholarly journals on late nineteenth and early twentieth-century social and political history. Formerly a Hertfordshire head teacher, he became a history lecturer, Masters programme director and then European Masters project manager in the University of Plymouth's Faculty of Arts & Education.

As part of the commemorations of the First World War he has written weekly articles for a Devon newspaper, given presentations across the county and contributed to BBC TV and Radio Devon programmes.

Dr Parker is married with a grown-up son and daughter and lives in Exeter.

❧ *Previous Books* ☙

John Newsom (University of Hertfordshire Press, 2005).

Hertfordshire Children in War & Peace: 1914–39
(University of Hertfordshire Press, 2007).

The People of Devon in the First World War (The History Press, 2013).
Winner of Devon History Society's W. G. Hoskins Book of the Year 2013.

Great War Britain: Exeter, Remembering 1914–1918 (The History Press, 2014).

European Stamp Issues of the Second World War:
Images of Triumph, Despair & Defeat (The History Press, 2015).

ACKNOWLEDGEMENTS

I am very grateful for the help many people have given me as I researched and wrote this book. My thanks are given to Axe Valley Museum in Seaton, Bovey Tracey Heritage Centre, Crediton Museum, *Country Life*, Dawlish Museum, Devon Heritage Centre in Exeter, the North Devon Athenaeum in Barnstaple, the North Devon Local Studies Centre in Barnstaple, Plymouth Central Library, Plymouth & West Devon Record Office, Tavistock Museum, Torquay Library and the Valiant Soldier Museum in Buckfastleigh.

I remain grateful for the time and ready assistance afforded me by Kathryn Burrell of Beaford Arts Old Archive Bank; Su Conniff and Margaret Knight of the Devon & Exeter Institution; Sara Hodson of Ilfracombe Museum; Nigel Canham of the *Mid Devon Advertiser*; Peter & Aileen Carratt in Newton Abbot; Felicity Cole of Newton Abbot Town & GWR (Great Western Railway) Museum; Paul Hambling of Okehampton Museum of Dartmoor Life; Jocelyn Hemming and Julia Neville of the Poltimore Estate Research Society; Raymond Bartlett, archivist of Seale-Hayne College Alumni Association; Pippa Griffith, Pamela Sampson and Bernard Swain of Tiverton Museum of Mid Devon Life, and Catriona Batty of Topsham Museum.

I have greatly appreciated the willingness of Bill Leedham and Tony Ovens to discuss numerous aspects of the period with me during my self-imposed obsession with it. Any errors in the book, though, are wholly mine. My special thanks go once again to Tony Ovens for photographing many of the illustrations and often painstakingly refining them from poor quality originals.

NOTES

❧ *Money Values* ☙

In 1901 British money included pounds, shillings and pence. Twelve pence were equated with one shilling (represented as 1*s* 0*d* or 1/-), and twenty shillings with £1. Nominally a shilling is equated with 5p today, sixpence (6*d*) with 2½p and one penny (1*d*) with less than ½p. In this book whole shilling values are written as 5/- and values including both shillings and pence as 5*s* 3*d*.

At the highest end of the monetary scale in Edwardian times were guineas – one guinea being worth £1 1*s* 0*d*. Prices in guineas usually meant that one was in a high-class retail establishment or on the racecourse. At the lowest end of the scale a penny was divided into four farthings or two halfpennies (called ha'pennies). These coins cannot be equated with any monetary values today, but in 1901 they could buy scraps of food for poor families.

Using the estimated percentage increase in the retail price index, the purchasing power of a shilling in 1901 was equal to about £5.40 today, and £1 to about £95. However, £1 would be worth around £350 today if average earnings are the basis for calculation, as people today have about three and a half times the real annual income of those living in 1901. Therefore, a shilling was far more precious to working-class families in 1901 than £5.40 is to people today.

A Devon farm labourer was paid around 16/- a week, but he might have a rent-free tied cottage with a vegetable patch; a skilled urban artisan might receive around 25/- a week but he had no comparable extras. In real terms housing was far less expensive than today, as a modest but new terrace house could be rented for 6/- a week, but most foods and new clothing were far more costly.

❧ *Sources & References* ☙

A list of sources is included, but limited space has precluded a lengthy list of references, running to well over 1,000 for this book. A number of references to particular newspapers, school logbooks and authors are included in the text, and through the publisher the author would be pleased to discuss particular sources with readers wishing to pursue themes further.

I

DEVON
The Background & the Boer War

Countless postcards sent across the nation, and indeed across the world, from Edwardian Devon captured the awesome beauty of its moors and rivers, the attractions of its bustling seaside resorts and high streets, and the glories of its historic castles, churches and mansions. They portrayed a county basking in its ancient landscapes, dramatic past and prosperous present, and they did not lie. And neither did the plethora of guidebooks describing the plethora of leisure attractions and facilities awaiting visitors. But not surprisingly, the truth about Edwardian Devon is far more complicated and a great deal more interesting.

The period 1901–14 is generally known as 'Edwardian', even though it includes the first few years of George V's reign (1910–36) as well as all of Edward VII's (1901–10). Throughout these years, the Union Jack flew over British imperial possessions across the world, the red 'duster' fluttered at the sterns of thousands of British merchantmen and the white ensign announced the arrival of British warships in every ocean and countless ports. But beneath these awesome signs of power and prosperity Great Britain itself was becoming discernibly less sure of its pre-eminence, less confident in its social order and less optimistic about its future.

This book argues that this important period possesses a character of its own, much like Edward possessed a character very different to Victoria and Albert, his parents. Indeed, the Edwardians found that many of the social and political issues vexing the Victorians were now demanding solutions, however controversial and costly those solutions might be. The book examines these turbulent years through the eyes of Devon society with all its variations in wealth, occupations, attitudes and lifestyles, and its primary aim is to highlight the hopes and fears, and convictions and doubts that led the people of Devon to interact as they did. It draws upon the plentiful evidence of the tensions and trends that lies tucked away in museums and archives across the county.

Devon County Council's minutes record the decisions reached regarding its steadily increasing responsibilities for highways, public health and, after 1903, most elementary and secondary schools. Head teachers' logbooks give insights into local lives with entries covering syllabuses, standards, inspectors' reports, managers' visits, pupil attendances, local epidemics and, sometimes, glimpses of parental attitudes, the gross inadequacies of school facilities and teachers' joys and frustrations.

Many local newspapers record verbatim, or as verbatim as the reporter and editor decided, the speeches made by the proponents and opponents of every major contemporary question. Most newspapers were avidly partisan, favouring either the Liberal or Conservative Party, but as we shall see, views on the suffragettes, Irish Home Rule and tariff reform often transcended party lines and rendered Edwardian party politics and elections even more confusing than usual. Generally speaking, editors claimed their preferred orators argued eloquently, sincerely and coherently while their opponents were hesitant, repetitive and unconvincing.

The newspapers also contain reports and letters on local sports events, theatre and seaside entertainments, the seasonal condition of agriculture, the many fetes and sales on behalf of charities and political parties, naval and military exercises, church and chapel affairs, court cases and the interminable meetings of school boards, boards of guardians and city, town and borough councils. Advertisements give invaluable information on the range of goods and prices and the frequency of trains and trips by sea.

Other important sources are directories, magazines, pamphlets and memoirs. *Kelly's Directory* is a mine of local information, as are the 1891, 1901 and 1911 census summaries. Church magazines provide further evidence of local societies and their aims, clientele and success, as well as the views of the clergy. An array of pamphlets and brochures survive promoting religious and temperance movements, political campaigns, the openings, extension and maintenance of hospitals and mental institutions, and the sales of great houses and estates. The memoirs of Earl Fortescue, Devon's Edwardian lord lieutenant, contain interesting perspectives on his family's interests and local trends, and the published and unpublished memories of villagers growing up around the turn of the century throw light, often unconsciously, on the social hierarchies surrounding them as well as the enormous efforts required to keep warm, clean and fed.

◈ *The Victorian Background* ◈

Queen Victoria reigned from June 1837 to January 1901, and during these sixty-four years her kingdom was buffeted by a bewildering variety of stresses and strains. A host of factories poured out an array of mass-produced goods as well as never-ending billows of smoke, and increasingly powerful locomotives heaved wagons and coaches across the rapidly expanding railway network.

The population almost trebled, and so did the nation's wealth, with the fanciful mock Gothic houses and fussy parterres of the newly rich matching the ancient, if substantially renovated, mansions and sweeping parkland of the older established grand families. The glittering reception halls and dining rooms were devoted to lavish parties, balls and masques where income and status were flaunted at a time when servants were plentiful and cheap.

The vagaries of markets and investments combined with unfettered expenditure meant that some notable families managed to bankrupt themselves, but there were others all too keen to buy their estates. And all the while the mass of the population crowded into the courts and tenements of the towns and cities or, if they were more fortunate, the serried rows of late Victorian terraced estates springing up on their outskirts. Some of these new houses were plain and flat fronted, and some had decorated brickwork and bay windows, as even working-class homes, like everything else in Victorian Britain, displayed the nuances of a family's place in the social pecking order. In the middle of the century the urban population outstripped the rural one for the first time, and the gap steadily widened.

Protected by the world's most powerful navy, British shipping companies and commercial enterprises sought raw materials and markets across the globe, and in doing so the British Empire grew ever larger. Amidst numerous colonial wars, sometimes fought with alarming incompetence although generally successful in the end, large parts of Africa were added to the older established colonies of Canada, Australia and New Zealand, and a racially and politically divided India remained largely secure in British hands despite a bloody rebellion in 1857.

But it was not only trade that made the empire important: as Victoria's reign drew to a close both France and Germany had become Britain's bitter rivals in empire building and its concomitant commercial exploitation, and equally important, in the fervent pride they possessed in this essentially Eurocentric age in exerting and flaunting their imperial influence as they jostled for international pre-eminence.

There was much for Victorians to be fearful about as the British economy changed for the better for some but the worse for many others. Towns became overwhelmed by thousands of migrant families lured by the widespread rash of vast new factories exploiting new technologies that offered regular work and wages. Many migrants had little choice as the new technologies, notably in the vast textile trade, rendered cottage industries such as the home-based handloom weavers redundant. Victoria's reign saw a transformation in the means of production and transportation, and a dramatic rise in consumerism for those who could afford the dazzling array of new domestic furnishings, clothing and gadgets on offer.

From the late 1870s rural conditions deteriorated as the vast plains of North America, India and the Russian Empire poured huge amounts of grain into British ports far more cheaply than it could be produced here. The imports were also tariff free. Arable farmers were forced to sell up, or to seek lower rents if they were tenants and then diversify into new markets and reduce labour costs. As a result yet more country families trudged to the towns to join the earlier migrants, or packed into the ill-serviced emigration ships sailing to North and South America, Australia and New Zealand, and South Africa.

To the growing consternation of Victorian churchmen, humanitarians, local officials and national politicians, the vast working-class areas in the ever-expanding towns appeared as mounting threats to law and order, and to health and morality, with their plethora of slums, public houses, criminal gangs and brothels, and chronic lack of clean water, sewage, churches, police and schools. Charities moved in with varying degrees of generosity, boards of guardians created vast workhouses run with varying degrees of efficiency and humanity, and with varying degrees of success the rival Anglican, Nonconformist and Roman Catholic churches made huge efforts to build places of worship, provide clergy and attract new congregations. Gradually, too, public health authorities sought to cleanse and drain the streets, but all these tasks were far from complete at the turn of the century, and abject poverty, overcrowding and epidemics remained commonplace.

Poverty was endemic in both town and country, and many working families' wages provided a mere subsistence standard of living that was always under threat from death or disease removing one of the wage earners, be it the husband, wife or older children.

The very poor had two sources of support – local charities drawing funds from legacies and subscriptions, and boards of guardians drawing on the rates. The former varied widely in their availability, resources and willingness to support those they suspected of being feckless or dissolute; the latter were as much guardians of rate-payers' pockets as they were of the poor, and the stigma of being labelled a 'pauper', along with the workhouse uniform and discipline, went a long way to ensure that only those who had fallen to the very bottom of the social scale applied for admission.

Many upper and middle-class commentators were scathing in their indictment of the poorest members of the working classes as being largely responsible through drink, idleness and debauchery for their own misery. Many people also found the idea of the State intervening in essentially private family affairs abhorrent on ethical grounds. Such widely held views clashed vehemently within and beyond the Houses of Parliament with contrary arguments put forward by reformers for a greater degree of State support for those who had fallen on hard times – often, they boldly claimed, through no fault of their own. Arguments attempting to define 'deserving' and 'undeserving' poor and surrounding the right and duty of the State to interfere in people's lives, and the likely expense, raged to and fro throughout the nineteenth century, and in doing so prevented more than minimal welfare legislation passing into law.

Victorian Britain was never free from popular dissent and protest; indeed it was a violent age. The angry but futile protests of the handloom weavers against the machines of the textile magnates had been mirrored in the 1830s by the equally unsuccessful attacks of rural workers on the new threshing machines. Huge civil disturbances accompanied the campaign for electoral reform before the 1832 Franchise Act was grudgingly passed and also the Anti-Corn Law crusade which secured the abolition of import duties in the 1840s. Around the same time the Chartist movement fought aggressively, but ultimately unsuccessfully, for even greater parliamentary reforms, notably universal male suffrage, secret ballots and the removal of property qualifications for parliamentary candidates. Election contests were often violent, and accusations of corruption were commonplace and often proved justified.

By 1901 two further bitterly contested reform acts in 1867 and 1884 had extended the vote down the social scale to 60 per cent of adult males, and parliamentary constituencies had been substantially realigned to ensure their more even distribution. As each bill struggled to become law many politicians and commentators prophesied the downfall of constitutional government and the degeneration of politics into outright class warfare. As we shall see, such Jeremiahs were not completely wide of the mark, but were no doubt comforted as the new century approached that although women could vote in local school board and board of guardians elections, and even become members of them, they remained firmly barred from voting in general elections.

Nevertheless, virtually all of Britain's national institutions, and most notably the House of Lords, were soon to be subject to immense and prolonged public scrutiny and criticism. And thrown into the boiling cauldron of Edwardian controversies were the additional and equally hotly contested issues of giving women the vote, finally granting Ireland Home Rule and imposing tariffs on foreign imports.

The deep antipathies between the Church of England and the various Nonconformist sects became more sharply focused, especially over working-class education as it became inextricably entangled in economic, sectarian and political arguments over its value, cost and content. In Devon, as elsewhere, most, but not all, Anglicans leaned towards the Conservatives, and most, but not all, Nonconformists preferred the Liberals. As we shall see, the various overlapping alliances proved a recipe for even more confusion and bitterness.

If the period's newspapers are to be believed, everyone had views on all these issues. The people of Devon were certainly actively engaged in every trauma, as the verbal and intermittent physical violence characterising the keenly fought general elections revealed. Change, ominous to some but welcome to others, was said to be 'in the air'. Liberals and Conservatives largely agreed that things were not as they should be – though not, of course, on the causes or the solutions. As Hamlet said of Elsinore – 'the times are out of joint'.

❦ *The Long Shadow of the Boer War* ❧

The final war in the long list of wars in Queen Victoria's reign heightened the relevance of Hamlet's bitter assessment, and cast a lengthy shadow over both home

German pro-Boer postcard mocking British military prowess, 1899. The caption reads, 'How the Boers take snapshots of the British army arriving in Durban'. (Author's collection)

and overseas affairs throughout the Edwardian era. It was fought against the small Dutch-Boer controlled republics of the Orange Free State and Transvaal in South Africa, and lasted from 11 October 1899 until 31 May 1902 – far longer than anyone in Great Britain anticipated. In this respect it foreshadowed the greater conflict in 1914, a mere dozen years later.

Diamonds and gold had been discovered in the two Boer republics some years earlier, and their lure had intensified the long-standing antipathies between the independent-minded Boer leadership and British aspirations to control the whole of southern Africa. Great Britain won the war, but the price was heavy. Over 21,000 British, Canadian, New Zealand and Australian soldiers died in battle or from disease. Just over 9,000 Boer combatants died, but so did 28,000 white civilians and unknown thousands of black Africans.

The war had three phases, each of them casting grave doubts on British military competence, political sagacity and moral integrity. At the outset, the Boers struck rapidly into British-held Natal and Cape Colony, and laid siege to Ladysmith, Mafeking and Kimberley. As General Sir Redvers Buller, the British commander, sought to extricate the garrisons in these key towns, his forces suffered three costly defeats in a single week in December 1899 among the rocky outcrops and scrub of Stormberg, Colenso and Magersfontein, and a fourth in January 1900 at Spion Kop.

Modern telegraphic communications ensured that British newspapers were full of the latest military advance or, more commonly, setback. The *Devon & Exeter*

Gazette provided its readers with maps and details of the defeats, and an early editorial gave a prescient analysis of the Boers' ability to pick off British soldiers at long range while scorning the efficacy of any return fire. 'What is the use of firing a volley against the face of a rock,' asked the *Gazette*, in its condemnation of the superannuated tactics of ill-trained British officers.

British troops crossing the Tugela River prior to their defeat at Spion Kop, January 1900, from the *Illustrated London News*. (Author's collection)

With the British nation stunned, and its French and German rivals gloating, the government sent lavish reinforcements together with a new commander-in-chief, Field Marshal Lord Roberts, and phase two began. The three sieges were relieved to hysterical rejoicing back in Britain, and by June 1900 Buller had driven the Boers from Natal and the Cape Colony and Roberts had invaded the Transvaal and captured Pretoria, its capital. This was the high tide of British military success and secured iconic status for Lord Roberts, but to the nation's surprise and dismay the Boers felt far from defeated.

Phase three was a bitter and frustrating guerrilla war with Boer commando-style groups harrying troop columns and attacking railway lines, storage depots and telegraph links, while the British, now under Lord Kitchener, resorted to a scorched earth policy of burning farms, imprisoning civilians and hunting down the raiding parties. It was a desperate time in South Africa, and also back in Great Britain where the vocal minority of people hostile to the war from its outset was reinforced by the mounting number of critics of the army for imposing suffering on thousands of Boer families herded into crude insanitary encampments – 'concentration camps' they were called – often with grossly inadequate food and medical provision.

The war, and the new century, sent a chill through Great Britain. The stubborn Boers were still defying British forces when Queen Victoria, the personification of imperial might and glory in her old age, died, and many suggested her passing symbolised a time, perhaps imminent, when Great Britain might not maintain its international supremacy or occupy the high moral ground in world affairs. Her son's involvement in various social scandals, and predilection for horse-racing, gambling, good living and the company of raffish nouveaux riche, did not endear him, at least initially, to the middle classes. The new king seemed to be the embodiment of a worrying new age that was less stable, less reassuring and fundamentally less admirable than his predecessor's.

As the army licked its wounds, its commanders and their political masters pondered the causes of its poor performance. After due inquiry, in 1907 the government restructured the Regular Army, created the mobile Expeditionary Force, and reorganised county militia and yeomanry into a far better co-ordinated Territorial Army. In 1909 the Imperial General Staff was established.

At the same time, the need for a more extensive nursing and ancillary service linked to the Territorials was recognised with the creation of county-based Voluntary Aid Detachments (VADs) comprising men and women willing to be trained in an array of support roles. In Devon, Earl and Countess Fortescue and other notable families ensured the county was covered with well-trained and self-sufficient VADs while Earl Fortescue and Lord Clifford, as respective commanding officers of the Royal North Devon Hussars and Devonshire Regiment Volunteer battalions, set about overseeing their restructuring.

After one in four Boer War recruits had been rejected as unfit by the army, an Inter-Departmental Committee investigation confirmed the appalling physical condition of many young men. Amidst great controversy, in 1906 this led to public money being spent on midday meals for 'necessitous' children, although the bureaucracy attached to this pioneering initiative meant its clauses were rarely invoked. The following year the School Medical Service was established and henceforth all elementary school children were examined each year, their 'defects' identified, and their parents ordered to seek treatment – either by paying their doctor or through charitable support.

The nation also shifted its attitudes towards its overseas possessions. They remained a source of profit as the provider of raw materials and the market for Great Britain's finished goods, and also the means of consistently 'out-trumping' France and Germany in imperial prestige, but the empire became far more emotionally embedded in the nation as a source of pride. Rather perversely, after the hard won victory in South Africa many more people felt enhanced by the knowledge that their country still ruled the largest empire ever known and could fight off all challengers.

Devon was deeply involved in the war, not least because several battalions of the Devonshire Regiment – the 'Devons' – were involved in prominent battles. Most people celebrated its outbreak, believing the intransigent Boers deserved speedy chastisement. With bands playing the 'Georgia March', in October 1899 the Devonshire Regiment's 2nd Battalion Reservists were cheered through the streets of Exeter to Queen Street Station. Other units sent out to reinforce the battered army were still being cheered a year later.

In October 1899 Private Orchard wrote home describing the alarming advance of the 1st Devons over open country towards the Boer trenches at Elandslaagte. It was a small British victory but cost fifty-five dead and 205 wounded. Surveying the British and Boer bodies, he wrote, 'It was a great slaughter. I never saw such an awful sight before.' In November, a soldier with Lord Methuen at the Modder River wrote home to Lynton saying, 'We have had three dreadful fights in six days', and told of a ferocious bayonet charge in which twenty-eight of his colleagues were killed and 107 wounded before the Boer position was taken.

In January 1900 the Devon County Volunteer Fund started to collect money to provide equipment for new volunteers, and within a few days had accrued £5,000. All subscribers were listed in the *Western Times*, in order of their donations, starting with £1,000 each from the Honourable Mark Rolle of Stevenstone and Mr Thornton West of Streatham Hall in Exeter. Across the county, collections were launched for needy wives and dependents of soldiers. By January 1901, for example, the people of Cullompton and Tiverton had donated £771, of which £547 had been given out already.

Late in February 1900 the surrender of the Boer General Cronje was celebrated across the county – with the *Western Times* reporting on the bells rung, flags hoisted, bands playing and cheering crowds in Ashburton, Barnstaple, Cullompton, Dawlish,

Bradworthy celebrates the relief of Mafeking. (Beaford Arts)

Ilfracombe, South Molton, Teignmouth, Tiverton and Totnes. The British entry into Ladysmith on 1 March caused further rejoicing, not least because the 1st Devons had charged and routed a Boer force threatening the town from Wagon Hill.

In May 1900 Mafeking was relieved, and once again the county went wild with excitement. In Exeter, streets were hung with flags, shops closed early and cheering people carried Union Jacks and pictures of Colonel Baden-Powell, the hero of the hour. In honour of the famous naval brigade that hauled 4.7in guns from HMS *Powerful* on hurriedly made carriages in support of the hard-pressed army, a vast procession was formed behind men dressed up as sailors pulling a mock cannon. Accompanied by torch bearers and bands from army units in the city barracks and also the Church Lads and Boys' Brigade, the City Fire Brigade and Post Office, everyone gathered at the Guildhall in the High Street where the National Anthem was played. Then everyone marched off to the County Ground in St Thomas for more patriotic songs and speeches.

The battles were still raging, though. In May 1900 Private Newberry, an Exeter footballer in the 2nd Devons, wrote home about being shot in the right side – 'but thank goodness it only grazed my liver'. In May, too, Trooper Sid Braund from Barnstaple wrote to a friend from hospital after being laid low with dysentery. It had struck down many others, and so had enteric fever. Throughout the war, *The Times* correspondents in South Africa had little good to say about the primitive medical care, especially the lack of nurses. But there was bravery too.

In October 1900 Major Edward Brown of the 14th Hussars, a resident of St Marychurch, won the Victoria Cross for rescuing three colleagues under heavy fire during a fierce skirmish around a farmstead at Geluk during the advance into the Transvaal.

William Hems, the son of Harry Hems, the renowned Exeter sculptor and wood carver, lived not far from Ladysmith and in 1901 he witnessed the adoption of the scorched earth policy as soldiers drove thousands of horses, sheep and goats out of the Orange Free State. 'They are all in the most awfully wretched condition, and driven almost to death. One continuous string of them is left along the road to die ... But the troops seem to care nothing.'

Sergeant Basting of the 1st Devons wrote of his wearisome observation duties in one of the block houses erected to restrict Boer forays, and the ever-present danger of Boer sniping. 'I should like to have half a pint of good old Devon cider now,' he added. Trooper W. P. Hamlyn from Buckfastleigh told how he was help-ing turn families out of their 'filthy, dirty' farms, sending them to camps and then removing all items of furniture and food. 'We leave nothing edible in the houses'. In June 1901 Trooper Stewart Ferris wrote home to Paignton, just before he was killed, that his troop was engaged in escorting wagon convoys and searching every farmstead and kopje for infiltrating Boers.

The appalling conditions in which Boer families lived, and died, in the makeshift British camps became common knowledge long before the end of the war, but many articles refuted the charges. In August 1901, for example, the *South Molton Gazette* published a report attributed to Reuters claiming the Klerksdorp Camp, holding 3,000 people, had plentiful supplies of fuel, water, food, cooking facilities, bedding and clothing. It said a midwife lived on site, a doctor visited daily and the children received free schooling. In March 1902 another upbeat report, again attributed to Reuters, used sporting terminology to describe a British raiding party descending upon a Boer farm at dawn. The cavalrymen 'shouted to each other out of sheer enjoyment, and spurred on their horses like men finishing a race rather than like men galloping to a possible death or wound'. When some Boers managed to escape the trap, they were chased 'like foxes for several miles'. The report marvelled at the cavalry's 'astonishing energy and marvellous activity'. Many readers in Devon would have related sympathetically to the hunting analogy.

Returning servicemen, whatever their rank, were treated like heroes. In November 1900 crowds at Barnstaple Junction Station welcomed home Captain Sir Edward Chichester RN, the chief naval transport officer at Capetown. He was 'cheered to the echo' at a Guildhall reception, especially when he praised the Devons. Even greater crowds assembled that month to welcome Sir Redvers Buller back to Devon. Exeter presented him with a silver casket with an inscription marking 'the eminent services he rendered to the Empire during the war in South Africa 1899–1900'. At the gates of Downes, his home outside Crediton, his tenants

General Sir Redvers Buller VC, of Downes, Crediton. (Devon & Exeter Institution)

removed the horses from his carriage and pulled it up the drive to the specially decorated house. The violent attacks on his leadership after the defeats in late 1899 were bitterly resented locally, and far greater emphasis was placed on his subsequent successes in relieving Ladysmith and reclaiming Natal and the Transvaal.

In June 1901 the Devon Volunteers returned home and exploding fog detonators placed on the railway lines as a tribute by company employees announced their arrival in Exeter, where a cathedral service followed by luncheon in Victoria Hall awaited them. As the troopers dispersed to their homes each community organised its own welcome. A horse brake met the three men from Chudleigh at Newton

Abbot Station, and a band accompanied them through the crowded village streets. They were guests of honour at the Globe Hotel, then presented with gold watches, briar pipes and an inscribed pendant at a parade in the Drill Hall, and finally attended a smoking concert in their honour.

And still bad news filtered through from South Africa. Arthur Bowden from Butterleigh wrote to the rector about a surprise Boer attack on a nearby British camp at Tweenfontein on Christmas Day 1901 in which seven officers and seventy-five men were killed and another sixty-three wounded out of a complement of 300. 'There must have been something wrong with our camp,' he thought, 'but it is difficult to say who was to blame.' Trooper Welby, a medical orderly from Chelston, survived the attack, and told his sister:

> I had just cut a man's breeches down who had got hit in the thigh, when a bullet struck the doctor in the arm; he went on, however, till he suddenly cried, 'My God', and rolled over. He had again got hit, the bullet missing his heart by half an inch and coming out on the other side just above his hip.

Not surprisingly, in June 1902 the vicar of Seaton noted 'the spontaneous outburst of thankfulness', and also his packed church, when peace was finally announced. Soon afterwards Sir John Kennaway unveiled the memorial plaque in the town to Troopers Bernard Salter and Percy Jones and said they had died 'in the cause of justice, liberty and humanity'. A year later a memorial window and tablet to the fallen from the county were dedicated in a service in Exeter Cathedral attended by men from the Devonshire Regiment and also Lord Clifford and Viscount Ebrington, the 3rd Earl Fortescue's heir and brother of Major the Hon. Lionel Fortescue killed in South Africa on 11 June 1900. The dean said the memorial would be 'one of the most precious possessions of their great ancestral Cathedral', and Lord Ebrington trusted that the moving tribute to the 460 men named on it would help 'their sons, and their sons' sons, whether in the navy, army, or civil life, to be strong and brave men'.

The images in the window reflected prevailing attitudes towards the victory, although perhaps the heavily loaded analogies hinted as much at the uncertainties surrounding the nation's pre-eminence as at the more public assumption of a God-given triumph. One pictured Abraham receiving bread and wine from the high priest after a victorious campaign; the second showed Joshua with the approving Captain of the Lord's Host after the fall of Jericho; the third pictured King Alfred and the Treaty of Wedmore he signed with the defeated Danes; the fourth contained the warrior king Edward I being nursed by Queen Eleanor after an assassination attempt, and the central image showed the Resurrection and Christ defeating death. Indicative of the strength of feeling for the hitherto generally unloved British Army, 18,000 subscribers enabled four silver drums to be presented to the 2nd Devons that same evening in Exeter's Higher Barracks.

A Winkleigh family in best clothes outside their house decorated
for King Edward VII's coronation. (Beaford Arts)

In August 1902 lavish celebrations in Devon's towns and villages marked the coronation of King Edward VII. It was as though there was a collective sigh of relief at the end of the war and Edward's recovery from a serious illness, and an accompanying determination to put on a show of national pride and confidence. Streets were decorated, churches were packed and returning volunteers filled many pews. Collections were given, at the king's request, to local hospitals. School children marched through the streets with accompanying bands, sang patriotic songs and were given medals, mugs and tea. 'No one could have failed to observe,' wrote the vicar of Seaton, 'the loyalty and affectionate feeling towards His Majesty and the Queen which animated all classes.'

2

OPENING UP TO THE WORLD
Travel & Tourism, Commerce & Consumerism

The growth of steam-powered railways, shipping and factories, the increasing globalisation of trade and production and the spread of tourism down through the social classes had a dramatic impact upon the towns and villages of Devon, not least in laying bare the conflict between those avidly promoting new developments and those steadfastly opposing them.

The threats and opportunities posed by steam power in all its manifestations began to strike Devon not long after the accession of Queen Victoria, but only during the reign of her son did it become clear that the onslaught of mass tourism and mass production had changed the nature and structure of Devon's economy forever.

The Railways: Commerce, Consumerism & Convenience

In 1901 a Devonian aged 60 might have remembered the county without any steam locomotives pounding along railway lines. Anyone younger would have grown up with the constant sights and sounds of new cuttings, tunnels and bridges transforming the landscape as the spider's web of lines covered the county. Indeed, in 1901 much of the vast network was new, and its influence was still growing.

The Great Western
By May 1844 Isambard Kingdom Brunel's Great Western Railway (GWR) had passed Bristol and Taunton to reach Exeter St David's, and as the excited newspapers reported, people marvelled that they could lunch in the county town and have supper in London on the same day. Within a year the fastest journey was reduced from five and a half to four and a half hours, and the death knell began to sound for the Grand Western Canal between Tiverton and Taunton.

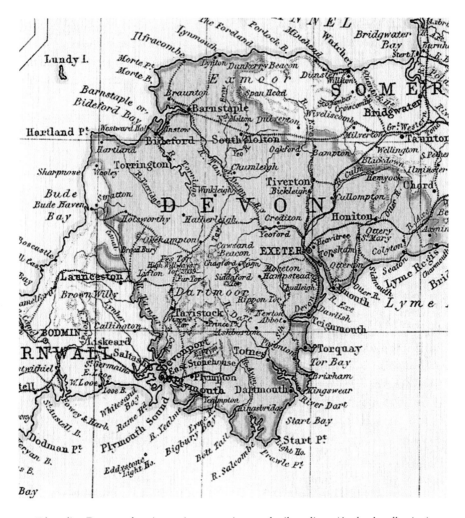

Edwardian Devon – showing main towns, rivers and railway lines. (Author's collection)

At Exeter, as almost everywhere else, the first trains were welcomed with rousing bands, lengthy speeches and tables groaning with food and drink for the crowd. As the newspapers gleefully reported, the occasions could get joyously out of hand. Thanks largely to Thomas Latimer of the *Western Times*, local newspapers enthusiastically equated rail transport with growing prosperity, but the canal and stagecoach companies, fearing annihilation, and some clergy and landowners who equated mass travel with unruly and licentious behaviour, were far less keen.

Amidst all the excitement and anxiety the GWR advanced down the Exe, along the coast past Dawlish and Teignmouth, and then inland to Newton Abbot, around the fringes of Dartmoor to Totnes and Ivybridge and then on to Plymouth where it arrived in April 1849. The lure of profits led subsidiary companies to build branch lines off the main east–west route. In August 1859 one from Newton Abbot reached Paignton via Torquay, and went on to Kingswear in 1864. The line had a dramatic impact. Torquay's reputation as an upper-class winter resort came to an end, and the town experienced a distinct decline in its fortunes until the middle classes took to it as a summer destination. The line, though, was the making of Paignton at the cheaper end of the market and brought in thousands of visitors – and hundreds of wagons of coal for domestic and commercial consumers, including in due course the huge new gas works. Dartmouth, on the opposite bank to Kingswear on the River Dart, was the planned destination of the line, but a major landowner successfully fought off the idea. All Dartmouth ever got was a rail-less station and a ferry connection with Kingswear.

Other branches also tapped into local industries. In February 1868 a spur off the Torquay line reached Brixham, and most days saw the dispatch of several well-packed fish wagons. In July 1866 a branch opened from Newton Abbot to Moretonhampstead, and secured considerable traffic in incoming coal and outgoing farm produce and clay from the Bovey Basin pits and adits along its line. Fewer clay barges used the Stover Canal connection with the Teign Docks, and by Edwardian times it was clear its profitability was coming to a close. From May 1872 a line out of Totnes grew profitable serving Buckfastleigh's textile mills and Ashburton's cattle fairs and gas works.

There were, though, less shrewd investments. The 1893 branch line from Brent to Kingsbridge owed its precarious survival almost entirely to the late Victorian and Edwardian summer holiday traffic rather than any goods contracts. Conversely it was mineral and agricultural traffic from the Teign Valley rather than passenger numbers that saved a belated inland route between Newton Abbot and Exeter via Heathfield, Ide and Christow. Beset by money worries, troublesome landowners and hilly countryside, work began in the 1880s but it took until July 1903 for the line to reach Exeter.

By 1901 numerous lines snaked through Plymouth, Devonport and East Stonehouse, serving both commerce and commuters. The GWR built docks at Plymouth near its Millbay Station, and in 1851 inaugurated a monthly steamship service to Australia, China and India, thereby starting a running battle with Southampton. In May 1859 the opening of Brunel's Saltash Bridge made access to and from Cornwall much easier. A month later a GWR line from Plymouth reached Tavistock and in 1865 this was extended to Launceston via Lydford, adding significantly to Plymouth's commercial links. In 1883 a winding line to Princetown aided the troubled granite trade and excited tourists with views of Dartmoor.

The London & South Western

Meanwhile the rival London & South Western Railway (LSWR) had been far from idle. Its shorter line from Waterloo via Salisbury, Axminster and Honiton arrived at its centrally sited station in Exeter in 1860. For the next thirty years Devonians lived with two different gauges of railway – the GWR's idiosyncratic but possibly more

The LSWR's large, centrally sited Queen Street Station in Exeter, *c.* 1905. (Author's collection)

cost-effective 7ft ¼in favoured by Brunel and the LSWR's far more widely used 4ft 8½in which had served miners for generations. In 1892 the narrower gauge triumphed, and over a weekend in May that year thousands of families enjoyed watching well-rehearsed gangs turn 177 miles of broad track west of Exeter into 'standard' gauge.

By 1874 the LSWR had secured access to GWR's Exeter St David's Station and worked its way around the north of Dartmoor to Okehampton and then south to Lydford where a troublesome mixed gauge agreement with the GWR allowed the LSWR access to Plymouth in 1876. This finally ended in June 1890 when a separate LSWR route from Lydford to Plymouth, via Bere Alston and Bere Ferrers, belatedly opened up the Tamar Valley, boosting the prosperity of local market gardeners but creating a menacing rival to the river boats.

Other LSWR lines from Exeter wound through the Taw Valley villages to reach Barnstaple in August 1854, Bideford in November 1855 and, rather belatedly, Great Torrington in July 1872. Each intermediate station possessed sidings, goods sheds and cattle pens, most had coal yards, and several, such as Eggesford and Barnstaple, had slaughterhouses nearby. Goods trains hauling cattle and horseboxes, milk tankers and meat vans, and wagons of apples, coal, hay and straw, manure, animal feed, timber and stone became regular sights. In 1879 a slow and winding branch from near Okehampton rambled through the sparse north-west countryside to link Halwill, Holsworthy and Cornwall's Bude with the wider world.

There were losers as well as winners. The railway eroded Bideford's prosperity when freight handling became concentrated at Barnstaple's bigger and better-serviced goods depots. Shapland & Petter's large Raleigh Cabinet Works was sited

Halwill Junction, a country station with sidings and goods wagons, 1907. (Beaford Arts)

not far from Barnstaple's LSWR Station and possessed its own siding for incoming coal and wood and outgoing finished furniture. Crediton failed to take full advantage of its station and yard, and continued to decline as Exeter's trade increased. Probably Chulmleigh, bypassed by the line, suffered most when its auction house and market transferred to Eggesford Station.

North Devon tourism received a further boost later in the century. In July 1874 a line opened from Barnstaple to Braunton, the stopping point for Saunton Sands and Croyde Bay, and went on to a windswept terminus high above Ilfracombe from which families, depending upon their means, were ushered to a reserved hotel carriage, paid a public carrier or walked to their holiday accommodation. As late as May 1898 Barnstaple acquired another line when a 1ft 11½in gauge railway opened to Lynton, 20 miles away across Exmoor, in the face of vociferous opposition by Sir Thomas Acland and other lovers of the area's stag hunting, isolation and exclusivity. No doubt to their satisfaction, it struggled to survive, making more money delivering coal than carrying passengers. Yet more local lines linked Bideford to Northam in May 1901 and the shipbuilding port of Appledore in May 1908. The commercial traffic never materialised, but tourists enjoyed the scenery.

In 1873 a long GWR branch line from Norton Fitzwarren near Taunton reached Barnstaple via South Molton. Heavy expresses used it as well as local passenger and goods services, including the celebrated 'rabbit specials' destined for the London and Midland markets. Joining this line in May 1885 at Morebath on the Devon–Somerset border was the winding Exe Valley line from Stoke Canon, a few miles outside Exeter. The textile, brewing and market town of

Tiverton was on this route, but its more important connection was with the main GWR London and Exeter line at Tiverton Junction. Local landowners and farmers invested in a branch line eastwards from this junction towards Hemyock. It opened in May 1876, but did little business until a textile factory at Uffculme decided to use it.

Short but costly branches were hacked through the hills and valleys between the LSWR's main Waterloo–Exeter line and east Devon's seaside resorts. They made a significant difference to some communities, but not others. A line along the Exe estuary reached sandy Exmouth in May 1861 and gave immediate impetus to the development of its docks, guesthouses and residential estates. Coal, timber and fish became important traffic, and the railway also helped Topsham Quay to stay commercially active, but far greater profits came from passengers using the line's well-sited intermediate stations.

A branch along the Axe Valley to Seaton opened in March 1868 with plans to develop Axmouth Harbour that came to nothing. Seaton itself remained a minor resort, although its historian records it charmed one holidaymaker in 1894 who delighted in the quietness 'far away from the madding crowd', adding, 'if one wanted entertaining one would go elsewhere'.

Another branch reached Sidmouth, or rather a terminus a mile outside it, in July 1874. The townsfolk had divided loyalties; for well over fifty years Sidmouth had grown used to its select and wealthy visitors, but many traders and hoteliers warmly welcomed the hundreds of less elevated families regularly deposited on its outskirts. In May 1895 a branch off the Sidmouth line reached the small town of Budleigh Salterton, and in 1903 it went on to connect with Exmouth. Day trips from Exeter proved popular, and so did cheap excursions from London, but Exmouth's sand was much preferred to Budleigh's shingle.

Cost & Convenience

In Edwardian times most of Devon's small towns were well served by trains. In 1912 Okehampton's station was considered a disgrace, with narrow, frequently congested platforms and hardly any shelters, but there were eleven passenger trains a day to Exeter and nine back, and ten to Tavistock and Plymouth with eleven back. The railway companies often offered 'cheap day returns' and advertised the easy accessibility of many destinations. In the summer of 1911, for example, Exeter day trippers could go for 1/- to Exmouth, 1s 6d to Budleigh Salterton, 2/- to Sidmouth, Seaton and Okehampton, 2s 6d to Bridestowe, Lydford and Brentor, 3/- to Lyme Regis, 3s 3d to Tavistock, 3s 9d to Plymouth and Devonport, 4/- to Bude and Barnstaple, 4s 6d to Bideford and Braunton, 5/- to Ilfracombe, Mortehoe and Torrington, and 5s 3d to Lynton. A few of these places still retain stations, and price comparisons indicate that in real terms the 1911 day return tickets cost about the same as those today – not especially cheap.

Comfort began to accompany speed in Edwardian times, at least on express trains. In 1901 the GWR's world-famous *Cornishman* reached Exeter in three hours and thirty-eight minutes and Plymouth in five hours. When the shorter route from Paddington via Castle Cary opened in 1906, the *Cornish Riviera* reached Plymouth in four hours and ten minutes. The first express serving meals appeared on the Waterloo to Exeter route in August 1901. Dinner was 3*s* 6*d* and afternoon tea 1/-. The first train fitted throughout with corridors, on-board lavatories, electric lighting and heated compartments left Waterloo for Ilfracombe in July 1904. Three years later, all express trains leaving Waterloo for the West Country had corridor carriages and also dining cars available to all classes.

Rivers, Seas & Sailors: Struggling Against the Tide

In general, the railways enhanced the efficiency of local ports rather than competed with them, but they could not halt the steady decay of Devon's seagoing trade. Despite this, waterborne occupations provided a living for thousands of Edwardian Devon families. The 1901 census showed that there were 2,028 fishermen, 3,135 male and eight female merchant seamen and pilots, 392 barge and lightermen, 676 dock and wharf labourers and officials, 606 coal heavers and 3,502 shipwrights and 'other workers in metal and wood on ships and boats'.

Fishing Communities
Each port had its tale of slow decline. In 1820 there were thirty sailing trawlers working out of Plymouth's Sutton Pool. As a result of rapid rail communications and new markets, numbers had grown to sixty-six in 1872 with another couple of hundred arriving in the mackerel and pilchard seasons. At busy times in the 1890s 300 fishing boats crowded the harbour and approaching 500 handcarts waited on Barbican Quay to handle the catches. Over two days in January 1901, 1,000 tons of herrings were landed, admittedly a rare bonanza.

In 1896 a new market was built, significantly easing the congestion. But it did so just as a lingering depression set in. New large steam trawlers from Britain's east coast brought in vast catches from the North Sea and Atlantic and began to put the West Country's sailing fleet, whose owners had insufficient resources to invest in comparable vessels, out of business. The huge hauls nationally brought down the price of fish, as shown by the value of Plymouth's catches – £85,850 in 1886; £162,900 in 1890; £101,000 in 1900 and £72,000 in 1904.

Ironically this meant the popularity of fish and chip shops soared in Plymouth and other Devon towns. One local business closely associated with this trade was short lived, though, as the stench from Mount Batten's dogfish offal processing plant that had opened in 1906 forced its closure in 1912.

The Barbican Quay, Plymouth, *c.* 1907. (Devon & Exeter Institution)

By 1901 Brixham's sailing trawlers, too, had been crowded out of the North Sea. Its larger vessels began concentrating along the Devon and Cornwall coast, the Bristol Channel and the Irish Sea; the smaller smacks stayed more local, generally between Start Point and Portland Bill. The catches included sole, turbot, plaice, cod, gurnard, mackerel and conger eels. About 200 boats still called Brixham home but numbers slowly declined in Edwardian times, as did the port's population. Nevertheless, the women still wove the nets and knitted warm clothes, the ships drew on their crews' children and local orphanages for their young apprentices, and many of the men no longer at sea made sails and repaired the weather-beaten vessels on their visits home.

Fishing for crabs, and for crab bait, was a delicate, arduous but historic occupation in Start Bay and around Start Point, especially by men from Beesands and Hallsands. Using small sailboats, the crab fishers – or 'potters' – dropped a series of baited, weighted and rope-connected willow baskets with narrow funnel entrances on the seabed. Brixham's smacks were banned from Start Bay, but during the 1890s the crabbers constantly complained of the damage wrought by illegal trawler fishing there. The erection of lights on Berry Head and the Skerries to mark the areas protected for crabbers had little effect. So angry became the confrontations that the Devon Sea Fisheries Committee inspector had to take armed coastguards with him on patrols. When prosecutions were brought against several trawler skippers in 1896 a naval gunboat was ordered to visit the bay to enforce the regulations. The trawlers were undeterred, and the newspapers continued to report prosecutions and hefty fines of £20 or more – a sure indication of the profits at stake. In a celebrated case in 1911 one trawler resorted to covering its identification marks and the crew, with blackened and masked faces, used oars and spikes to repel fishery officers attempting to board it.

Local trawlers were also under further pressure from foreign steam trawlers fishing off the coast, but secured little redress. All that was gained by a Devon deputation in 1907 to Lord Tweedmouth, First Lord of the Admiralty, was his sympathy for the loss of profits and jobs alongside his regret that owners were not investing in steam power and his refusal to increase the number of Channel gunboats.

Steamships, Sailing Ships & Cargoes

In terms of overall seaborne trade, Plymouth reigned supreme in Devon. It could accommodate the largest vessels, and far more of them than Dartmouth and Teignmouth, and its waterfront provided vast spaces for warehouses and railway sidings and stations. While Sutton Pool concentrated on fishing, Millbay Dock was developed to service ocean steamships, and Cattewater handled the burgeoning trade in grain, timber, clay, fertilisers and oil. The annual tonnage of cargo shipping at Plymouth soared from 200,000 in the 1840s to over 750,000 just before the First World War.

The contrast with the rest of Edwardian Devon was startling. Appledore had been a successful Victorian trading centre, especially under the aggressive entrepreneurs James and William Yeo, but along with nearby Barnstaple and Bideford its businessmen eschewed involvement in steamships. During the Edwardian era all three trading communities relied upon their aging sailing ships to carry goods such as coal, limestone, fish and agricultural produce around the coast and across the Bristol Channel. They remained busy, if not as prosperous as a generation ago, as revealed by the fifty-five vessels arriving at Bideford Quay during the final quarter of 1900. And in just one week of September 1904 thirteen ships docked at Barnstaple with coal from Wales, wheat from Bristol, salt from Gloucester, slate from Carnarvon, flour from Liverpool and oil cake from London. A few hardy schooners still braved the Atlantic Ocean to bring home cargoes of salt fish, thereby maintaining the region's historic connection with Labrador and Newfoundland.

William Slade was born in 1892 and *Out of Appledore*, his memoirs as a seaman, mate and finally master of commercial sailing ships, completely ignores any beauty they possessed and expresses no regret for their general passing. At times, he wrote, life in them bordered on the intolerable. His book is full of the horrors of storms, the narrow escapes from rocks, the loss of sails and masts, the sudden injuries that could occur, the frustrating delays caused by becalming and the arduous work of winching heavy cargo.

Lives continued to be lost. In January 1900, for example, four ships out of Appledore foundered in a gale, seven men were lost and several others injured. In July 1908, all five crew were killed when the trawler *Fear Not* was rammed and sunk by the steamship *Irak* off Bishop's Lighthouse. On 16 December 1910 a terrible storm in the Bristol Channel claimed seven Brixham smacks and eighteen men, leaving many widows and thirty children fatherless. It was some comfort that £6,500 was raised across south Devon to support them. The following December the Appledore schooner *Agnes* was wrecked off Falmouth in a gale and two local men drowned. The only Seamen's Orphan Boys' Home in Devon was sited in Brixham; it housed around forty lads in 1906. It survived with a struggle on charitable donations and church collections, and some funds from the Royal Navy for the care of its orphans.

Several south coast ports remained active in Edwardian times, some more so than others. Along the Exe estuary three ports battled for trading supremacy – and thereby survival. However, Exeter was several miles upriver and Topsham had no large dock; both were superannuated as far as larger steamships were concerned. When Exmouth's secure and well-serviced docks at the mouth of the river opened in 1868 it was in prime position to handle most of the area's surviving overseas trade in Baltic timber, American petroleum, South American hides and Iberian wine and spirits.

Teignmouth Harbour, *c.* 1907. (Devon & Exeter Institution)

Nevertheless, the coastal trade that kept small ports in business remained important. Sailing ships still brought in such popular commodities as the rice, sugar and tea they had loaded from warehouses in the great international trading port of Liverpool. Teignmouth regularly unloaded barley and stone from Portland in Dorset, and china clay, slate and bricks from Charlestown and Padstow in Cornwall. Much of the china clay, along with other clays extracted locally, was shipped on to the Low Countries, Germany, Scandinavia and Spain. Nevertheless, Edwardian investment in Teignmouth's port facilities and dredging was negligible, and its trading figures, except for clay, slowly declined.

In the nineteenth century the River Tamar provided numerous families with livelihoods from tourism, agriculture and industry, but by Edwardian times the balance between these sources had changed dramatically. The traffic downriver in lead, copper and manganese from local mines had faded as world commodity prices plummeted, and this meant the upriver traffic in coal, pig iron and pit props fell away too. There remained, though, the ships bringing fertilisers to enrich the acid soil of the valley's market gardens, and ferry the early season soft fruit and flowers down to Plymouth. The steamers also carried thousands of tourists to admire the scenery and enjoy the farmers' wives' strawberry and cream teas.

Coal merchant's advertisement picturing a collier unloading at Kingsbridge and company coal wagons, *c.* 1906. (Devon & Exeter Institution)

Coal from South Wales and the north was the major import nearly everywhere. It was vital for the increasing number of steam-powered warships, the thousands of new terraced houses, the steadily modernising potteries, textile factories, paper mills and iron foundries, and the numerous gasworks spreading across Edwardian Devon. Coal dust covered many of Devon's docks and railway sidings, and palls of smoke dirtied factories, workshops and towns. Each port jealously guarded its trade, and relations between Brixham and Dartmouth were constantly soured by alleged attempts to steal each other's coaling contracts.

Ironically, it was coal and the engines it drove that brought about the late Victorian and Edwardian decline in West Country commercial shipbuilding. Investment was not forthcoming and Devon's yards remained restricted to sailing ships – notably the barques and schooners that continued to ply the coastal routes. Indicative of changing times, some well-known firms, notably Holmans of Topsham, chose not only to switch from shipbuilding to ship owning but to move their operating bases out of Devon. In Holmans' case this was London.

Most famous of all was William Reardon Smith from Appledore who went on to create a major shipping line in South Wales. Among the few exceptions were Phillips' Yard and Simpson & Strickland on the Dart, but they were dealing with small vessels. Nevertheless, historian Ray Freeman notes how busy they were throughout the Edwardian era with contracts for steam yachts, pleasure craft, naval pinnaces and patrol boats, many for customers overseas.

Devonport & Dartmouth: The Naval Bases At Their Height

The little fishing village of Hallsands hugged the cliffs, and by 1901 it was in great danger of collapse through the constant dredging of a protective gravel bank just offshore by contractors working on improvements to Devonport Dockyard. The 100 or so residents, asserted the *Devon & Exeter Gazette* that year, 'live in constant dread of a south-easterly gale' sending the sea crashing against their homes.

Throughout the nineteenth century the great naval dockyard at Devonport was in a state of constant modernisation and expansion as warships grew ever more complicated and powerful. In 1889 a jittery British Parliament passed the Naval Defence Act to ensure the Royal Navy's strength was equal to that of the combined strength of its two nearest rivals, still seen as France and Imperial Russia. It provided for ten new battleships and several dozen cruisers, and in 1895 the Naval Works Act authorised huge improvements to dockyard facilities and defences at Devonport, Chatham, Portsmouth, Portland, Gibraltar and Hong Kong.

In due course, the vast Keyham Extension with its enclosed basins, several docks, numerous wharves and accompanying stores, fitting shops and coke and coal depots was opened by the Prince and Princess of Wales in February 1907. The base was at its height, employing over 13,000 men in a vast array of trades. In addition, the 1911 census recorded over 18,000 servicemen in Plymouth and Devonport. Although most of the dockyard's plate, machinery and guns were brought in from outside the county, Hamlyns at Buckfastleigh supplied textiles, Vicarys at Newton Abbot produced hides and leather, Candy near Bovey Tracey supplied firebricks, and firms in Bideford, Exeter, Crediton, Plymouth and Devonport itself undertook specialised joinery.

The number of massive warships constructed at Devonport in the early twentieth century reveals the yard's capacity and importance and also the heavy demands of naval defence at a time of never-ending international tensions. Between 1900 and 1914 it constructed the battleships HMS *Montagu*, HMS *Queen*, HMS *King Edward VII*, HMS *Hibernia*, HMS *Temeraire*, HMS *Collingwood*, HMS *Centurion*, HMS *Marlborough*, HMS *Warspite* and HMS *Royal Oak*, the battlecruisers HMS *Indefatigable* and HMS *Lion*, and the cruisers HMS *Encounter*, HMS *Minotaur* and HMS *Aurora*. Launches, often by the wives of local aristocrats, were proud, formal and well-publicised ceremonies. In March 1902 Queen Alexandra herself launched HMS *Queen*, and in due recognition of rank the local newspaper noted that King Edward shook hands with the admirals, touched his hat to other officers and 'nodded' to the men.

If increasingly complex warships were needed, so was training for the new generation of officers. Since the 1860s two gloomy, claustrophobic and unhealthy naval hulks named the *Britannia* and *Hindostan* had been moored in the river at Dartmouth to provide intensive training to the nation's future naval officers,

Countess Fortescue arriving to launch the battleship HMS *Temeraire* (18,800 tons with ten 12in guns) in August 1907 and (inset) the completed warship. (Author's collection)

something that hitherto had been largely left to midshipmen to pick up on the job while serving at sea. After years of debate and delay, in March 1902 King Edward VII laid the foundation stone of the new *Britannia* Royal Naval College on the banks of the Dart. It opened in September 1905, bringing significantly enhanced prestige, trade and tourism to the town, as well as continuing dismay that its railway station saw no trains. As one magistrate stated in 1902 when lamenting the rowdy behaviour at the coronation festivities, the 'town would long ago have sunk into insignificance but for the Royal visits and *Britannia*'.

A third hulk, HMS *Marlborough*, moored near Devonport, housed the first generation of trainee engineering officers from 1877 until their purpose-built Keyham College opened in 1880. In 1877 yet another hulk, the *Mount Edgcumbe*, had moored on the Tamar and was still in use in 1914. It was run by a charity chaired by the Earl of Mount Edgcumbe and accommodated, trained and eventually sent to sea boys whose miserable early lives had placed them 'at risk' but who had not been convicted of any crime. Its strict discipline was as renowned as its polished drill and accomplished band.

The Resorts: Anxieties & Aspirations

In the eighteenth century the fashionable habit of visiting spas to partake of their mineral-laden spring waters led to a belief in the even more beneficial effects of bathing in and drinking seawater. Thus Sidmouth, Exmouth and Dawlish began their slow rise to prosperity. As Continental travel was impossible during the long war against France between 1793 and 1815, other wealthy tourists looked to the West Country as a pale but acceptable reflection of the Alps, and fell for the new eulogies of sea and mountain air. In imitation of the spas, shrewd developers built rows of genteel housing, and then classically styled assembly rooms, baths and libraries. A seafront promenade 'to take the air' and view the quaintly spoken and attired locals in their working environment was essential.

Edwardian guidebooks perpetuated the trend. The south Devon climate, claimed William Pollard, was 'invaluable in inflammatory bronchitic afflictions, in scrofula and also in some forms of dyspepsia', and 'especially in the irritable state of the lungs which so often precedes the development of consumption'. Unlike other parts of the country it 'did not depress the functions of the liver'.

Torbay
Arthur Ellis's magisterial history of Torquay records the central role played by the Victorian Palk family, and especially its entrepreneurial agent, William Kitson, in creating new properties for the upper and aspiring upper middle classes; developing Fleet Street and the Strand; constructing the great outer harbour; building

the prestigious Imperial Hotel and still keeping the resort exclusive. Wealthy invalids abounded, as did senior officers, often with connections to Devon's naval or military establishments.

Sir Lawrence Palk was raised to the peerage as Lord Haldon in 1880 just as the debt-ridden family was descending towards bankruptcy in 1891. The Carys of Torre Abbey, another notable property-owning family, were also entering a decline in their fortunes and Torquay Corporation welcomed the chance to take more effective control of local developments. However, as the new century neared, the town fractured between those anxious to preserve a genteel environment in which to reside and those determined to create a more commercially attractive and profitable holiday resort. As the *Torquay Times* explained in January 1902, 'there are many residents who have passed their eightieth year, whilst septuagenarians are quite numerous'. They 'fight like cats', it lamented, 'if any new ideas are mooted'.

Torquay Corporation acquired the harbour in 1883 and, amidst further accusations of unnecessary expense, a new sea wall and Princess Pier and Gardens were completed in the mid-1890s. However, memories of an ill-fated Winter Garden complex in Torwood Street that had opened in 1881 and closed the following year haunted development plans for a generation. They helped to limit the ideas for a grand pier head entertainment centre to a modest concert hall in 1902, and then confuse and delay proposals for a larger hall that eventually became the famous, if poorly designed, pavilion in 1912. Horror stories of drunken and licentious behaviour at Torquay Races continually fed the fears and arguments of those hostile to adding further visitor attractions.

The agitation to make Torquay more attractive to visitors never ceased throughout the Edwardian era. In January 1903 the *Torquay Times* carried a heartfelt article on the town's inadequacies. It was 'the home of unrelieved boredom in winter', the station was 'a mile from the town' and the access road was drenched by the sea in a south-east wind, there was no transport 'but inferior cabs', and after dinner there was nothing to do 'but go to bed'. It noted, too, the frequent complaints that the roads either raised clouds of 'aggravating dust' or were topped with a layer of glutinous mud. After years of wrangling a limited omnibus service was introduced in 1903, and in 1907 a tram circuit opened linking Torquay and Torre stations with the town centre and the road to Babbacombe and St Marychurch despite all the lamentations about likely electrocution and pandering to the unruly masses. It proved popular with residents and tourists alike.

Nevertheless, in 1907 the organiser of a Lancashire holiday outing to Torquay berated the town for its 'deadly dull' evenings and lack of 'amusements on the sands and palaces of entertainment in which to spend a restful hour'. Soon afterwards the *Torquay Times* sarcastically welcomed, 'after deliberations of almost sufficient length to decide the fate of a nation', the corporation's decision to engage a band for six weeks each summer. Various bands were hired, but the German ones – notably that of Herr Karl Kaps – were much preferred, as they were elsewhere. In August 1908 the *Torquay Times* provocatively reprinted an article in Lincolnshire's *Boston Guardian* that condemned Torquay's chokingly dusty streets, surprising number of slums, sad unwatered gardens and excessive tram charges.

Despite these issues, mass arrivals were already common. In September 1901, seven trains organised by the Industrial Co-operative Society transported over 3,000 people from Oldham to Torquay for their holiday, and each succeeding year other industrial conurbations did much the same. In July 1910 the town's first summer carnival was held, with numerous eye-catching floral cars and tableaux such as 'Neptune', 'Cupid's Garden', 'Old Times Coach', 'The Happy Family', 'Faith, Hope & Charity' and the 'Empire'. The *Torquay Times* announced it a great success, but only after its promoters had 'contended with difficulties and prejudices quite unknown to the general public'.

Finally, a travelling fair – complete with clowns, stilt walkers, snake charmer, fortune-teller, magician, a fat lady, escape artist and boxing booth – was allowed to visit each year when the sailing regatta was held. The regatta itself was a popular spectacle. Indeed, in 1913 the Centenary Regatta was honoured by the King's Yacht *Britannia* and Kaiser Wilhelm's yacht *Meteor* participating in races – but not against each other.

Looking back on 1913 the *Torquay Times* was gratified to see civic amenities – notably the grand town hall complex – and visitor attractions receiving adequate attention at last. 'A remarkable feature of the year has been the enormous growth and popularity of entertainments.' For better or worse, the transformation had been largely an Edwardian affair.

One of Devon's abiding attractions were the visits of warships to various resorts. Each summer one or more moored off Ilfracombe, the crews engaged in displays and sports ashore and the ships were open to visitors. In 1906 the battleship HMS *Montagu* created particular horror and excitement when she struck a treacherous ledge of rocks known as the Shutters on Lundy Island in fog during a radio signalling trial. No one was injured, but all attempts to refloat her failed and she became a total wreck.

Besides this, the most awe-inspiring sights were the massive gatherings of the Channel and Home Fleets in Torbay during exercises. In July 1902 no less than sixteen battleships, flanked by seventeen cruisers, nine destroyers and around thirty torpedo boats filled the bay. In the evening Torquay and Paignton seafronts were illuminated with Chinese lanterns and fairy lights, and huge crowds enjoyed the ships' searchlights playing across each other and the towns.

In May 1907 the *Torquay Times* was suitably impressed by the 'world's greatest battleship', HMS *Dreadnought*, armed with ten 12in guns, leading the fleet to its Torbay anchorage. The greatest spectacle of all was the Coronation Review in July 1910 by King George V and Queen Mary. Over 200 ships from the Home, Atlantic and Mediterranean fleets were involved and many thousands gazed upon

Souvenir postcard of the royal review in Torbay, July 1910. (Author's collection)

'the finest fleet the world has ever seen'. The royal yacht came close enough inshore for all to see, the warships thundered a twenty-one gun salute, and bugles sounded and crews cheered as the *Victoria & Albert* steamed past each vessel. The town was less thrilled with the brawling and drunkenness that accompanied the naval shore parties during visits, notwithstanding the determined efforts of churches and charities to provide wholesome leisure activities in alcohol-free establishments.

In a prophetic announcement, the *Torquay Times* described the flight of Claude Grahame-White's biplane over the Coronation Review as a foretaste of things to come. If he had used some 'yet to be invented explosive', it said, he could 'have put the whole of the fighting fleet out of action'. The contemporary fascination with flying machines ensured Henri Salmet's displays in Torquay, Paignton, Plymouth and Exeter in the summers of 1912, 1913 and 1914 thrilled thousands of onlookers, and particularly the fortunate few he took aloft in his fragile Bleriot XI-2. The visits were all part of Grahame-White's 'Wake Up England' campaign to alert the nation to his vision of the commercial and military future of aircraft.

Paignton grew in the shadow of Torquay. Its main nineteenth-century developer, Arthur Hyde Dendy, recognised the difference, and said, 'Torquay was built for Paignton to look at'. The centrally sited station was a boon, and Dendy built two hotels and the pier with its hall offering concerts, dances and shows, started the local newspaper and ran a bus and steamship service to Torquay. He died in 1886, but his successor as the most influential local citizen was already in residence. Isaac Singer, of the Singer Sewing Machine Company, had moved there in 1870 and it was his background in trade rather than his disreputable lifestyle that led to his chilly reception in Torquay, although Paignton welcomed his lavish benefactions. He built the original Oldway Mansion, which was later transformed into a miniature Versailles, complete with lake, grottos and hot house, by his son Paris in 1904–07. The Singers were rarely in residence, but they helped make Paignton famous although never as genteel or decorous as Torquay. And its climate was never as salubrious.

Hardly any Edwardian guidebooks mention sea bathing, perhaps because of its Victorian associations with nudity. The habit of bathing naked had descended down the social scale during the nineteenth century, much to the condemnation of many Devon residents and visitors. However, the use of bathing machines for changing clothes gradually became more widespread, and by the Edwardian era local resorts had won a hard-fought campaign for universal swimming costumes. Once public decency had triumphed, the unhappy separation of families into separate male and female bathing areas on Victorian beaches could end. Mixed bathing was once again permitted, and soared in popularity.

Guidebooks highlighted more elevating and instructive activities. Pollard's *Guide to Exeter* is a good example. For those seeking outdoor exercise the Exe was commended for its fishing, rowing, canoeing and yachting, while the city itself offered tennis, golf, a large library, a YMCA gymnasium, numerous historical buildings to admire, programmes of lectures at the Literary Society, and plays and concerts at the Theatre Royal and other halls. As always, the cathedral and city churches occupied several pages. Local gardens were a major feature of the guidebook, with the renowned Lucombe, Pince & Company's Nurseries and Veitch's Royal Exotic Nurseries to the fore, alongside the city's well-manicured

Bathing costumes and bathing machines at Woolacombe beach, *c.* 1900. (Beaford Arts)

public parks and the exotic glasshouses and ornamental gardens at Streatham Hall and Bicton. In a passage probably included to occupy the high moral ground rather than solicit a personal visit, readers were informed that the Girls' Recreational Club and YWCA afforded the city's factory and shop girls a range of 'music, dressmaking, and cookery lessons', together with 'social pleasures and enjoyment'.

North Devon

The rugged north Devon coast had attracted visitors who were wealthy and hardy enough to cope with arduous and expensive journeys along ill-kempt roads long before the railways arrived. In 1830 the fastest, and very costly, mail coach from London took over twenty-eight hours to reach Barnstaple, whereas Exeter could be reached in nineteen hours. It was the paddle steamers that started to arrive from Wales and Bristol around that time that really boosted the fortunes of the north coast resorts, and notably Ilfracombe with its small but secure harbour.

These communities, or at least many of their influential citizens, shared Torquay's worries about mass invasions. In 1899 Ilfracombe banned Welsh excursion steamers on Sundays, thereby limiting the working-class crowds to bank holidays. Lynton and Lynmouth rejected proposals to build a better pier to allow steamships to tie up rather than oblige trippers to be ferried ashore in small boats. The canny owner of Clovelly forbade any overt commercialisation and, although easily accessible by sea, the striking village remained undeveloped but popular because it seemed frozen in time. At Woody Bay a conservative landowner was only too ready to bring developments to a crashing halt by purchasing the estate of a neighbour whose attempts at building a pier and hotels in the 1890s had collapsed in a spectacular case of fraud.

Nevertheless, the heady mix of rail travel, sea trips, dramatic scenery, places to explore and healthy exercise ensured increasing numbers of tourists poured in. Two Edwardian accounts of holidays highlight north Devon's allure. On 31 July 1907 a family of six boarded the 11.10 train from Waterloo, and arrived at Ilfracombe at 5.20 p.m. – 'an hour late', wrote one of the children in a record of their holiday. The family was energetic, and explored local towns, churches and museums, walked along the cliffs admiring the magnificent views and thought cream teas were admirable. They were, though, frequently caught in sudden downpours, 'which appears to be not uncommon in this part of the country'. The paddle steamer *Gwalia* took them to Clovelly where the awkward landing in little boats was a highlight rather than an annoyance. Less pleasing, though, was the boat trip to Lynmouth, as the *Normandy* was forty-five minutes late getting underway and took an hour to offload the trippers into two small boats.

One trip relied entirely on the railways. First they went to Barnstaple Junction where they joined a train to Bideford. After exploring the town they took another train to Westward Ho! and had a 'bracing' walk to Appledore. A ferry took them to Instow where they joined a train back to Barnstaple, which they still had the energy

Ilfracombe's harbour showing the pier, paddle steamers and, in the background,
superior clifftop hotels, *c.* 1906. (Devon & Exeter Institution)

to explore before catching an evening train to Ilfracombe. They attended church
on Sunday, as did Lily Phillips and her family when they holidayed with relations
in Ilfracombe in June 1910. Her account was more earnest in tone and content
as she sought to learn as much as possible about local life – the array of flowers,
vegetables, fruit and dairy produce in the market, the dialect of the children singing
in the church, the seemingly isolated farms tucked into the Chambercombe Valley,
the clarity of the tumbling streams, the ways in which cider and clotted cream were
made and the stories of ancient Celtic heroes.

Ilfracombe and north Devon was changing fast. During Easter 1904 the *Gwalia*,
Cambria, *Westonia* and *Albion* made repeated trips to Bristol, Cardiff and Barry to
bring thousands of trippers to Ilfracombe. During the August Bank Holiday in
1912 they landed 3,000 passengers from South Wales, the trains brought in hundreds more, the streets were packed and so were the numerous coastal cruises and
the performances of Maximes, the White Coons, the Jolly Boys and Mr Henry
Clay's concert parties. Rowdiness was not unknown; the town had lost its exclusivity, but profits were high. The heyday of the exclusive, expensive, but magnificently
furnished and serviced Ilfracombe Hotel that had opened in 1867 was already over.

Clergy repeatedly deprecated the impact of tourism on Sunday observance.
Motor cars and excursion trains came in for particular condemnation by the archdeacon of Barnstaple during his visitations in 1907, the former for enticing families
away from church attendance, and the latter for obliging so many employees to
work on Sundays. However, with fishing, boat building and seaborne trade in obvious decline, Barnstaple and Bideford badly needed alternative sources of revenue.

Cycles, Cars & Charabancs

Cyclists proliferated, as did cycling clubs, shops and hirers, and several local newspapers, notably the *Crediton Chronicle*, contained weekly advisory columns. They ranged from recommended circular rides through the countryside, the safest way to overtake horses and wagons, and the dangers associated with farm entrances, blind junctions and humpbacked bridges, to the multiple benefits of gears, the foolishness of purchasing cheap tyres, the ways to replace brake blocks, how to use puncture repair kits and the key features of fashionable new cycling outfits. Elliman's Universal Embrocation saw a ready market and regular advertisements pictured happy cyclists who might soon be suffering from sprains, bruises, cramp and stiff joints.

By 1914 the *Michelin Guide* thought it profitable enough to describe Devon from the perspective of the motorist. It gave a comprehensive listing of the sites, facilities and opening times of garages, the good quality hotels offering covered car parks, and the numerous hazards to be faced on various routes. The roads from Paignton to Totnes, Exeter to Chudleigh and Plympton to Plymouth were considered particularly poorly maintained and dangerous. As early as 1904 some carriage builders, such as Saunders of Winkleigh and Prideaux of Barnstaple, had diversified into motor car servicing and repairs, and also into building motor car bodies into which they fitted engines and controls that they had purchased as kits.

Devon's census for 1901 lists just four car drivers alongside 10,000 domestic and commercial coachmen, grooms, stable keepers, carters and carriers. Ten years later the horse-drawn occupations had declined to under 8,000, while domestic motor car drivers numbered 487 and commercial motor car, lorry, van and bus drivers and 'attendants' had risen to 1,641.

Saunders' Garage at Winkleigh and the assembly of motor cars from kits, *c.* 1910. (Beaford Arts)

A postcard sent in July 1909 – with two extra horses, a tourist excursion coach labours up Countisbury Hill near Lynmouth. (Author's collection)

Exploring was de rigueur, but not cheap. The Ilfracombe paddle steamers were often packed, and if the newspapers are to be believed sometimes over packed. The famous *Duke of Devonshire* and *Duchess of Devonshire* paddle steamers were often equally crowded for their trips to and from Torquay, Exmouth and Dartmouth. The coaching companies based in Ilfracombe, Tavistock, Bovey Tracey, Torquay and Newton Abbot laid on numerous daily excursions along the coast and onto the moors. Copp's of Ilfracombe ran eight different excursions most days in the 1901 season. With stops at hotels and tea rooms, they wound their various picturesque ways to Heddonsmouth Valley, Lynton, Lynmouth, Lee-on-Sea, Combe Martin, Watermouth Caves and Barnstaple. Prices were at 5/- and 2s 6d for a whole or half day trip respectively, and an additional shilling if one wanted a box seat. It was a costly family treat.

Holidaymakers could sometimes buy combined rail and coach tickets. In 1908 a typical, and possibly exhausting, Hellier & Lee's day excursion from Bovey Tracey Station went to Haytor Rocks, Saddle Tor, Rippon Tor, White Gate, Buckland Beacon, Hazel Hill, Ashburton and finished at Newton Abbot Station. Clearly awed by a similar experience, one Edwardian visitor's description highlighted the 'desolate scene of peat, morasse, hills and valleys', the isolated cottages glimmering in the drizzle, the frightening legends attached to the granite tors, the guns of the guards watching over gangs of Dartmoor prisoners at work, and the need for the passengers to assist the horses on the steeper hills by walking with them. The moors rarely failed to feed the Gothic imagination so beloved of many Edwardian visitors.

Devon's dramatic and varying landscape was popularised by many writers and artists as well as the compilers of guidebooks and the publicity departments of the railway companies who delighted in such exotic phrases as 'singular granite crags', 'brawling rivers' and 'exuberant vegetation'.

In 1872 the Reverend Sabine Baring-Gould (1834–1924) inherited the family estate at Lew Trenchard and spent the remainder of his long life preserving, and sometimes sanitising, local folk songs and publishing numerous works on Devon's colourful history and legends, such as *Dartmoor Idylls*, *Devonshire Characters & Strange Events* and *A Book of the West*. His eclectic mix of erudition, romance and myth proved very successful commercially.

Beginning in 1898 Eden Phillpotts (1862–1960) published a series of eighteen immensely popular novels centred upon Dartmoor villages, farms and families. The evocative descriptions of rural lives, aspirations, anxieties and tragedies set within the dramatic moorland context found ready markets and attracted numerous visitors to the easily recognisable places within the novels. From 1897 Ernest Henham, using the pen name John Trevena, published his popular Dartmoor trilogy – *Furze the Cruel*, *Heather* and *Granite* – whose titles, the author claimed, represented the locality's dominant qualities of cruelty, endurance and strength. These qualities are mirrored in the characters he places within the landscape, making the moor itself as alarming and as alluring as its imaginary inhabitants to Edwardian readers and visitors.

Industries: Changing Times & Fortunes

The 1899 Factory Inspectorate's report on Devon revealed a significant trend of which it heartily approved. Many small, and often antiquated, dairies, laundries, clothing workshops, grist mills, breweries and paper mills were closing down, unable to face the competition of larger firms in the locality with their heavy investment in steam-powered mechanisation. The report praised the fortuitous combination of their faster and more cost-effective means of production and the significant improvement in workers' conditions, health and job security. Tradition meant nothing to the authors if it smacked of inefficiency.

Foundries & Mills: Casualties & Survivors

There were many signs of the change. By far the largest and most prosperous foundry was Messrs Willey & Company in Haven Banks and James Street, Exeter, that manufactured everything for the gas industry from domestic meters and cookers to complete gasworks – of which it designed and built at least fifty, many for Devon towns. By 1903 the company had 1,000 employees and had diversified into electrical equipment. However, by then two of Tavistock's hitherto buoyant iron foundries had closed down during the rural recession, although a third struggled on through a succession of crises and owners.

Beaten by major suppliers, Rafarel's Iron Foundry in Barnstaple closed in 1902 after many years providing the town with drainpipes, manhole covers, lamp standards, park benches and kitchen stoves. A few small works, such as Finch Foundry at Sticklepath, near Okehampton, weathered the competition from the mass manufacturers of hand tools and continued to do business at local fairs and markets. A number of agricultural engineers, such as Huxtable's in Barnstaple, continued to make and mend larger farm machinery, although repair work became more common in the face of competition from major manufacturers outside the county.

During the eighteenth and early nineteenth century numerous paper mills were established along the rivers of Devon, mostly around Plymouth and the South Hams and along the Exe and Culm valleys. Historian Alfred Shorter has identified fifty-three, but records that only twelve survived into the Edwardian period and by 1914 only nine were left – Stowford Mill at Ivybridge, Kilbury at Buckfastleigh, Tuckenhay on the Dart, Trew's Weir and Head Weir at Exeter, Etherleigh Bridge Mill at Silverton, Higher King's Mill at Cullompton, and Hele and Stoke Canon. He confirms that the competition from larger and more cost-effective steam-powered mills outside the county together with foreign imports were largely to blame. The railways played an important part too, inasmuch as they assisted those mills adjacent to them while damaging the competitiveness of those far from them.

Men, women and children leaving the Heathcoat-Amory Lace Factory in Tiverton. On the right is the elementary school built by the Heathcoat-Amory family in the mid-1840s. (Author's collection)

An elderly female lace maker in Beer. This is probably a tourist photograph, *c.* 1910.
(Author's collection)

The Edwardian era saw several textile mills close down. The surviving mills in Ashburton and Buckfastleigh remained busy, though, producing serges and blankets, and there was also the multi-storied and highly mechanised Derby Lace Factory in Barnstaple and Heathcoat-Amory Lace Factory in Tiverton.

William Huxtable's Heathcoat Lace Factory Log Book provides plentiful evidence of the dangerous conditions, but also the consideration of the owners. The numerous workers suffering torn, crushed or lost fingers received several shillings a week compensation during their convalescence, boys and girls passing trade-related courses of study received small pay rises, and in 1906 a pension fund was started with the company matching a 2½–5 per cent contribution from workers. In a demonstration of loyalty 500 employees attended a public meeting in December 1909 to challenge accusations they had heard that the factory was a 'sweat shop'. There was a general feeling that the Liberal Heathcoat-Amory family was being traduced by malicious Conservative supporters during the bitter campaign leading up to the January 1910 general election.

A few hand lace makers survived in Honiton, the famous centre for this once exclusive product, and also in Branscombe, Beer, Seaton, Colyton and Torquay. They were, though, already more part of the tourist trade than the textile industry. John Yallop records forty-five small hand businesses in 1885, thirty-one in 1902 and twenty-eight in 1910, and the industry was entering a terminal decline that even late Victorian and Edwardian training classes aided by the technical education committee and the county council could not stem. The fame gained by Devon lace adorning the wedding dresses of Queen Victoria in 1840 and Princess Alexandra in 1863 belied the lace makers' interminable labour in cramped, ill-lit cottages for the pitifully small wages paid by local merchants.

The shirt and collar factory in South Molton was typical of the modern factories welcomed by the Factory Inspectorate. A 1909 report noted it employed eighty people and turned out 12,000 finished articles a week. The building was clean, well ventilated and lit brightly with electricity, the hours were 8.30 a.m. until 6.30 p.m. with an hour's break, and the wages rose to 18 shillings for adults – 'distinctly in advance of those earned in many other classes of female industry'. Shirts and collars were separate items at this time, and collar factories also existed in Bideford and Exeter.

William Vaughan's Glove Works at Torrington had been purpose built in 1884 even though it resembled a converted chapel. Just like other major families running local businesses, such as the Hamlyns of Buckfastleigh and the Heathcoat-Amorys of Tiverton, William Vaughan was actively involved in both local and county councils, served as a magistrate and was a generous benefactor of the local hospital and schools. By 1912, though, the factory was not working full time. In common with the glove factory at Pilton, overproduction had accompanied the Edwardian decline in wearing leather gloves as a fashion accessory rather than just for warmth.

Mines & Quarries: Casualties & Survivors

Mining and quarrying were changing too. Coasters unloading limestone had been common sights, and limestone quarrying had abounded across north Devon – notably at Landkey, Swimbridge, Filleigh, South Molton and Combe Martin – with hundreds of lime kilns to feed to ensure an adequate supply of quicklime to counter the notorious acidity of Devon's soils. In the 1890s the use of artificial manures began to bring this dangerous, but essential, industry to a close. It had all but ceased by 1914. Just thirty-nine lime burners were recorded in 1911.

Richard Edwards has recorded that a little slate had been quarried near Buckfastleigh on and off since the fourteenth century, but finally ceased in 1908. A little whetstone, used to sharpen tools, was still mined around Blackborough and Kentisbeare in east Devon, and Beer Caves, active since Roman times, were still being worked for the hard limestone blocks for prestigious building schemes. Devonshire clays remained commercially profitable for domestic use as well as export, with major potteries at Barnstaple, Bideford, and Bovey Tracey, glazed brick and tile works at Annery, near Monkleigh, terracotta ware at Watcombe and a thriving kaolin export trade at Lee Moor. The 1901 census shows 1,083 people were engaged in stone quarrying, eighty-seven in slate, and 642 in extracting clay, sand and gravel.

Miners with work tools and strings of candles at Ramsley Copper Mine, South Zeal.
It was probably the last working copper mine in the county. (Beaford Arts)

In 1901 the vast numbers of already abandoned shafts, pumping houses and assorted works were a testimony to the historic searches across Devon for tin, copper, iron, manganese, silver and silver-lead. Edwards notes that in 1907 just 94 tons of tin was produced, and long before then the vast reserve of copper at the Great Consul Mine near Tavistock was abandoned in the face of overseas competition and slumping prices, and except for Wheal Friendship near Mary Tavy, which reopened in 1907, even arsenic ore mining had ceased. Near South Zeal, Ramsley Copper Mine struggled on until 1909, but copper mining at Heasley Mill near North Molton was only remembered in the village's name, and the miners' cottages were crumbling to the ground.

Only the very high quality of iron ore found near Brixham ensured it was still mined there, while many other iron mines had closed as profits plummeted. One of the last to be abandoned was at Combe Martin in 1906.

Lignite was still mined at Bovey Tracey, and culm near Bideford; both were used as cheap if malodorous fuel, the former in pottery kilns and for firing bricks, and the latter for burning lime in the surviving working kilns. Bideford culm also was used to make black paint. Another paint, impeding the rusting of cast-iron plate, was made from ochre found at Brixham. The ochre was also mixed with tar, tallow and powdered oak bark to protect canvas sails from seawater. They were dyed red in order to save money rather than excite the emotions of visiting artists.

The Towns: Commodities, Consumerism & Competition

Gas & Electricity Wars

By 1901 most Devon towns possessed gasworks with their massive cylindrical holders and sooty acrid smell. Operated by private companies, some had been in existence for several decades. By 1901, though, electricity was becoming a fashionable commodity, not least because the upper classes considered gaslight too harsh for domestic comfort, and especially the female complexion. Perhaps the alacrity with which they limited gas supplies to their servants' quarters and installed electric generators for their own use had not gone unnoticed. There were many complaints, too, of gaslights behaving erratically because companies could not maintain adequate output.

Electricity could be purchased through generating companies in Exeter, Okehampton, Plymouth and Torquay from the 1880s and 1890s, but its relatively high cost meant it was slow to spread. It was in the Edwardian era that most Devon towns saw public buildings, including schools and hospitals, and a minority of homes supplied through local generators – among them Dartmouth in 1902, Totnes in 1905, Paignton in 1909 and Tavistock as late as 1914. After a slow start, by 1914 Plymouth's vast Prince Rock generator was powering the tramway, all major public buildings and tens of thousands of street lights – but only 1,750 homes.

Heavy advertising and promotions were the order of the day. Typically, in 1903 Ilfracombe's new electricity company announced a series of open days and 'One Month's Free Lighting'. Advertisements highlighted electricity's silence, cleanliness, lack of smell and, especially, its steady soft white light. In 1905 the *Mid Devon Advertiser* gave fulsome praise to the vastly enlarged Newton Union Electricity Works, to the new lights adorning public buildings and streets, and to the company's promotion of wondrous inventions such as electric fires, kettles, irons, ladies' hair curlers and fans. It omitted to say that gas was far cheaper, and that in 1902 the electricity company had undercut the gas company's street light charges, and accepted the temporary loss, in order to secure the council's contract.

But across the county gas companies fought back, with exhibits and demonstrations of economical gas fires, cookers and lamps at local trade exhibitions, and large advertisements in newspapers complete with arithmetical calculations showing that domestic gas lighting was one-tenth the cost of electricity. And in 1909 Willey's completed a huge new gas holder for the St Marychurch and Babbacombe Works in anticipation of a growth in demand.

Retail Wars
Another lengthy battle was being fought by independent traders in Devon towns against the Co-operative Societies attempting to establish footholds in them. In 1910 the 42nd Annual Co-operative Congress was held in Plymouth and a book was written charting the battle-scarred history of the borough's Co-operative Society as it sought to provide the essentials of life at the lowest possible price to working-class families.

Starting in 1859, it steadily expanded its membership through bulk purchases and highly competitive prices, and then purchased farms and established processing plants to control as many stages of production as possible. By 1910 Plymouth's Co-operative possessed twenty-six grocery shops, nine dairies, twenty-two butcheries, seven boot shops, eight boot factories, six drapery, furnishing and ironmongery departments, two tailoring and outfitting branches, five dressmaking and millinery departments, a flour mill, two farms totalling 330 acres, an abattoir, market gardens, a grocery and packing warehouse, a fleet of delivery wagons, large stables, a saddlery department, a large public restaurant and had 1,147 employees. It also dominated local supplies of domestic coal.

All accusations that dividends were an underhand way of undercutting other traders' prices, and that massive bulk purchases by the society would reduce independent retailers to poverty, were ignored. Nevertheless, the monolithic Plymouth Co-operative remained surrounded by hostile rumours that it had dangerous Socialist motives and sought nothing less than commercial dominance. Interestingly, in 1916 its own employees went on strike, as much against its authoritarian management as for higher wages, and they nearly brought the city's supply of vital domestic goods to a standstill.

A Plymouth Co-operative Society's mobile greengrocery van. (Devon & Exeter Institution)

The 1910 *Congress Book* catalogued other Co-operative Societies in Devon. Notable successes were in Buckfastleigh, Chudleigh, Dartmouth, Exmouth, Kingswear, Newton Abbot, Okehampton, Sidmouth and Teignmouth. In Exeter, though, the grocery trade in the city united to challenge the Society and although its growth was severely retarded, members' loyalty saved it from collapse. In 1903 the Sheriff of Exeter had very publicly 'regretted' the dire threat the Co-operative posed to at least fifteen independent retailers. Similarly well-targeted actions, as well as some mismanagement, frustrated the growth of Torquay, Ottery St Mary, Paignton, Holsworthy and Brixham Societies, and succeeded in forcing Kingsbridge Society to close.

High Streets
Edwardian high streets were crowded and noisy places, not least because shops were fully stocked with goods from across the world and companies knew the value of special discounts, promotions and constant advertising in newspapers, magazines and on hoardings. Large plate-glass windows were growing in number and store advertisements avidly encouraged the new hobby of window gazing.

Consumerism was rife, and Christmas advertisements in particular reveal the huge range of goods on offer. In Newton Abbot in December 1905 Christie & Bennet advertised a range of cameras and optics; Missenden's, a host of seasonal fancy goods; Bartlett's, novelty presents and confectionary; Coomes', assorted cigars, cigarettes, pipes and tobacco; Townshend & Brealey's advertised crystallised fruits, nuts, chocolates, biscuits and cheeses; and Greenslade's offered wines and spirits. Leemon's promoted ladies' accessories, perfumes and jewellery, while Waddington's displayed the latest bicycles and motor accessories; Ford's, a range of 'prime' meat and poultry; Barnes', a host of patent medicines; Harley's, a plethora of photo frames, clocks, rings, chains, match and cigar boxes, brooches and lockets, and Looman Bawdon's advertised a wide range of furs, linen, children's clothes and servants' uniforms. At Christmas Walton's in Exeter advertised an array of toys – including boxes of soldiers, wooden railway trains, dressed dolls, sets of bricks, tea sets, magic lanterns, rocking horses and skittles. All pockets were targeted, as each range of toys varied from a few pence to several shillings in price depending on quality and size.

Food prices remained stable but high enough, for example, to oblige Exeter City Council's 270 manual workers, who earned £1 a week, to budget very carefully. In January 1902, H. W. Thorne of Tiverton advertised 'good family teas' for between 1*s* 2*d* and 1*s* 6*d* per pound and superior Mazawattee and Blue Cross blends for between 1*s* 6*d* and 2/-. Oranges were eighteen for 6*d*, prunes were 6*d* per pound, sultanas cost between 5*d* and 7*d*, muscatels were 3*d* and walnuts 4*d* to 5*d*. 'Best Cheddar' was 6½*d* per pound, fat bacon was 6*d*, lean bacon was 7*d*, smoked picnic ham cost 5½*d*, lard 6½*d* and Lyle's syrup was 6½*d* for a 2lb tin. Biscuits varied according to quality and ingredients, from 3*d* to 1*s* 3*d* per pound, white sugar varied according to its 'whiteness', from 1½*d* to 2½*d*, the 'best' lump sugar was 3*d* per pound and the ordinary variety 2½*d*. Vegetables were cheap throughout the era, with turnips and carrots around 1½*d* 'a bunch' and potatoes costing 1/- for

'Old Town Street', Plymouth, showing the tramway, street lights and
plate-glass shop window displays. (Author's collection)

20lb at markets, although meat was expensive, with beef and mutton around 8*d* or 9*d* a lb, rabbits at 8*d* to 10*d* each and chickens around 5/- a pair. No wonder urban back gardens often possessed chicken runs and rabbit hutches.

Chemists were important, then as now, and packed with products. In an age when doctors' bills were to be feared and advertising standards non-existent, the purveyors of patent medicines played fast and loose with people's fears regarding their health. Among numerous inflated claims, Bile Beans were held to cure constipation, indigestion, piles, rheumatism, flatulence and headaches, Holloways' Ointment and Pills cured diarrhoea, dysentery and cholera, Eade's Pills cured gout, rheumatism, sciatica and lumbago, and Dr Davis's 'Famous Pills' were 'the best known remedy for anaemia, giddiness, fullness and swelling after meals, loss of appetite, hysteria, palpitation of the heart, debility, depression, weakness, irregularity, and all female ailments'. Zam-Buk was an ointment that could be applied everywhere for virtually anything. 'Its healing property is as mysterious as it is far-reaching', advertisements asserted, and was unequalled 'for eczema, ulcers, bad legs, piles, ringworm, psoriasis, "chaps", chilblains, poisoned wounds, pimples, blotches, burns, scalds, cuts and bruises'. And then they added, 'Zam-Buk is also splendid for rheumatism, sore throat and cold in the head.'

Modernisation and enhanced consumerism brought problems. Letters, articles and court cases reveal the dangers posed by motor cars, lorries and wagons, the obstruction and noise caused by street traders and the unpredictable behaviour of animals being driven to markets which were still often held in the centre of country towns.

Road signs were rare and, although the Edwardian era saw the beginning of prosecutions for dangerous driving, the absence of legislation governing and defining road use made convictions difficult. Two early cases failed in Tiverton because no one really knew how to define 'reckless'. In 1912, though, a fine was imposed on a driver dodging in and out of carts strung along Exeter's high street at 14–16mph.

Also in that year, the constant complaints of litter and obstruction finally obliged the city council to ban carts plastered with advertisements and make it an offence to throw 'orange peels, banana skins or any other dangerous substances', notably bottles and broken glass, in the streets. Fearing the repercussions of limiting commerce, it deferred a decision on banning the traditional shouting, ringing of bells, banging of gongs and 'other noisey instruments' that street traders used to attract customers. Writing in 1952, Eric Delderfield recalled the organ grinder, the one-man band, the handcarts selling vegetables, fish, hot chestnuts, faggots and ice cream, and the shouts of the chair mender, rag and bone man and knife-grinder on the streets of late Victorian and Edwardian Exmouth.

Exeter's annual Cart Horse Parade was popular, and evidence of the continuing importance of horse power throughout the period. It was held first in 1896 when influential female figures such as Lady Rosalind Northcote, Mrs Thornton West,

Lady Audrey Buller and Lady Iddesleigh sought to enhance concern for, and pride in, the well-being of working horses – no doubt because so many were obviously in poor condition. The idea spread to other local towns and proved immensely popular. Entries were numerous, classes were carefully divided into urban and rural trades, and medals awarded to winners and runners-up. Nevertheless, worn out and neglected working horses remained common sights, although the RSPCA was active in seeking prosecutions. In just a few months in 1907 a Barnstaple baker was fined for working a horse whose back was covered in festering sores, a second trader there was convicted of working a horse with chronic ringworm, and a haulier was fined for making a lame horse pull a wagon loaded with a ton of timber.

Worries About Improvements

Better civic amenities and visitor attractions became greater priorities for urban councils, as succeeding editions of guidebooks reveal. Plymouth changed dramatically, as its historians have recorded. By 1901 its lamentable public health record had improved, and its epidemics became less frequent and less serious as the later Victorians pursued various drainage schemes, constructed a Dartmoor reservoir, founded more hospitals and supportive charities, imposed controls on market trading, made attempts to improve housing by cajoling landlords to renovate slum properties and built the first council houses, in Laira Road, in 1896.

The nineteenth century also saw the opening of Plymouth's large library, museum and art gallery in imposing pseudo-Classical style, and a Gothic civic centre built alongside the Guildhall. In 1898, however, after several decades of heady progress at great public expense, a rate rising to 7/- proved too much for voters and they rejected the 'progressive' majority on Plymouth Corporation, ushering in a lengthy period of more cost-conscious Edwardian Conservatism.

Probably the greatest achievement of this period was in 1914 when the 'Three Towns' of East Stonehouse, Devonport and Plymouth became the single Borough of Plymouth, embracing 214,000 people and finally ending the tiresomeness and expense of separation and competition. This pleased local commanding officers who were fed up with dealing with three often warring authorities, and brought together common interests in rail developments, public health and education.

In 1914 Exeter, too, considered costly city improvements. That March, T. H. Mawson, a noted town planner, submitted a radical long-term project for the easing of congestion, the creation of new vistas, the public enhancement of the city's status and the encouragement of tourism, especially, he said, from North America. He envisaged much of Queen Street becoming 'a great municipal centre' sited within ornamental gardens. Several narrow city crossroads would become spacious circuses, and further ancient buildings would be demolished to create wide walkways between the shopping centre and the cathedral green. It attracted much attention, largely for its likely cost and 'foreign appearance' rather than the

New Queen Street: part of T. H. Mawson's plans for the redevelopment of Exeter city centre.
(Devon & Exeter Institution)

widespread demolition of ancient properties, but was soon overtaken by world events and forgotten.

Perhaps the most obvious legacy of late Victorian and Edwardian builders is the vast array of speculative housing in most Devon towns. Long roads of terraced properties, some plain and flat fronted, others adorned with patterned brickwork and bay windows, stretched along the outskirts of most towns or formed dense estates serviced with narrow roads. Shorter roads contained a sprinkling of more highly decorated detached or semi-detached 'villas'. In 1902 the *North Devon Journal* praised the recent efforts of several developers in providing Barnstaple with around 200 new houses, many of them modest but cheap. The medical officer of health was less sanguine, asserting that only 'superior artisans' could hope to afford any; ordinary workmen earning around 16/– a week would still have to make do with the old 'back to backs' with two rooms upstairs and two downstairs.

Throughout the era local councils were wracked by bitter rows over the extent of slum courtyards and abject poverty, and the need to invest in council-controlled building projects. Some councillors, as in Exeter, minimised the problems or worried the authority would never get its investment back in rents, some thought private initiatives would resolve everything, and others believed the poor were content and would not, or could not, afford anything better.

Modest starts were made, though. In Exeter a gift of free land by H. A. Willey persuaded the city council to build forty-two homes in Isca Road between 1904 and 1907 with weekly rents of 4s 9d. And in Tiverton Mayor Gregory was proud that by 1914 nineteen well-constructed council houses could be let, with rents between 5s 3d and 5s 9d.

3

INTERWOVEN LIVES
The Great Estates & Their Families

❧ *The Hierarchy* ❧

In 1907 an expensive leather-bound volume appeared with photographs and biographies of several hundred men, but no women, whom the publisher William Mates thought dominated Devon's social, spiritual, political and economic life. More than 100 additional photographs pictured the impressive ancient and modern mansions of the more celebrated families – the aristocrats and country gentry – and many pages were devoted to the county's major rural leisure occupation of hunting.

Among the long-established Devon noble families with estates reckoned in tens of thousands of acres were the Earl of Devon at Powderham; Earl Fortescue at Castle Hill; Lord Clifford at Ugbrooke; Lord Clinton at Heanton Satchville and Bicton; and Lord Poltimore at Poltimore and North Molton. Others, with fewer acres, were the Earl of Iddesleigh at Pynes, near Exeter; Viscount Exmouth at Cantonteign; Lord Seaton at Beechwood, Plympton; Lord Churston at Lupton, Churston Ferrers; and Lord Coleridge at The Chanter's House, Ottery St Mary.

Just in case readers failed to appreciate the nuances of the social hierarchy, the chapters were in a specific order with pictures and descriptions of gradually diminishing size. The aristocracy, bishops and Members of Parliament were honoured with a whole page each, followed by 'county families' and 'country gentry' at two to a page, and then selected senior army and navy officers, clergy, men of business and major farmers at three a page. There were images of rolling hills and moorland streams, the gathering of hunts, picturesque churches and expansive manicured gardens, but not of arduous agricultural occupations or the inelegant trappings of urban industry and commerce.

Among the old 'county families' was Sir Thomas Acland, the 12th baronet, of Killerton – ex-MP, deputy lieutenant of Devon, senior officer in the yeomanry, county alderman and chairman of the education committee. Colonel Lucius Cary of Torre Abbey was another in this category, and his biography highlights his professional military career, especially in the Ashanti Campaign, and his prominence in Torbay institutions, notably its hospital. A third example was Richard Harold St Maur of Stover, near Newton Abbot, the illegitimate son of the heir to the Duke of Somerset, who served in Natal as a captain in the 1st Devon Imperial Yeomanry, and was also master of the South Devon Foxhounds. The book ignored Miss Rosalie Chichester, the redoubtable chatelaine of Arlington Court and 5,000 acres of north Devon, although several male Chichesters with lesser Devon estates *are* included.

The gentry were a little lower in Mates' scale, usually because they were relative newcomers to the county. They included John S. C. Davies of Ebberly House, Roborough, a retired senior Indian Civil Service official who was soon to administer and develop Devon's new VAD network, and Captain Ernest Morrison-Bell of Pitt House, Torquay, who served in the 9th Lancers in the Boer War and became a big game hunter before election as Mid Devon's stridently Conservative MP in 1908. Sir John Heathcoat-Amory, the owner of Tiverton Lace Factory, also appears in this section, no doubt because his mid-Victorian mansion, Knightshayes, its accompanying estate, and his total commitment to the gentlemanly sports of stag and fox hunting had lifted him out of the 'men of business' section. Not surprisingly, hunting, shooting and fishing were interests shared by numerous figures in these sections of the book.

At first sight the book suggests a county overwhelmingly given over to a myriad of country estates – some vast, some modest – with beautifully sited mansions at their social and economic centres. There is some truth in this suggestion, but whether consciously or not (and probably not) William Mates reveals another world beyond this apparently wealthy and leisured elite. The lengthy biographies accorded the aristocracy and gentry reveal their heavy involvement in agriculture, politics and commerce as well as the efficient administration of county and local affairs as JPs, county aldermen and councillors, militia and yeomanry officers and chairmen of key committees. However, just as the ranks of the aristocracy shaded off into the ranks of the gentry, so they shaded off into a host of other local dignitaries – gentlemen farmers, beneficed clergy and businessmen whose status, posts and property assured them of a marked degree of local authority and influence.

Mates honoured one squire with pride of place before all other entries. General Sir Redvers Buller VC had been a career soldier but he was also the popular squire of Downes. In 1900, his public reputation was in tatters, except in Devon where it soared. In 1905, he and his wife had the satisfaction of attending the unveiling of an imposing statue on the Crediton Road in Exeter of the general on horseback high above a granite plinth, tellingly inscribed, 'He saved Natal',

Crowds attend the unveiling of the statue of Sir Redvers Buller in Exeter
on 6 September 1905. (Author's collection)

and knowing that 50,000 subscriptions had been received. The people of Crediton
were a little aggrieved that the figure was facing the city, not the way home to
Downes. Crediton, though, had its moment of glory in 1908 when Buller died
and thousands watched units from all the regiments associated with him in South
Africa escort his coffin to the parish church.

◌◌ *The Great Houses: Fittings, Features & Fires* ◌◌

Vacant estates were advertised all the time as owners moved away, changed their
investment priorities, consolidated their holdings, became bankrupt or died. And
sales catalogues were always at pains to ensure the service facilities and lifestyle
opportunities were described as lavishly as the main family rooms. The one advertising Redworth, on the River Dart outside Totnes, in 1901 was typical. Although
the numerous bedrooms, wood-panelled reception rooms and service facilities
are clearly listed, it is the estate's potential contribution to the owner's luxurious
lifestyle, and especially country sports, that are highlighted in this age of conspicuous consumption. Among its delights were a billiard room, 'capital' wine and beer
cellarage, locally generated gas and electricity supplies, dog kennels, 'conveniently
placed' stabling along with several stalls, loose boxes, coach houses and staff living
accommodation, tennis courts and 'a productive and fully-stocked kitchen garden,
peach house, vinery, tomato house, stove house, cucumber and melon house (all
heated), [and] a range of forcing pits'. Yachting, hunting, fishing and shooting were

readily accessible, and the house was surrounded by the usual 'pleasure grounds' with their 'choice conifers', 'wide lawns' and 'broad gravelled terrace'.

Where furniture and fittings were sold with the houses they reveal both the necessities and luxuries of the times. The list for Timewell House outside Morebath in 1903 is typical. The bedrooms came complete with heavy curtain poles and thick curtains, huge iron bedsteads with spring and hair mattresses, elaborate cane chairs, fire guards and tongs, and dark mahogany washstands, wardrobes, chests of drawers, tables and swing mirrors. Each one possessed its own bedpans and slop pails. A plethora of china vases and ornaments, small tables, brass candlesticks and elaborately framed pictures and mirrors adorned the drawing and dining rooms. The service quarters possessed an array of china, glasses and cutlery for every dish and occasion, along with washtubs and mangles, clothes horses and hot irons, dressers and cupboards, tables and trays, a Dutch oven with jacks, fenders and fire irons, bread pans and cheese stands, coffee mill, scales and weights, assorted ladles, whisks and tongs, and there were properly fitted out rooms for fruit, game and dairy produce.

In an age of log and coal fires, assorted cooking ranges, candles and early electrical wiring, fire was a great danger. Not all estates possessed fire engines, let alone efficient ones, and most town machines were also underpowered both in terms of horsepower and water pressure to respond effectively to calls, whether coming via a newly installed telephone or a breathless rider on horseback from several miles away.

One afternoon in September 1906 the Quicke family found their ancient mansion in Newton St Cryes had caught fire. Mounted servants were sent to the fire stations in Exeter and Crediton, but the inevitable time delay, the prevailing breeze and the distance from the nearest water supply in the river meant much of the house was destroyed. Fortunately, with the help of servants, police and villagers, the family rescued some of the valuable furniture, pictures, jewellery and china.

In August 1908 Mr Carslake was talking to a gardener at Darracombe, his mansion at Highweek, Newton Abbot, when he noticed smoke billowing from the kitchen quarter. No one was in there at the time. A catalogue of mishaps – the new address of the fire station delaying the gardener in alerting the fire brigade, followed by further delays in gathering the men and finding a lost standpipe connection, compounded by the inadequate pressure from the mains and a strong wind – ensured the house was engulfed in flames and totally destroyed. 'The three maid servants lost everything, save the clothes they were wearing', lamented the local newspaper, and it trusted that Newton Abbot Borough Council would reconsider its refusal to invest in a steam-powered fire engine.

That November, the Waldron family at Bradfield was luckier. When the butler interrupted a house party gathered in the library to announce the house was on fire the men and servants rushed to the scene and stemmed the blaze with buckets of water until the fire engines arrived from Tiverton and Cullompton. The telephone connection had worked, and just a couple of rooms were damaged.

Hollerday House outside Lynton was built in 1890 and lavishly decorated and furnished by George Newnes, whose fortune had been made from popular magazines such as *Tit-Bits, Country Life* and serialising Sherlock Holmes stories in the *Strand Magazine*. He was a great benefactor of Lynton, paying for its town hall, cricket pavilion and Congregational chapel. He died in 1910 just as his company's fortunes declined. Hollerday was deserted, and in 1913 the suffragettes were suspected of starting the fire that destroyed the greater part of the short-lived mansion upon which its creator had spent so much time and money.

The Great House & the Community

Mansion grounds were often the scenes of community events. Local squadrons of the Volunteer cavalry and infantry sometimes camped in them and, in 1900 at Sir John Kennaway's Escot, near Ottery St Mary, thousands watched them engage in a mock battle defending the LSWR railway near Feniton from attack.

House grounds were often the venues for parties of Sunday school children, frequently numbered in their hundreds, enjoying the games and teas associated with their annual 'treats'. Some elementary schools were lucky enough to enjoy similar outings paid for by the 'big house'. Sir Edmund de la Pole, for example, welcomed Seaton's school to Shute from time to time.

Village 'at homes' were common. One afternoon in 1901 the local Volunteers' band accompanied the school children from Poltimore and Huxham as they marched to meet Lord and Lady Poltimore, and then mingled in the grounds with their families and other estate workers, tenants and parishioners during an 'at home' complete with tea, races, cricket, Aunt Sally, swings and dancing.

Village sporting events often took place on estate fields and, among many examples, the Honourable Mark Rolle provided a cricket ground at Stevenstone for the local team and also donated the tea at home matches. Knightshayes, too, had its own cricket ground, not least because several young Amory men at this time enjoyed playing. In August 1905 the *Crediton Chronicle* recorded their victory over Lionel Walrond's team from Bradfield, together with the additional illustrious names of Fortescue, Acland-Troyte, Lord Eliot and the Honourable Gerald Legge adorning their teams. A few days later Knightshayes played and lost to Bicton.

Charities could soar in both status and funds from the favour of wealthy families and the fetes and social gatherings they put on for their benefit. The historian of Payhembury notes Miss Gwen Venn's support of Ottery St Mary's cottage hospital through such events, with their sale of homemade goods and garden produce. She was, it is said, 'a very gracious old lady, aristocratic but kindly in manner'. Earl Fortescue's deer park at Castle Hill hosted the East & West Buckland

A garden party at Fremington House, 30 June 1909. (Beaford Arts)

Cottage and Garden Show and the Annual Festival of the Filleigh Branch of the National Deposit Friendly Society, as well as the village sports days. Castle Hill itself was thrown open most years for guided tours in aid of Barnstaple Infirmary. The Heathcoat-Amorys opened Knightshayes to help Tiverton Hospital, and Lady Churston and her daughters were the prime movers behind the annual fetes at Lupton for Brixham Hospital. The Tiverton Girls' Friendly Society cel-ebrated its annual festival at Mr and Mrs (later Sir Edwin and Lady) Dunning's Stoodleigh Court.

Christmas remained a traditional time for charitable acts. In 1901, for example, the Earl of Portsmouth at Eggesford, 'with his usual kindness', said the *Devon & Exeter Gazette*, donated £12 to the Chawleigh and Cheldon Clothing Club. Mr Moulton Barrett gave a joint of beef to every poor family in Chawleigh, the Honourable Mark Rolle of Stevenstone gave every employee one, and so did Sir Redvers Buller at Downes and Miss Yeo, the 'lady of the manor' at Fremington. No doubt other wealthy families did much the same.

Influential families rarely hesitated to influence others. In October 1900 the vicar of Seaton wrote a respectful description in his parish magazine of Lady Peek's 'kindness' in bringing women from Rousdon, Colyton, Beer and Seaton together to learn more about the Mothers' Union, with particular regard to its teachings on the training of children 'in habits of trustfulness, obedience, kindness to one another, and prayer'. In 1903 another deferential entry in the magazine noted

Lady Peek's talk at the union to give 'those who were so fortunate as to be present some wise and sympathetic and kindly counsels'. Lady Peek also became closely involved with the voluntary Devon Nursing Association alongside compatriots from the Acland, Coleridge, Courtenay, Fortescue, Fursdon and Iddesleigh families as they strove to increase the numbers of trained nurses and midwives in hospitals and local communities. The status and wide-ranging connections of these women ensured their voices were heard.

The late Victorian restoration of many Devon parish churches owed much to the injection of funds by wealthy local residents, and the habit lingered into the Edwardian era. Sir Henry Peek, for example, restored Rousdon church. In April 1905, St Andrew's parish church in Moretonhampstead was reopened after a complete restoration paid for by Frederick Smith, MP for Westminster (later 2nd Viscount Hambleden), of the famous book and stationery store family, W. H. Smith. The family was soon to reside, at least for some weeks each year, in the vast new manor house they were building at North Bovey.

Equally interesting to some influential worshippers were the religious practices of local Church of England clergy. In November 1905 a deputation led by Earl Fortescue, Lord Poltimore and Sir Thomas Acland presented a petition to Dr Archibald Robertson, Bishop of Exeter, signed by 600 patrons of livings, county councillors, churchwardens and members of the Diocesan Synod against 'the disorders and irregularities' prevalent in some parishes in the diocese. Discomfited by this high-profile opposition to Anglican incumbents straying too close to Roman Catholicism and stung by the implicit criticism of his inaction, the bishop took refuge in a policy of tolerating a 'divergence' of ceremonial practice as long as it remained 'within the limits of the Book of Common Prayer' – which the petitioners clearly thought in some churches it did not.

A high-profile case had been 'exposed' at St John's church in Bovey Tracey that summer when a *Mid Devon Advertiser* reporter, no doubt well-primed, saw images of the Virgin Mary and Christ Crucified adorned with flowers and witnessed a High Mass, complete with numerous tall candles, the priest in a gold-embroidered cope and acolytes in cassocks and Roman cottas swinging thuribles. The militant Protestant Reform Society was outraged and, in 1907, secured extensive publicity for its accusations that 'Popish' vestments were worn in sixty-five Anglican churches within the Diocese of Exeter, their services had moved illegally out of the Anglican 'fold', and the bishop was failing to discipline errant priests. It warned of 'the disastrous effect … Roman doctrines and practices would have upon the character and morals of the nation.' A Reform Society meeting in Newton Abbot specifically targeted the 'offences' perpetrated at St Paul's there. Controversy raged on, notably around St Mary Magdalene's in Barnstaple in 1906 and All Saints in Plymouth in 1914, but episcopal cautions and evangelical outrage failed to discourage the Anglo-Catholic clergy and their devoted congregations.

◑ *Gentlemanly Sports* ◐

Devon's countryside abounded with gentlemanly sports. Game birds were slaughtered in their thousands during house parties specially invited in the season, and Devon's newspapers revelled in news of the frequent deer, fox and otter hunts. The Earls Fortescue were keen huntsmen, generally with the Devon & Somerset Staghounds, and for a time the Honourable Mark Rolle was actively involved in their North Devon and Exmoor hunts. Around the turn of the century the proliferation of deer led to the Barnstaple and Tiverton packs being established, the latter under Sir John Heathcoat-Amory (1829–1914). The former did not last long, largely due to the determined opposition, to the point of threatening court action to transgressors, of Miss Rosalie Chichester, the owner of the extensive Arlington Court estate, to hunting on her land.

Elsewhere, local newspapers gave notice of the regular meets, usually three or four a week in the season, and published reports of the more dramatic kills or escapes, lavishing praise on the skill of both the leading huntsmen and the animals providing them with such pleasure. The annual hunt dinners and formal presentations were lavish affairs attended by great landowners, squires, gentlemen farmers and clergy.

Sir John Heathcoat-Amory and his son Ian, later the 2nd Baronet, hunted regularly and any dramatic forays were avidly reported. For example, in April 1908 the hunt met at West Worlington and pursued a stag through Burridge Wood to Hansford and Toneyfield, then across the Taw where it backtracked to Burridge

The Honourable Mark Rolle's foxhounds meet at Stevenstone House, 2 November 1905.
(Beaford Arts)

and was hotly pursued down the Little Dart Valley towards Chawleigh and then Park Mill at Chulmleigh. Leaping from one field to another it crossed the river to Dartridge, and went through the grounds of Leigh House towards Horridge before doubling back to head for Rashleigh. It took to the water again where, after another half a mile, the hounds seized it. The *South Molton Gazette* noted the usual appreciative crowd had followed the hunt, and concluded, 'Good sport has resulted from each meet in this neighbourhood this season'. In March 1910 Ian Heathcoat-Amory took his father's hounds by train to Okehampton where a particularly fine stag had been observed. Two hundred horsemen and 1,000 followers in cars, on bicycles and on foot gathered for the chase. The stag led them for 17 miles and nearly two hours around Inwardleigh, Hatherleigh, Meeth and back towards Okehampton before the hunt, not the stag, gave up. The report happily concluded, 'It is believed the stag will make its way back to its old lair to provide another day's hunt.' Afterwards, members of the hunt enjoyed a hearty dinner with numerous toasts, not least to the king, the master of the hunt and the deer.

Fox hunting was endemic in Devon, with twelve large packs spread across the county. In January 1913 the *Crediton Chronicle* reprinted a *Sporting Life* eulogy of the Tiverton Hunt, saying, 'they are men who know how to get the maximum of pleasure out of their hunting, and are careful to do the minimum of damage to the farmers'. It added that most local farmers were huntsmen, 'men respected and liked by their neighbours, men of a type that England could do with more of'. In the same edition, the *Chronicle* described the Silverton Foxhounds pursuing their prey in an article similar to many others throughout the period. 'A real good fox was found by the banks of the River Culm' and the hounds chased him over Bradninch Common, down and along the valley to Chapelhaies, across the Silverton road nearly to Dorweeke, and then across streams and fields to Exeland. After 7 miles and seventy-five minutes of pursuit the hounds 'pulled down an old dog fox in the open'. It was the twenty-sixth kill in twenty-one days.

Some meets were less exciting for the human participants, as when the East Devon Foxhounds caught a fox 'napping'. 'Within fifty or sixty yards he was caught, and had to pay the penalty of his unwatchfulness. It was nobody's fault but his own, yet much to be deplored.' In 1913 Bideford's Public Rooms were adorned with fifty mounted 'masks and brushes' to add atmosphere to Stevenstone Hunt's New Year's Eve Ball attended by the Fortescues, Clintons and local clergy, army officers and gentlemen farmers.

Otter hunts provided excitement too, and most rivers had a pack somewhere along their freshwater length. In August 1900 the Cheriton Hounds trailed a dog otter along the Taw to a mill leat just below a weir. It became 'too hot for the otter, who was forced to leave this holt for the river. Here, in a fairly deep pool, it showed some excellent sport in full view of the whole field, once getting a hound under water.' It took half an hour to kill it. During the same hunt, another otter was luckier and escaped over the weir and through a hedge. A few years later, in 1904, the Culmstock Hounds trapped a large otter in deep water on the Coly when suddenly it charged the ring of men 'nearly upsetting one man and went through', but 'the hounds were too quick for him'. Such tales regularly filled newspaper columns, and also several books celebrating the history of particular packs.

☙ *Garden Parties* ❧

Garden parties were de rigueur. For one and a half hours one August day in 1908 'long lines of carriages and motor cars', some of which had collected guests from Tiverton and Cullompton railway stations, 'filed up the stately avenue of oaks' leading to Bradfield House and 'set down guests at the main entrance where they were received by the Hon. Lionel and Mrs Waldron' and then passed through into the Italian garden. The list of those invited filled a complete column in the *South Molton Gazette*.

Exactly a year earlier, Mr and Mrs Harold St Maur had held an even more exalted garden party at Stover. The rapturous description in the *Mid Devon Times* was typical of reports on such grand occasions across the county:

> For an hour or so the usually quiet and secluded drives and avenues leading from different parts of the neighbourhood through the picturesque estate to the house had quite an animated appearance as the well-horsed equipages and smart motors passed to and fro. The large proportion of the latter was very noticeable, showing how general this new form of locomotion has become.

Bradfield House near Uffculme, east Devon, *c.* 1907, with visitors arriving and lanterns on the terrace. (Devon & Exeter Institution)

The hostess, 'charmingly dressed in brown, received her guests on the lawn', and they included numerous titled families, including the Earl of Devon and other Courtenay family members, the Poltimores, Cliffords, Churstons, Iddesleighs and Exmouths, and a number of knights and their ladies, notably General Sir Redvers and Lady Buller, and many notable but untitled guests such General Kekewich, the defender of Kimberley in the Boer War. Probably to the chagrin of many unmentioned guests, the list tails off with just 'etc.' 'Afternoon tea was provided al fresco on the lawn', and all the fruit on the tables had been grown in the estate's kitchen garden and greenhouses. The St Maurs' grapes, peaches and apples had won first prizes at Taunton Show the previous week. Golf, croquet and bowls competitions ran during the afternoon, with silver sugar tongs, trays and table centres being awarded to the winners. Guests also:

> … spent an enjoyable time in wandering about the beautiful grounds, inspecting the greenhouses, etc., the host pointing out with pardonable pride the very picturesque rock Alpine garden, with the beautiful arrangement of mountain scenery in miniature, streams splashing gently through the cool rocky grottoes, and ponds with their beautiful water lilies … Immediately above them is the large lawn, from which a magnificent panorama of moorland scenery is viewed, and on which there are the well-appointed croquet and tennis lawns.

Stover, near Newton Abbot, *c.* 1907. (Devon & Exeter Institution)

Large gatherings sometimes had an avowed political agenda and cut across the social classes. The 2nd Lord Poltimore (1837–1908) was a devoted Liberal for much of his life, but by Edwardian times he had broken with them over Irish Home Rule and become an avid Unionist and Conservative. In May 1908 his obituary in the *North Devon Journal* noted his shift of allegiance:

> His close association with the affairs of the Primrose League brought him into more intimate relationship with his party, and at times stirred him into quite unwonted activity, particularly when the League held any demonstrations. The Devonshire habitations, and especially those in the vicinity of Exeter, never sought his assistance in vain, and the knights and dames of that organisation have more than once carried out most successful fetes in his beautiful park, which specially lent itself, by reason of its spacious character and picturesque surroundings to this form of holiday-making and propagandist work.

Frederick Bampfylde, 2nd Baron Poltimore (1837–1908), deputy lord lieutenant, JP, Devon County Council alderman, master of foxhounds and president of Exeter & County Hospital and Barnstaple Infirmary. (Devon & Exeter Institution)

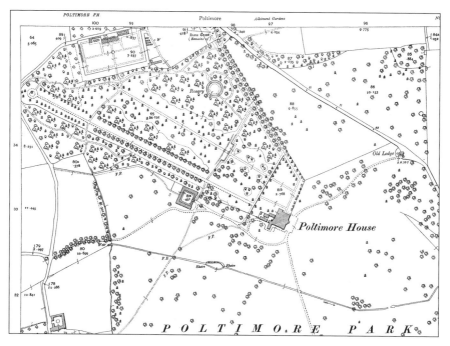

OS map of Poltimore House and its pleasure and kitchen gardens, 1905.
(Devon & Exeter Institution)

The ladies' hat stall at Hatherleigh Conservative Fete, July 1909. (Beaford Arts)

NOTICES.

RECREATION GROUND, NEWTON — ABBOT. —

WHIT-MONDAY, 20th MAY.

MID-DEVON
LIBERAL CLUB FETE,

**Horse Jumping Competitions,
Pony Races,
Driving Competition,
Cart Horse Parade,
and Foot Events.**

PRIZES £25 IN VALUE.

PROGRAMME OF EVENTS:—

Horse Jumping Competition (for horses that have never won a 3rd prize). Entrance fee 1s., post entries 2s.

Ditto 15 h.h. and under, ditto.

Pony Race (one mile), 14 h.h. and under, for ponies that have never won a first prize.

Ditto, any height (1½ mile).

Cart Horse Parade.

Driving Competition, for best Harness Horse.

Basket and Potato Race.

Tradesmen's Turn-out (dray horses excepted) for cleanest horse, vehicle, and harness; vehicles to bear owner's name.

FOOT EVENTS:

220 yards Boys' Flat Race (under 12 years of age).

440 yards ditto (under 15).

Entries close to the Secretary on Wednesday, 15th May. The Secretary will be in attendance at the Club each evening prior to this date, between the hours of 8 and 9 p.m., for receiving entries.

Prizes will be distributed by Mrs S. Hacker, who will be supported by H. T. Eve, Esq., K.C., M.P., William Vicary, Esq., J.P., C.C., and other prominent Liberals of the West.

To be followed by an Illuminated Al Fresco Ball and Confetti Fete (special dancing enclosure 3d extra). The Newton Band (under the conductorship of Bandmaster Gilpin), will be in attendance. Refreshments at popular prices. Teas from 3d each during the afternoon.

Look out for the Procession, leaving the Ground at 12-30.

Swings, Shooting Galleries, and other attractions

EXCURSION TRAINS WILL RUN.

Doors open for judging 10-30 a.m., and for the Fete at 1 p.m.

Admission to the Ground 6d ; Grand Stand 6d ; Reserved Seats 1s.

Entry Forms and for further particulars apply
A. TRUMAN, Secretary.

Liberal Club, Newton Abbot, 4th May, 1907.

Advertisement publicising the multiple attractions of the Mid Devon Liberal Club's fete. (*Mid Devon & Newton Times*, 11 May 1907)

Lord Poltimore had been made chancellor of the ultra-Conservative Primrose League, named after Benjamin Disraeli's favourite flower, in 1895. The league reached an apogee in the Edwardian era with well over 2 million 'associates', in 'habitations' or branches, with key adherents elevated to honorary knights and dames. The league's fetes, like the rival Liberal ones, made every effort to attract whole families.

Both major political parties had active youth organisations, and ensured they were fully engaged in public events. The fetes had the usual sideshows of 'skittling' for a pig, bowling for a duck, roundabouts, swings and shooting galleries, with attractive prizes for race and completion winners, and, of course, tea was provided. It was only when a good mood prevailed that the political speeches rammed home the key messages of the day – taxation and social reform, battleships and the defence of empire, and the merits and perils of Irish Home Rule, female suffrage and the House of Lords.

In June 1911 the Conservative Fete at Luscombe Castle, the banker Peter Hoare's estate above Dawlish, was preceded by a noisy procession from the town centre led by bands and cheering members of the Union Jack Boys' Association, followed by an open carriage carrying Captain Morrison-Bell, the local MP. Devon's wealthy families were highly politicised, and everyone knew it.

Continuity & Coming of Age

Not surprisingly the fortunes, and misfortunes, of estate owners significantly influenced the comfort and security of their employees and tenants. Changes could be for the better or worse, and as much depended upon the character of the owners as upon their accumulating or declining wealth.

The lingering habit of customary deference, and no doubt the community's desire to get relationships off to the best possible start, meant the arrival of new owners was a major local event. Tenants and their families made a show of cheering them at the gates of their estates, and often there were speeches of welcome overtly interspersed with professions of loyalty. When the banker Charles Cave (from 1896, Sir Charles) inherited Sidbury Manor from his brother in the 1880s, the tenants of his 6,500-acre estate presented him with an illuminated address, and in return a few weeks later all their families and the local school children and other 'cottagers' were invited to the manor, where they sat down to tea in the coach house, drank each other's health, enjoyed the gardens, listened to the church bells, heard Mr Cave praise the local Anglican school and watched a firework display.

Such events, replete with mutual reassurances of loyalty and respect in these uncertain political and agricultural times, were to continue into the new century. In August 1912, Sir Edmund de la Pole died suddenly at Shute, the estate he had rescued from dilapidation seventeen years ago. Significantly, two years earlier his relieved tenants and employees had recognised this achievement with a 'handsome presentation'. He had been a generous supporter of local hospitals and horticultural societies, and each year augmented subscriptions to Shute's Coal and Clothes Club by 25 per cent. Not surprisingly, there were hopes that the new baronet, his brother from Ilfracombe, would show 'the same geniality'.

It was customary for tenants and villagers to honour the 'coming of age' of the son and heir of the owner of the estate. In July 1898 a typical ceremony marked the 21st birthday of the Honourable Geoffrey Duke Coleridge, the only son of Lord Coleridge. The church bells 'rang forth merry peals', and the bands of the Ottery St Mary Volunteers and the Church of England Temperance Society 'discoursed pleasing selections in the streets'. Houses hung decorations, and the Coleridge family welcomed 'a large number of townspeople', along with local clergy and Sir John Kennaway and his family from nearby Escot. The vicar of Ottery praised the Coleridges' generosity to the parish, and presented Geoffrey with 'a massive two-handled loving cup' inscribed with the family's coat of arms and the town's dedication to 'his future prosperity and happiness'. The tenants made a separate presentation of a silver inkstand.

Two years later, Sir John Kennaway's son received a similar 'coming of age' presentation, this time an illuminated address and 'a massive silver lamp with four candlesticks to match, all beautifully chased'. The address, and vicar's speech, initially paid greater attention to Sir John than his son, praising his stalwart services as the local Conservative MP and abiding concern for the community, and only then wishing his son 'no higher distinction than to win among your neighbours and your countrymen the same eminently honourable position which his Christian character, his zeal in all good works, and his devotion to duty have won him'.

In July 1909 the *North Devon Journal* expended several columns on the majority of Lord Ebrington, son and heir of the 4th Earl Fortescue. In typically Edwardian vein he was presented with a pair of inscribed silver rose bowls by his father's tenants, a hunter pocket watch by estate workers, and a dressing case from the town of Barnstaple. Significantly, the tenants' speech expressed the hope that Lord Ebrington would continue his father's obvious interest in the well-being of the estate and, equally significantly, Earl Fortescue took it upon himself to acknowledge the ravages of the rural depression. 'The year 1875 was about the crest of the wave of prosperity,' the earl recalled, 'and since then all connected with the land have been in the hollow!' He added, 'I am afraid few of you find times quite as good as you did twenty or thirty years ago', and he highlighted the serious decline in the estate's rentals under his own father, even though £100,000 had been spent in 'repairs, upkeep and renewals'. He did, though, think agricultural prices were recovering and hoped this 'would enable the landowners who in some cases have had to let their places to resume living on their estates'. He was cheered when he said landowners like himself should manage their estates first hand, as it was

Hugh, 4th Earl Fortescue (1854–1932), known by his courtesy title of
Viscount Ebrington until succeeding his father in 1905. He was a Liberal MP
1880–1902, lord lieutenant 1903–28, and for many years chairman of Devon
County Council, JP, master of Devon & Somerset Staghounds, and lieutenant
colonel of the Royal North Devon Hussars. (Devon & Exeter Institution)

'as much a matter of business as a mill or a factory', although his hint of necessary adjustments in relationships since his own father's death in 1905 might have caused some tenant farmers to worry that he was considering rent reviews.

Lord Fortescue was a member of the Central Lands Association, a recently created national pressure group promoting major landowners' interests in the face of the Liberal government's higher taxation proposals. In 1909 the Earl of Portsmouth addressed a meeting in Exeter to create a county branch. Owning 76,000 acres in several counties, he condemned the iniquity of depleting the 'pockets' of all those who owned land, lived in its neighbourhood 'and were the centres of local life and in many cases of the charities throughout the country'. At an Eggesford 'at home' that year he told his tenants that the Liberal government's vicious attacks on landlords would hurt everyone in the countryside. Despite the mounting national unrest, he hoped co-operation, not conflict, would prevail across all social classes in the countryside.

Perhaps Portsmouth was recalling a grating incident with one disgruntled tenant in 1907 that prompted his open letter to the *North Devon Journal* clarifying the significant reductions in rent from £670 in 1881 to £287 10s 0d in 1896 that he and his father had granted him. Despite the *Journal* recording the 'hear, hear' that greeted Portsmouth's 'at home' speech, his tenants and employees would have recalled that the earl had sold off numerous farms in recent years and were perhaps, with justification, anxiously pondering his lordship's future intentions.

Most tenants, estate workers and local tradesmen considered continuity in land ownership, and stability within the family that owned it, to be considerable blessings. In 1901 Lord and Lady Coleridge celebrated their silver wedding, and their tenants and employees duly presented them with an illuminated address reaffirming their loyalty as well as offering congratulations. In 1905 over 700 tenants and villages assembled at Killerton from across Devon and Cornwall to mark the silver wedding of Sir Thomas and Lady Acland with gifts. The Aclands, like the Coleridges, provided everyone with tea and a band. In 1908 Mr and Mrs Harris, the squire of Halwill Manor and his wife, celebrated their golden wedding three times – first at a private house party, then with local traders, and finally with their tenants.

☙ *Daughters of the House* ❧

For a daughter, her presentation at court was all-important as a sign of social status and a widening of the events she could attend as an adult. In a typically glowing report, in March 1912 the *Ilfracombe Chronicle* missed no details of the outfits worn by Miss Katie Soares and her mother, Lady Soares (the wife of Sir Ernest Soares, the recently knighted ex-Liberal MP for Barnstaple), when they visited Buckingham Palace. Lady Soares wore 'a gown of empire blue chiffon over clair-de-lune satin, with a band of rich blue and gold embroidery on the underskirt, partly veiled with an overcoat of chiffon edged with gold embroidery, and finished above with a smaller coat of cream and gold needlerun lace'. Her train was 'Empire blue and gold brocade lined with old gold chiffon'. Her daughter wore:

> … a dress of white Charmeuse satin, with a tunic of Brussels net embroidered with an uncommon and artistic design in shaded silver spangles. The train of crepe mousseline was veiled entirely with the net, on which spangles figured at intervals, and it had a large scroll in one corner of the same design as that used for the tunic and bodice, with a lining of chiffon.

Weddings of the social elite were grand local occasions, involving all social classes but in carefully orchestrated ways. The wedding of Sir John and Lady Kennaway's daughter at Talaton, near Escot, in August 1901 took place in a village adorned with flags, and as she neared the church 'a very pretty archway composed of ever-greens and flowers' greeted her with the inscriptions 'Long Life and Happiness' and 'Health and Prosperity'. Three other decorated archways had spanned the drive from Escot House, and yet others adorned the entrance gate and the road to the railway station. As the bridal pair left the church local school children strewed flowers in their path. The major guests included a roll call of south Devon's notable families – the Aclands, the Acland-Troyes, Caves, Coleridges, Courtenays, Iddesleighs, de la Poles, Rolles, Shelleys and the Walronds – and some 600 tenants and local residents were invited to tea in the grounds. The cake was displayed and cut on the terrace so everyone could witness this key moment.

The *Devon & Exeter Gazette* found space to describe the clothes worn by some of the distinguished guests. 'Broad brimmed hats' were popular, and 'of toques there were none'. One evening gown was of 'pale mauve satin, lined throughout with white silk', another of 'black esprit net, made simply over black silk [and] a series of little frills edged the skirt'. 'Of blouses the number seemed unlimited, those of soft white silk with transparent lace being much favoured.' Others were 'more elaborate' and one 'of soft rose pink with under-sleeves and vest of Swiss embroidered muslin' was deemed 'extremely fascinating'.

Later that month the wedding of Sir William and Lady Walrond's daughter dominated Bradfield in east Devon. Sir William, like Sir John Kennaway, was a long-standing local Conservative MP, and was serving as Parliamentary Secretary to the Treasury in Lord Salisbury's final administration (1895–1902). The wedding day became a local public holiday, the school closed and numerous arches were constructed and decorated with flowers and streamers under the watchful eye of the estate manager. 'Thousands', said the *Gazette*, watched the public part of the festivities in the park when the bride and groom were presented with gifts by the local school children, the church choir and Sir William's tenants and employees.

A thousand guests attended the wedding of Miss Edith Dunning, the daughter of the squire of Stoodleigh Court in east Devon, in May 1903. Colourful streamers hung between the village trees, and houses were decorated with bunting. Distinguished guests ate in the mansion's dining room; the less distinguished ones in a vast marquee on the lawn. The *Crediton Chronicle* highlighted the popularity of the bride due to her kindness to the sick and poor and the children of the village school, '… and in the hunting field and other scenes of rural life she is equally popular'.

It was a much quieter affair when Lord Churston's son and heir, the Honourable John Yarde-Buller, married Denise Orme, an actress and singer, two years earlier at Kensington Registry Office. The new Mrs Yarde-Buller happily told *The People* that her husband first saw her at London's Daly's Theatre in the immensely popular operetta, *The Little Michus*. For several successive nights he had taken a box, and then persuaded a mutual friend to introduce him. 'We fell in love. We were later engaged, and now we are married … Only a few personal friends attended. That is the whole story.' The newspaper could not resist adding that it thought Miss Orme had been engaged recently to Baron von Ernsthausen, a notable sportsman and wealthy London businessman, but he had denied it.

The Impact of New Money

The Aclands, Cliffords, Courtenays, Fortescues, Poltimores, Rolles, Walronds and Yarde-Bullers were well-established Devon dynasties, but the Dunnings epitomised the 'new money' buying into county society. Edwin Dunning had amassed his fortune mining and dealing in the gold and diamonds found in South Africa, and around 1885 he purchased Stoodleigh Court, built just four years earlier for Thomas Carew Daniel (whose wife disliked it), along with its 5,000 acres.

Dunning remained a director of the African & European Investment Company and various South African mining concerns, but also became a landlord, country gentlemen, Mayor of Tiverton for a year, an active supporter of the local Liberal Party and the founder of the local agricultural show. He was duly knighted for 'public services' in 1904. He appreciated that his arrival and success had not made him universally popular. Speaking to his tenants soon after his knighthood he acknowledged, 'there were some few in the neighbourhood whose merits, for some reason or the other, His Majesty had not yet recognised, and that they were – perhaps not unnaturally – lacking in enthusiasm over the elevation of one who had been more fortunate than themselves'. Nevertheless, he went on, to cheers and applause, to praise the estate's production and profitability, and to promise that he and his agent would listen sympathetically to requests for farm improvements.

However, by the middle of 1908 the Stoodleigh estate had been sold again, primarily, said the *Devon & Somerset Weekly News*, because Dunning needed to be in the Transvaal and Orange Free State 'to direct big undertakings with which his name is prominently associated'. The newspaper highlighted his investment in his tenants' farm repairs, and also Lady Dunning's generosity towards the 'sick and needy', her Christmas gifts to cottagers and her funding of village school 'treats'. They had become instant squires, landowners, country house hosts and local benefactors in their whirlwind occupancy – and, of course, secured a title.

Writing in 1932, Alfred Gregory, a long-standing mayor and editor of the *Tiverton Gazette*, clearly disliked Dunning's public displays of charity and the pressure he put on the local newspaper. His memoirs acidly assert that Dunning himself largely paid for a portrait that local farmers presented to him at a public dinner. There lingered, too, a suspicion that he had paid for his title. Local evidence that such degrading deals were well known comes from the *Torquay Times* in July 1908 when Mr R. J. Parr, the NSPCC's director, lamented the lack of honour given to the society's founder, the Reverend Benjamin Waugh, and added, 'it is said that the current market-price of a peerage was £25,000, and that baronetcies cost somewhat less'. Parr was correct; the honours system was entering a particular shabby phase.

Dunning's successor was Hugh Burdett Money-Coutts (later 6th Lord Latymer), a partner in the renowned Coutts Bank and nephew of Baroness Burdett Coutts, reputedly the richest woman in England. The villagers of Stoodleigh dutifully turned out to greet them, a welcoming arch straddled the gateway, the long drive was decorated with flags, Mrs Coutts was presented with a bouquet and the rector made a short speech. As no doubt expected, the family was soon engaged in local affairs – Liberal meetings and fetes, sports days and flower shows, charities and tea parties. However, ten years later they too had gone, and the estate was sold to a breeder of racehorses.

Another example of the influx of new wealth was the vast neo-Jacobean North Bovey Manor House built by Frederick Smith in 1907. His father, W. H. Smith, had purchased the 5,000-acre estate with its thirty farms, but more importantly its shooting coverts and fishing rights on the Bovey and Teign, from the Earl of Devon in 1890. In high contemporary fashion, the mansion's interior mimicked the early seventeenth-century predilection for massive wooden staircases, decorated plaster ceilings, oak-panelled rooms, open fireplaces with stone surrounds and a minstrels' gallery in the great banqueting hall.

With their main properties in Buckinghamshire and London, Frederick Smith saw his Devon estate primarily as a showpiece sporting retreat for family members and suitably impressed friends. Their intermittent arrivals in a private carriage by train at Moretonhampstead with their horses in special boxes, followed by their departure in a fleet of carriages or motor cars to the manor house, was an awesome sight drawing large crowds to the station. However, the house's Edwardian heyday was brief, as were the years of the Smiths' local beneficence. In 1913 Smith inherited the Hambleden viscountcy from his mother and served as an officer in the Royal 1st Devon Yeomanry in the Boer War and First World War, but after 1918 the family's interest in the mansion quickly faded, and after his death in 1928 it was sold to help pay death duties.

✑ Funerals & Obituaries ✑

Funerals, like most occasions in wealthy families' lives, were usually grand affairs. Typically, when Sir Cuthbert Peek died in July 1901, Rousdon school children, 'all of whom wore some token of mourning', lined the path from the church gate to the porch. Tenants and villagers gathered around the church as dignitaries arrived from near and far, revealing how interconnected such families had become through wealth, rank, politics and marriage.

The mourners included not only the Kennaways and de la Poles, but from further afield the politically influential Brodrick family, headed by Viscount Midleton, and the Fremantle family headed by Lord Cottesloe, both of whom had intermarried with the Peeks. The Peeks were *nouveau riche* too. Sir Cuthbert's father's grocery import business had created the family's wealth and secured him a baronetcy in 1874. He had purchased the east Devon estate, including the village of Rousdon itself, and built the vast mock-Tudor Peek House.

Peek House, Rousdon, built in the 1880s, complete with banqueting hall and minstrels' gallery.
(Devon & Exeter Institution)

Lengthy obituaries were commonplace. In November 1903 the unexpected death of Charles Seale-Hayne, the wealthy Liberal MP for Mid Devon, evoked several black-edged columns in the *Exeter & South Devon Advertiser* and paeans of praise for his role in revitalising Dartmouth's economy through the construction of a new embankment and pier despite all the inertia and objections, his very active chairmanship of the Dartmouth & Torbay Railway, and his determined promotion of technical education and evening continuation classes in Newton Abbot. His final benefaction had been in his will, which reserved much of his fortune for the creation of a major agricultural college duly named after him.

The death of the aged 3rd Earl Fortescue in October 1905 attracted similar newspaper coverage, even though his wish for a simple funeral without flowers was honoured. A keen Liberal, he had supported Gladstone until 1886 when, like many other Liberals, he had become a Unionist in opposition to Irish Home Rule.

He drew his wealth from his extensive West Country and Lincolnshire estates, but when his son, the 4th earl, came to write his memoirs, he intimated that some of his father's various enthusiasms had dangerously reduced the family's wealth at a time of prolonged agricultural depression in the late nineteenth century. He wished he had invested more in pedigree cattle, and suspected in particular that 'both his time and money were largely wasted' in continuing the 2nd earl's avid support for the middle-class, agriculturally biased school he had established, primarily for farmers' sons, in nearby West Buckland in partnership with its equally enthusiastic parish priest, the Reverend Joseph Lloyd Brereton. The 4th earl had a point. Whether it was the high fees, the social ambience or the elevated curriculum, West Country farmers displayed little interest and by Edwardian times West Buckland School's survival depended on its reinvention as a mainstream grammar school.

The 3rd earl had also restored Filleigh church, donated land for a north Devon convalescent home, supported Barnstaple Infirmary, chaired the local Quarter Sessions and played an active part in the Western Provident Association, North Devon Athenaeum, the South Molton board of guardians and North Devon Yeomanry. The *North Devon Journal* was probably right in its comment that the 3rd earl 'was as lavish of his means as of his personal energy in the service of the movements he supported'. His son, the more cautious 4th earl, resolutely shouldered many of these duties, and epitomised the traditional role of wealthy estate owners as social leaders, patrons of morally sound institutions, leading supporters of charities and local guardians of law and order.

The Honourable Mark Rolle, the greatest landowner in Devon, died from complications following influenza in 1907. The second son of the 19th Lord Clinton, in 1856 his uncle, Lord Rolle, had bequeathed him over 45,000 acres together with Bicton House near Budleigh Salterton. Between 1868 and 1872 Mark Rolle had built Stevenstone, a vast square French-Italian style mansion at St Giles in the Wood in North Devon, but as he had two daughters but no son everything he owned reverted to the 21st Lord Clinton on his death. On his arrival half a century earlier, Torrington, St Giles in the Wood, Bicton and Budleigh Salterton had resounded with congratulatory addresses and welcoming bonfires, peals of bells, fireworks and tea parties.

The Stevenstone gardens he created with his wife were typically lavish, fashionably fussy, inevitably and maybe deliberately labour intensive and greatly admired. One visitor noted the variety of fir trees gracing the park, the beds of bamboos and acanthus and especially the large flowering paulownia brought as seed from the

The Honourable Mark Rolle. (Clinton Estates, Bicton)

South of France. There was a 'distinctly rich' avenue of fuchsias, and a remarkable 'collection of climbing roses and arches and standards of ironwork leading to an open arbour covered with roses and clematis'. 'Fan palms' gave part of the garden a tropical air, and the 'lower garden' possessed beds of salvias, fuchsias, begonias, petunias, verbenas and heliotropes. Large and complex rockeries and fishponds gave further entertainment for those strolling the pleasure park.

Half a century later muffled bells and 'deep gloom' marked his passing. The *North Devon Journal* recorded his generosity towards Torrington through giving it the common; improving the market; allowing fishing on his river; converting the old canal into a road alongside the River Torridge; getting the railway extended from Bideford to Torrington; donating land for a new cottage hospital; giving the town a public drinking fountain and clock; supporting and improving the Blue Coat School; maintaining the almshouses and subscribing generously to the parish church restoration and Additional Curates' Fund. He had also paid for the complete restoration of the parish church at St Giles in the Wood. He had been generous towards the East Devon Hunt, the Royal Devon Yeomanry, the Royal Devon & Exeter Hospital and other infirmaries, and funds for the west window and Boer War memorial window in Exeter Cathedral.

One sentence in the *Mid Devon Times* obituary reveals how sensitive relationships could be between landowners and local families when it remarked, 'In politics a strict Conservative, he was never known to attempt to interfere with the absolute freedom of the many tenants and employees of the estate to vote as they thought right'. It was an important point. Against considerable opposition by many landlords who saw nothing wrong in telling people in their power how to vote, the secret ballot had been introduced in 1872, and in 1884 the franchise had been significantly extended to include all men paying an annual rent of £10 or holding land valued at £10.

Changing Attitudes & the Breaking Up of Estates

In March 1910 a motorcar brought the Honourable George Bampfylde, eldest son of the 3rd Lord Poltimore, and his bride to the gates of Poltimore House a few miles outside Exeter. They had been married in Eaton Square, London, not in Devon. In warm welcome, estate employees pulled the car by ropes up the drive to the decorated front porch of the mansion where they were met by a large crowd. In traditional vein, the couple received presents from local tradesmen, tenants and the indoor and outdoor staff at Poltimore, but beneath the gaiety uncertainty pervaded the locality as, just a year earlier, Lord Poltimore had begun to sell farms, fields and cottages in nearby Whipton and Heavitree. Perhaps the sales helped pay for the 1908 extensions to the house, and the creation of a fashionable Chinese water garden, but in 1911 many more small holdings between Exeter and Pinhoe were auctioned off.

Poltimore House and formal garden, *c.* 1907. (Devon & Exeter Institution)

Poltimore House, the saloon, *c.* 1907. (Devon & Exeter Institution)

Lord Poltimore had inherited the title and properties only in May 1908, but static rents, rising taxation, long-term mortgages, jointures protecting elderly relatives and perhaps a loss of interest in this particular estate had started a process that his son would continue when he became the 4th Lord Poltimore in 1918. By 1921 Poltimore House was an empty mansion that no one wished to buy and all the land but its immediate gardens and woods had been sold. The Poltimores retreated to their London house and to their Court Hall estate near North Molton.

The countryside could be far from tranquil for those dependent upon tenancy agreements and upon employment as estate workers and domestic staff, and Lord Poltimore was far from alone in selling off large portions of his estate at this time. Among many examples, in 1901 Mr Legassicke Bellews' estate in East Anstey and Stockleigh English was auctioned in ten large lots, mainly complete farms of 50–100 acres. In the same year Mr Justice Kekewich sold off 2,000 acres of farms, fields and cottages around Black Torrington in thirty-one lots, and in 1905 Lady Walrond's Dunchideock House and estate totalling 3,700 acres was auctioned in twenty-two lots.

Such sales, of course, were not uncommon for various family reasons but during the Edwardian era several major county landowners decided to dispose of tens of thousands of acres and hundreds of properties. It was the beginning of the largest redistribution of land since the Tudor Dissolution of the Monasteries.

In 1909, soon after inheriting Mark Rolle's estates, Lord Clinton sold 6,500 acres around Stevenstone in north Devon. In 1912 he disposed of the vast mansion itself, and in July 1914 hundreds of farms, cottages, fields, inns and smiths around Yarnscombe, Roborough and Romansleigh were auctioned. In 1909 the *Crediton Chronicle* reported the anxiety that the break-up of the estate was causing tenants, and especially estate workers whom Mark Rolle had treated generously regarding housing and 'perks', but it quoted Lord Clinton's blunt explanation that the sales were 'necessitated by the heavy estate and succession duties I have to pay'.

In 1909 the Conservative *Exeter Flying Post* reprinted the *Church Family Newspaper*'s article praising Lord Clinton's 'personal interest' in his tenants, his fervent defence of landowners in the House of Lords against the bitter attacks of Lloyd George, the Liberal Chancellor of the Exchequer, and his care in selecting the incumbents for the twenty Church of England benefices on his estates. At the 1914 sale the auctioneer explained that a number of lots had been withdrawn as Lord Clinton had responded sympathetically to the concerns of anxious tenants about the volatile nature of auctions and agreed to sell some farms direct to them. Lord Clinton had no use for Stevenstone, which only a generation ago Mark Rolle had built and furnished with every luxury imaginable. It never again became the centre of a traditional landed estate; indeed parts of it were soon demolished.

Charles John Robert Hepburn-Stuart-Forbes-Trefusis, 21st Baron Clinton (1863–1957).
(Devon & Exeter Institution)

This was a momentous event in the Devon countryside, but not unique in the management of Lord Clinton's estate. As early as 1905 he had decided to consolidate his holdings, and raise capital, when eighty-six lots of individual farms, fields, cottages, shops and blacksmiths and wheelwrights' workshops around Ashburton were auctioned. The timing was good. 'There was a large attendance,' said the *Torquay Times*, 'and bidding was very brisk, nearly every lot being disposed of.' Only Ashburton's Market Hall and Pannier, Fish and Corn Market failed to reach its reserve price.

The 6th Earl of Portsmouth also resumed his extensive sales and quit Devon altogether. Early sales in 1905 and 1908 were followed by greater ones in 1911 and 1914 that included many dozens of farms, thousands of acres of wood and moorland, and numerous cottages, hostelries and workshops in and around Burrington, Chawleigh, Chulmleigh, East Worlington, Eggesford, North Tawton, Wembworthy, Winkleigh and Witheridge. In some cases tenants bought their farms, but the newspapers noted that competition was keen and many properties fell to new owners.

For a decade tenants and estate workers had remained uncertain of their futures as the earl pondered his own. A succession of advertisements sought the highest prices by highlighting the proximity of railways, the 'good rentals' paid by tenants, the region's fishing, shooting and hunting facilities, and the opportunities for capitalist investment. The only property failing to find a buyer in 1914 was Eggesford House itself, when the earl finally consolidated his property around his other mansion in Farleigh Wallop, Hampshire. Unsubstantiated rumours circulated about the earl's gambling debts, but consolidation around a preferred home, ridding oneself of unprofitable holdings, fears of punitive Liberal taxation and raising capital for different investments are other reasons that guided many major landlords at this time.

All of these factors, except perhaps gambling, applied to the immensely wealthy 11th Duke of Bedford who, in 1911, ended the connection his family had had with Tavistock since his ancestor was granted lands from its dissolved abbey in 1540. He had inherited the title and vast estates in central London, Bedfordshire and Devon in 1893, but soon recognised and bowed to the social, political and economic pressures bearing down upon the landed aristocracy. Death duties would take no account of all the improvements made to their properties, and public opinion generally was succumbing to the incessant charges made by radical politicians that the aristocracy was an impediment to progress due to its possession of the House of Lords' veto on House of Commons Bills, and its domination of so many national and local institutions.

A widening electorate, especially since 1884, was increasingly seeing, just as Lloyd George hoped it would, social and institutional reforms being inextricably linked to the erosion of the wealth, power and patronage of the aristocracy and great landowners. Their benefactions were becoming evidence not so much of their generosity and concern for the community as of an outmoded and highly personalised authority and control. In 1900 the duke sold several London properties to the London County Council for housing development, in 1909 his large Thorney Estate was sold to tenants, and in 1911 so were nearly all of his thousands of acres of land and properties in and around Tavistock.

Still hugely wealthy, everything else was concentrated around Woburn in Bedfordshire with just an enclave for shooting and fishing around the family's Swiss-style 'cottage' tucked away at Endsleigh in Devon. The *South Molton Gazette*'s sympathies were strongly with the tenants who faced the choice of paying full market prices for their properties or finding significant increases in rent imposed by new owners, as well as higher rates as a result of the mandatory reassessment at the point of sale. As always, the sales meant some tenants prospered as owners while others endured greater costs or dispossession.

The Courtenay Earls of Devon proceeded cautiously but ultimately successfully through both the late Victorian depression and the Edwardian era of Liberal hostility. A. J. H. Jackson, the historian of their Powderham estate, has shown how its acreage was maintained between 1870 and 1890 with various sales and purchases cancelling each other out. Afterwards, though, total acreage and gross rentals fell dramatically from 15,733 acres and £26,805 in 1890 to 6,233 acres and £13,954 in 1900. This was primarily through sales in South Hams and East Dartmoor and gradual contraction to the family heartlands adjoining Powderham Castle on the Exe estuary, around Wolborough in Newton Abbot where, shrewdly, some parcels of land were sold for housing, and around the Courtenays' second home near Whitchurch.

Jackson suggests that the earls had chosen to raise money – £273,160 between 1890 and 1895 – for more lucrative investments than land, and to settle various mortgages. From 1900 to 1915 agriculture made a slow but steady recovery, and the Courtenay acres increased to 7,421 in 1915, and their gross rentals to £16,128. In 1910 the estate made a net profit of £6,514 and in 1915, £9,074. In 1911 the earl even bought around 500 acres near Whitchurch from the Duke of Bedford when he disposed of his Devonshire holdings. The Powderham estate, like the Clinton estate, survives to this day.

Throughout the Edwardian period two of the most splendidly built and furnished Victorian mansions, complete with their costly and intricate gardens, lay unwanted within a generation of their inception. In different ways both were testimonies to the vast wealth of their creators and their desire to flaunt manifestations of that wealth in huge and complicated buildings, crowded furnishings, costly works of art, exotic gardens and sweeping landscapes offering the best possible sports.

In the late 1860s John Bryce ordered the demolition of Marley Lodge, a modest house on an estate he had purchased on rising land offering spectacular views above the seaside village of Exmouth. He replaced it, historian June Coulson wrote, with probably the most costly and grandiose Victorian mansion and exotic gardens in Devon.

The Bryce family fortune came from the vast profits of mining and shipping guano, the mineral-rich droppings of sea birds, from the coast of Peru using hundreds of 'coolie' labourers imported from China. Much of it was spent on the new Italian-Romanesque Marley with its numerous square and curved bays, high tower and marbled staircase, columns and fireplaces. Coulson notes the building cost £40,000, and suggests that the interior decorations, including painted pictorial ceilings and the richest Continental furnishings, and the 40 acres of gardens, with their height of fashion terraces and balustrades, Italian sunken garden, aviaries, archery ranges and tennis courts, cost ten times more.

A *Country Life* view of a fashionable terrace: Streatham Hall, Exeter. (*Country Life*, 22 April 1899)

Heated glasshouses were common features, but Marley's were huge. The vinery measured 100ft by 12½ft, the banana house measured 40½ft by 7½ft, the peach and rose house was 162ft by 11¾ft and the cucumber, melon and pineapple house was 100ft by 13½ft. The extensive coach houses and stables were equally grandiose to satisfy the aura of conspicuous consumption so beloved of newly wealthy Victorian entrepreneurs. By all accounts, though, the family rarely stayed there, and in 1875 the staff was reduced and Marley let out. By 1902 it seems it was empty for lengthy periods at a time, although kept in good repair by the Bryces, who had an equally grand house in Paris that they seem to have preferred.

In 1904 the sale of Marley's contents attracted many buyers, but nobody wanted the building itself when it was advertised the following year. It had no supporting estate and great country mansions were not the ultimate family trophies and fashion accessories they had been in previous generations. Marley remained a massive and costly 'white elephant' throughout the Edwardian era until the family finally got rid of it in 1919. It passed through various hands until it was demolished for its materials in 1930. One family story Coulson includes suggests that Marley's sole purpose had been to entice the immensely wealthy Peruvian heiress, Mercedes Gonzalez de Candamo, sister of an influential politician, to marry John Bryce's son, John Pablo, which she did in or around 1871.

The fate of another vast mansion, Membland near Noss Mayo in South Hams, epitomises both the vaulting ambitions of wealthy late Victorian and Edwardian families and their estates' perilous vulnerability to changing fortunes. In 1871 Edward Baring, from the famous banking family, acquired the Membland estate and immediately enlarged it to include thirty-seven bedrooms and all the necessary facilities – electric light and bells, water closets and baths, billiard and smoking rooms, vast dining and drawing rooms, tennis courts with changing rooms and water closets, private cricket ground and pavilion, yacht house and private quay, trimmed lawns and flower beds, vast hot houses and pits growing exotic fruit and numerous kennels and stables – to ensure his extended family and guests were comfortable, and impressed.

Equally energetically, he bought up numerous farms and improved them. For a time Membland was well used, with frequent hunting, shooting, sailing and numerous house parties, and many local people given employment as a result. In 1885 Baring became 1st Lord Revelstoke, but five years later his fortunes and reputation crashed in a South American investment disaster. In 1895 Membland was put up for sale, but no buyer for such a grand house was found. In 1899 its contents were sold, and soon afterwards a north country shipping magnate, William Cresswell Gray, purchased the estate primarily for its extensive sporting opportunities.

The 1st Lord Revelstoke's mansion, Membland, above the estuary at Noss Mayo.
(Devon Heritage Centre)

Gray's main homes were in Durham, and it seems Baring's great house remained largely unused throughout the Edwardian era. The impact on local communities seemingly secure in Baring's employment and enjoying his patronage must have been acute. From 1915 onwards Gray failed several times to sell the house, although his son was more successful in 1924 when his company's fortunes were also in decline. By then, nearly all the supporting 5,000 acres of farms had gone and in 1928 Membland was reduced to rubble.

However, just when Eggesford, Marley, Membland and Stevenstone were fast losing their eye-catching grandeur and vitality, yet another wealthy family was commissioning an equally vast house on the cliffs above the Teign outside Drewsteignton. Designed by the fashionable architect Edwin Lutyens, in 1911 work began on Castle Drogo, a granite castle commissioned by Julius Drewe, whose fortune had been made by the Home & Colonial grocery chain. It was the last monumental 'trophy' house to be built in Devon, but within a few years it would become more of a mausoleum than a home when Julius lost his eldest son in the Great War.

4

ENDURANCE & RESILIENCE
The Countryside & Farming

❧ The Tourists' Countryside ☙

In 1904 Arthur Norway's guide asserted that 'Devon contains scenery of a beauty which is not surpassed, and of a variety which is nowhere equalled in all England'. There are:

> … deep and fertile valleys, through which flow streams and rivers of extraordinary beauty, now flashing down swift and brown and foam flecked from the moors, now gliding among richly wooded pastures, now issuing in harbours where the great tradition of sea power has lain unquestioned during untold centuries.

The exotic past so beloved of such writers surfaced again when he eulogised the 'stern and rugged upland of vast extent, all glorious with furze and fern and purple heather, a wonderland of tradition and romance, the background of almost every landscape in Devon – could anyone look out over such a noble country without some swelling of the heart'.

At the height of the tourist season in August 1906 the *South Molton Gazette* waxed equally lyrical about the deep cut meandering lanes, higgledy-piggledy villages, churches filled with historic memories, 'the never-ceasing pageant of the seasons', valleys filled with buttercups, bluebells and anemones and villages bustling with the work of skilled craftsmen and the carts and carriages connecting with local stations and market towns.

Thus spoke ardent publicists, and no doubt their words were welcomed by all those who ran boarding houses and inns, operated coach and charabanc businesses, produced and hawked souvenirs and sold strawberry and cream teas. But they all knew the uncertainties of making a living in such a dramatic landscape, especially in such tumultuous economic times. Indeed, in 1904 Devon was just emerging from a generation of rural depression and the painful restructuring of its agriculture.

Late Victorian Anxieties & Resolutions

The problems had begun a generation ago. In the middle of the nineteenth century agriculture had prospered, and across Devon traditional sheep rearing remained popular and there had been a massive increase in arable acreage for oats, roots and green crops. Then, in the mid-1870s several successive years of appalling weather and poor harvests were compounded in the early 1880s by sheep rot, a deadly internal disease caused by liver flukes that proliferated in the sodden fields.

By then, however, the shortages hitherto caused by low yields were no longer being compensated by high prices as fleets of steam ships were bringing in vast quantities of American, Russian and Indian grain. In 1872 this amounted to just under 28 million hundredweight, but by 1904 it had grown to over 118 million. The average wholesale price of wheat in Britain dropped by 60 per cent from around 58s 8d a quarter in 1873 to 26s 2d in 1896. Barley prices declined from 40s 5d to 22s 11d, and oats from 25s 5d to 14s 9d. Meat prices fell, too, as refrigeration techniques enabled frozen carcasses to be imported from America, Australia and New Zealand, but this fall was less severe. Beef slumped from around 5s 5d per 8lb lot in 1873 to around 3s 9d in 1896, mutton from 5s 11d to 4s 5d and pork from 4s 6d to 2s 11d.

Farmers concentrating upon cereal production, as many did in Devon, were hardest hit and were forced to cut costs (notably on labour), to seek rent reductions and to diversify. Many Devon farmers turned to livestock farming, and one benefit from the drop in cereal prices was it also reduced the cost of animal feed. And as imported meat was largely considered to be best suited to the lower end of the market, British farmers, including those in Devon, concentrated on high-quality production.

Another key factor was the size of farms. Most in Devon were small, and where possible worked primarily by family members, thereby reducing their reliance on hired hands. In 1913, 2,824 were only 1–5 acres in size, 6,680 between 6 and 50 acres, 5,136 between 51 and 150 acres, 2,222 between 151 and 300 acres, and just 315 with over 300 acres. Around 55 per cent, therefore, were less than 50 acres in size, and less than 2 per cent were over 300 acres. The 1901 census reveals that there were 9,588 male and 641 female farmers in Devon, with another 5,082 male and 1,215 female family members assisting them. Overall this was 3,000 more than in 1891, and may represent the creation of more small holdings as large landlords disposed of properties – and perhaps more children were surviving to working ages.

The 1901 census lists 11,649 men and fifty-one women employed as general agricultural labourers, with another 5,713 men in charge of horses, and 2,653 men and 144 women in charge of cattle. Although the census categorisations in 1891 and 1901 differ slightly, there had been a substantial fall of around 5,000 hired hands over the decade. With 17,526 farming family members assisted by 20,210 hired workers, the move towards greater family self-sufficiency was clear.

By 1900 wheat and barley acreages across England and Wales were down by 39 per cent since 1875 and root crops by 18 per cent, although many farmers, especially in south and mid-Devon, still mixed animal husbandry with some grain and root crops, partly for sale and partly for feeding stock. In 1881, 277,716 acres across Devon were devoted to corn but only 205,901 acres in 1911. Over the same period green crops and roots declined from 140,605 acres to 110,833 acres.

In contrast, animal numbers soared. In 1881 Devon's Agricultural Returns showed there had been 82,369 dairy cows and 151,040 other cattle; in 1911 there were 110,898 and 196,085 respectively. In 1881 there had been 745,030 sheep; by 1911 numbers had recovered and soared to 915,519. The breeding and rearing of beef cattle became common, notably in South Hams, the Exe Valley and north Devon. Pigs, too, were proving profitable, especially in east Devon. In 1902 there were nearly 96,000 in the county.

Westcott Farm, Thelbridge, *c.*1909. (Beaford Arts)

Railways and tourism stimulated the growth of market gardening and dairy produce. The early harvests of strawberries and other soft fruit went from the Tamar and Exe valleys to London and the great conurbations of the Midlands and north, as well as to Plymouth and local river trippers. Profitable crops of early potatoes were exported from the Taw Valley and north Devon, and around Moretonhampstead, to urban South Wales. Every station, whether great or small, had its sidings and loading bays awaiting the wagons and carts of farm produce.

Leaving the Countryside

Overall, between 1871 and 1911 the number of full-time farm labourers in England and Wales dropped by 23 per cent from 891,000 to 688,000. Devon's unemployed agricultural workers had the choice of seeking 'poor relief', trudging towards distant industrial towns, or, clutching tickets often paid for by local benefactors, heading towards Plymouth and the emigration ships going to Canada, Australia and New Zealand. The exodus was never-ending, even though Edwardian agriculture was clearly on the road to recovery.

Throughout the period local newspapers contained eye-catching advertisements encouraging rural workers to settle in the dominions. In March 1903, for example, the *East & South Devon Advertiser* advertised a promotional visit to Devon by the Canadian Farmers' Delegation. Against a picture of rolling farmland, a wooden signpost adorned with a notice saying '160 acre farms in Western Canada free' pointed to 'Golden Canada'. The headline shouted out 'Free Farms! No More Rent for Farmers!' In May 1910, a comforting advertisement in the *Crediton Chronicle* reassured farm workers and domestic servants that Canada was safely within the empire and all its 'institutions are built on British Models'. In the same edition, an advertisement by the High Commissioner for Australia offered 'Land and Cows at easy prices' and 'regular employment and good wages' for men and women seeking work in the dominion's thriving dairy industry. Another advertisement promoted reduced fares to New Zealand.

The *Western Times* gathered figures for 1912, revealing that there had been 2,114 emigrants from the eighty-three Devon parishes sending back returns. Although towns such as Barnstaple (265 emigrants), Crediton (109), Exeter (400), Newton Abbot (150), Paignton (100) and Tavistock (110) headed the list, numerous villages were still losing families. Chittlehampton, for example, lost nine that year, East Budleigh lost eight, Kenn lost six, Lustleigh lost twenty, North Molton lost ten, East and West Ogwell lost thirteen, Sandford lost fourteen, Sheepwash lost four and Witheridge lost eleven.

Between 1801 and 1901 the population of the United Kingdom quadrupled; in Devon it merely doubled. In 1871 it was 606,102, in 1901 it was 662,196 and in 1911 the population reached 699,703. The relatively modest increases occurred primarily in the towns, notably Plymouth, but there were few major industries to encourage massive urban growth and immigration, and many villages, whether large or small, were in continuous decline. Broadhempston, for example, fell steadily from 661 in 1861 to 437 in 1911, Buckland-in-the-Moor fell from 113 to 80, Hennock went from 1,004 to 733, Ilsington from 1,209 to 989, Manaton from 415 to 286, Stokeinteignhead fell from 628 to 461, and Widecombe-in-the-Moor fell from 854 to 633. Only those with good communications, reputations as popular market centres or near to major towns, or better still all three, withstood the trend. Thus, Chudleigh fell only from 2,108 to 2,006 between 1861 and 1911, while Moretonhampstead grew a little from 1,468 to 1,561, and Bovey Tracey rather more, from 2,080 to 2,809.

In June 1901 rural depopulation dominated the Archdeacon of Exeter's visitation to deaneries around Tiverton. Clergy and laity lamented the empty properties but noted, too, the 'comfortless, cramped and miserable cottages', the 'rough, hard, plodding work of the agricultural labourer under the trying conditions of bad weather', the natural desire for the 'pleasures and holidays' that townsfolk enjoyed, and the need for better wages and better opportunities for rural children. They noted, too, the 'gaudy and attractive' image of Devon's countryside that misled the general public about its true state. The discussions led nowhere except to pious hopes that schools would adopt a rural bias and villages would be equipped with reading rooms, club houses and evening classes.

No one seriously thought that higher wages were possible at this time, or that much investment would be made in improving workers' cottages. In 1905 the *Crediton Chronicle* sneered that 'the pick of young men' had deserted the villages for employment in 'any occupation which offers higher wages in the present and some hope for the future' while the 'ne'er-do-well, the idle and the unenterprising remain to grumble that the farmer cannot pay them more than their labour is worth'.

☙ Devon Agriculture Reinvents Itself ☙

Historian Jeffrey Porter has described a Russian visitor's observations on the changes in Devon's countryside between visits in 1890 and 1912. In 1890 Prince Peter Kropotkin noted, 'In every direction I could see abandoned cottages and orchards going to ruin.' He lamented that field after field was covered in grass 'and thistles in profusion', and that the labour of previous generations in clearing, fencing and draining the land was being wasted. In contrast, though, in the same year William White's *History, Gazetteer and Directory of the County of Devon* perceived some signs of regeneration with new investment in drainage schemes; the levelling of hedges; the trials of artificial manures; the extension of meadow and grazing land, especially on hillsides; the scientific breeding of Devon cattle and the move towards longer leases for tenant farmers.

Eight years later the *Western Times* described a journey through mid-Devon from Crediton to Witheridge and Cruwys Morchard, and noted the variety of farms on the way. At Creedy there was a herd of 100 North Devon Ruby cattle, near Sandford, fields of mangolds and potatoes, and around Stone's Hill plenty of fields of grass and clover. In and around Kennerleigh both grass and wheat were doing well, near Thelbridge there was dredge corn and some oats and peas, and surrounding Hele Barton were fields of wheat, oats, clover and mangolds. Between the Gidley Arms and Witheridge wheat dominated the scene, and then copious fields of grass. With the exception of some windswept fields around Witheridge all the crops were deemed fine.

By 1912 Prince Kropotkin had nothing but praise for the energy and inventiveness of Devon's farmers, and cited in particular the market gardens supplying Covent Garden and the fame of the county's early potatoes. *Kelly's Directory* for 1914 confirms the diversity contributing to the recovery. Wheat and barley maintained significant presences at 48,984 and 38,726 acres each, but were far outstripped by oats covering 123,239 acres. Rape accounted for another 10,344 acres. The profitable potato fields now stretched over 10,783 acres, turnips and swedes continued to be important with 44,901 acres, and so did mangolds with 32,950 acres. Approaching 1 million acres of land, of widely varying quality, were now devoted to animal grazing and growing grasses, clover and sainfoin for hay. Taken together, water meadows and other grassland reaching up into the hills had increased by around 60 per cent since 1881. In addition, the intensive production of fruit included apples, largely for cider production, covering 25,045 acres, currants and gooseberries 322 acres, strawberries 300 acres, cherries 299 acres, raspberries 198 acres and 'mixed soft fruits' 467 acres.

The success of Devon's market gardeners proved particularly noteworthy. In June 1901 the *North Devon Journal* highlighted the 'sunny slopes' of Combe Martin, from where as many as 'twenty cartloads of strawberries' had been dispatched in one day to South Wales via the steamer service from Ilfracombe. Two years later the *Torquay Times* noted the fields of fruit trees achieving maturity and 'the hundreds of bunches of grapes' together with the peaches, strawberries, asparagus, tomatoes and cucumbers in the vast commercial glasshouses of the Devon Rosery Company near Cockington Court.

In 1904 *Trewman's Flying Post* compared the sad decay of Topsham's ancient port with the recent success of the market gardens that now covered 300 acres of the parish. 'Hundreds of tons' of gooseberries, plums, apples, strawberries and raspberries were sent to nearby Exeter, and modern rail transport and steamer ships had helped secure ready markets as far afield as France, Holland, Belgium and Germany. At peak harvest times numerous families were employed in Topsham's orchards and glasshouses, and well into Edwardian times local officials turned a blind eye to many children absenting themselves from school.

William White would have approved of these officials. In 1890 he condemned a major trend that he thought would be the death of rural prosperity. This was the 'abolition of apprenticeship, by which a young labourer had a practical training and became a skilled workman in husbandry, and the girls in cookery and domestic work'. He was referring to the controversy surrounding the extension of education for the rural working classes. 'The pernicious effects of this system,' he thundered, 'are the growing up of a race of boys and girls in a state of rebellion to their employers, ignorant and incapable of conducting the commonest work of the farm and household.'

A Snapshot of One Village

A decade later Rider Haggard, more famous nowadays for his novels, surveyed rural Devon and identified similar views. In June 1901 he interviewed Sir Thomas Acland's agent, Mr Stevens, and toured Broadclyst, a village owned by Sir Thomas, who resided at nearby Killerton. He was impressed with the 'well built and commodious' cottages, many of them recently restored after a fire, and by the numerous well-tilled allotments. Several cottages with gardens were reserved, with rentals of merely 1s 6d a week, for widows of estate workers.

The village had other attractions. The grass from 70 acres of water meadow was auctioned to villagers in small lots each year, and, very unusually, the profits from the Red Lion public house were 'spent for the general advantage of the community'. Rider Haggard cautioned that Broadclyst was exceptional, and 'the reader must remember that all Devonshire villages are not so fortunately placed or so well cared for'. From conversations with the Husseys, the Exeter auctioneers, Rider Haggard came to the cautious conclusion that east and south Devon's rich grasslands enabled farmers to 'earn a rent and a living, if no more'.

Stevens, the agent, confirmed this, but added that even with rents 20–30 per cent lower than twenty years ago few farmers or even landlords could afford any capital investment or improvements. Rider Haggard cited the universal complaint of farmers against the lack of tariffs on imported flour and barley meal and 'other animal feeding stuffs', but personally he thought tariffs would merely cause rents to rise and domestic competition to intensify. To him the greater problem was the lack of a strong rural bias in education, and he condemned as utterly useless the drawing lesson on 'cones and cubes' he had seen in Broadclyst's school. Stevens, too, bemoaned the quality as well as the quantity of farm labourers. Lads found it unappealing and became surly: 'Now even youths of seventeen treated the "master" as nobody, and would become abusive if rebuked'. He added, 'it was common in riding about the estate to find the men smoking and talking instead of doing their work. They were simply robbing their employer.'

In 1896 Ruth Whitaker's father became vicar of Broadclyst. In her memoirs she portrays the Edwardian village as largely free from abject poverty but nevertheless held uncomfortably in the grip of a closely stratified social hierarchy only slowly coming to terms with social, economic and political change. Despite their benefactions, she thought the strongly Liberal views of the Aclands did not endear them to the staunchly Conservative local gentry, tenant farmers and villagers. Broadclyst church was full each Sunday, with the gentry still firmly accustomed to sitting on the raised seats on the east side. One 'somewhat pretentious family' made their 'black-clad bonneted maids' walk a mile to church while 'the master and mistress bowled up in a brougham', but other families were beginning to allow their servants to worship 'in their pretty Sunday best'.

The memoirs give other glimpses of Edwardian life and hierarchies. In common with many country parishes, the vicarage was 'large and comfortable in the minor-country-house style', although often so cold that everyone developed chilblains. The Whitakers could afford to keep two, sometimes three, maids, a gardener-groom and a garden boy. The large garden and greenhouse provided vegetables, apples, pears, figs and peaches. The family got around the locality on bicycles and a governess cart pulled by their pony, but the family rarely dined with the Aclands. Her father gave religious instruction in the village school three days a week, but Ruth and her brothers kept apart from the village children and attended private schools in Exeter and Honiton.

❦ *Stemming Disenchantment: Attracting the Young* ❧

There is substantial evidence that in the Edwardian era depopulation had ended up causing a labour shortage. Newspapers were full of advertisements similar to these in the *Western Times* and *Devon & Exeter Gazette*:

WANTED BOY or LAD (indoors) to make himself useful on farm – Apply Hallett, Halsdon, Exmouth.

WANTED steady Girl as GENERAL SERVANT in farmhouse; able to milk if required – Apply Mrs Reddaway, Bathe, Northtawton.

WANTED a SHEPHERD: also a MAN to look after hacks, milk and make himself generally useful; good houses and gardens – Wm. T. Thomas, Fluxton, Ottery St Mary.

WANTED, RABBIT TRAPPERS, from now to Lady Day: catch at 2*d* each: board and lodge found: Isaac, Seed Stores, Winkleigh.

WANTED MAN to drive horses; must be a good ploughman; good cottage, garden and potato ground – FOALE, Smallacombe, Ilsington, Newton Abbot.

In 1902 Rider Haggard recorded Devon farmers' views on the growing labour shortage. A few admitted the inadequacies of local cottages and wages, a few blamed recruitment to the army and navy and many others blamed the lure of the facilities and opportunities offered in the towns. Certainly Rider Haggard found wages were poor in South Hams at about 15/- a week, with a shilling a day extra during the corn and hay harvest, together with the use of a cottage and its garden and, usually, permission to forage for firewood.

In 1913 Sir Daniel Hall's *Pilgrimage of British Farming* recorded that Devon's wages, and the extras, had not changed since the turn of the century. He added that a couple of quarts of cider a day were often customary, although on many farms this 'perk' was being commuted to an extra 1s 3d a week. In 1913 Devon farmers were perturbed when the Board of Trade asked for details of workers' wages to inform its decision on a minimum wage, but seemed to be ignoring the extras they received in kind. An anxiety-ridden farmers' meeting in east Devon revealed wages ranging between 13/- and 17/- with carters receiving around a shilling more than ordinary labourers. The average was 15s 6d, much the same as a decade earlier.

In 1902 Rider Haggard visited Mr W. P. Vosper's unusually large 1,000-acre farm near Plympton. He employed fifty men and bitterly lamented the reluctance of school leavers to work on the land. And those that did start on farms, he complained, soon departed for the towns. He said the Earl of Morley, the landlord, was improving the cottages, but Vosper thought better cottages and higher wages would not stem the drain of young men from the villages. The wages were already good, he claimed, 'averaging 16/- a week, with cottage, manure, milk, and sundries, which bring them up, perhaps, to the value of £1'. He shared the view of Stevens, the Aclands' agent, that farmers could find their rent but otherwise just 'rub along'. Nevertheless, Rider Haggard obviously thought Vosper's farm was particularly successful, and perhaps suspected he was protesting too much. The land was fertile, and his fields of cabbages, herds of 250 cows and 100 or so other cattle, flock of 800 sheep, and modern dairy turning out clotted cream, found ready markets and good prices in Plymouth and London. And as Vosper said, there was no shortage of new tenants for vacated farms.

Most farmers, Rider Haggard said, blamed the overly literary and academic syllabuses in rural schools for leading children to scorn hard practical work. Many farmers turned up to hear Walter Runciman, president of the Board of Agriculture, speak in Newton Abbot in November 1912. He said he had been pleased, as president of the Board of Education between 1908 and 1911, to encourage a rural bias through the extension of school gardens and studies of local farms, plants and animals, and he trusted this would manifest itself soon in Devon. He hoped that the programmes of the new Seale-Hayne Agricultural College would attract local interest, and complement the rural courses offered through the county council. Outside these hopes, Runciman promised very little. He expressed sympathy with the problems tenant farmers experienced trying to buy their farms but fell short of promising low-interest government loans.

Since Charles Seale-Hayne's death in 1903 it had taken all the influence and energy of his executor and friend, George Lambert, a gentleman farmer and Liberal MP for South Molton, to summon up much enthusiasm within the agricultural and educational communities for the project. In February 1910 the *Western Times* criticised the Devon Farmers' Union for its members' smug complacency – many, it asserted, 'feel quite convinced that no one either knows or can discover any better method'. It mocked their heated complaints about high rents, taxes and Poor Law rates and their ignorance of scientific innovations likely to improve crop and cattle yields. In a hugely complicated series of negotiations Lambert masterminded the purchase of the Howton estate outside Newton Abbot, and eventually brought together the Boards of Agriculture and Education, and Devon and Cornwall County Councils to ensure Seale-Hayne College was built and would offer courses at several levels. Construction started in 1912, but the first students were women volunteering as emergency farm workers during the Great War.

Devon County Council's 'Practical School of Agriculture' was already up and running, having been founded in the 1890s in partnership with the governors of Ashburton's ancient grammar school. Through fees or scholarships local boys over the age of 13 could receive an education that included practical and theoretical approaches to agricultural engineering, chemistry, mechanics, crop production and animal husbandry – although always alongside religious instruction and the humanities. The school was well staffed and equipped, and well connected with a variety of farms and agricultural businesses and included Lord Clinton, Lord Clifford and Sir Thomas Acland among its governors. Even so, in 1902 Sir Thomas was disappointed at the lack of interest in the scholarships, just as the lack of farmers' support for West Buckland School had disappointed Lord Fortescue.

Prior to 1903 the Technical Education Committees across the county had provided a number of well-received short courses in particular skills. In 1902, for example, sheep shearing classes took place in sixteen north Devon villages, and poultry keeping, ploughing, thatching and hedging in several others. Attendances ranged from ten to around thirty.

From 1903 the county council took over responsibility and covered Devon with five- to ten-day courses run by itinerant instructors. In 1908, a typical year, there were twenty courses on sheep shearing, nineteen on cheese and butter making, nineteen on horticulture, eighteen on poultry keeping, seventeen on manures and feeding stuffs, ten on hedging and ditching, four on thatching and three on ploughing. The classes were popular, no doubt because they were relevant, short, intensive, accessible and cheap. In 1908, 267 students attended the evening horticultural classes, 205 completed the butter- and cheese-making courses, and an average of twenty-five attended each poultry keeping course.

✑ *Poor Housing & Services* ✎

There is substantial evidence that a significant proportion of rural housing was grossly inadequate when judged against the gradually rising standards of public health authorities. The problem, though, evaded solution as nobody accepted blame, or responsibility.

In 1901 Mark Rolle's agent neatly explained another dilemma when Torrington Rural District Council served a notice to improve the drainage of some ancient cottages at Weare Giffard. As the cost would be greater than the value of the properties the agent threatened to demolish them, but argued that as the tenants preferred the very low rents, which was all they could afford, to living in the workhouse, it would be iniquitous to evict them if the properties were declared uninhabitable.

The 1905 annual report of the medical officer of health for Barnstaple Rural District detailed all the major issues. It confirmed that overall there was a sufficiency of housing, but overcrowding was a severe problem. 'Large families are frequently found occupying cottages with only two bedrooms, the disadvantages of this are obvious, and are bound to have a bad effect, both morally and physically, upon the younger members of these families.' In common with many other medical officers he had a low view of the standards of working-class families, and noted that 'neglect and indifference' quickly led some modern properties to become as dirty and disease ridden as ancient ones.

He condemned, too, the continuing acceptance of cesspits sited 'dangerously' near cottages, and the 'privies' projecting over streams or adjacent to 'manure heaps'. Although cesspits remained common in the district, by 1905 some larger communities such as Braunton, Combe Martin, Instow, Mortehoe and Woolacombe had modern sewerage systems discharging, quite acceptably then, straight into the sea. All these places had reliable pure water supplies too, except Instow, which joined the numerous other places across the district relying on wells and springs, many, the medical officer said, of dubious reliability regarding quantity and quality. Elsewhere, too, erratic supplies were condemned. The springs supplying Abbotswell, Bampton, Bishopsteignton and Hennock, for example, and servicing the village tank above Bovey Tracey church, often ran perilously low and sometimes dried up. Gradually some local councils secured contracts with larger authorities such as Torquay, Paignton and Plymouth for improved supplies from their massive reservoirs, although charges and piping and pumping costs were high and, not surprisingly, the cause of considerable argument within and between the councils. No wonder great relief, a formal ceremony and a public dinner marked Ipplepen finally drawing its first water supplies from Paignton's reservoir in 1907.

In 1913 the Diocese of Exeter surveyed rural housing and deemed 44 per cent of cottages 'inadequate'. Another 33 per cent were 'adequate', but barely so. Overcrowding was 'very bad' in 15 per cent of parishes, with further cases observed across another 50 per cent. The problems were compounded by the profitable letting of many cottages to tourists that effectively deprived local families of them. The report believed only about a quarter of rural properties were owned by major landowners; most belonged to 'small shopkeepers, widows, spinsters, and others' for whom improvements would far exceed the rental income. There was a long list of inadequacies. 'Many old cottages are very badly lighted, the windows small, the bedrooms wretched.' Sanitation was 'good' in just 12 per cent of parishes; in most other cases it was 'primitive'. The majority of cottages possessed only two bedrooms, and the report joined all those from district medical officers condemning girls and boys of all ages sleeping in the same room.

In the same year the local government board inspector, Dr T. Carnwath, surveyed several rural districts, and found them all wanting. Around Bideford there were many 'rudely built' cob buildings, damp at ground level, with cracked and crumbling walls and in dire need of rethatching. There were usually two small bedrooms, one living room and occasionally a back scullery. The floors were often 'rubble, brick or earth', larders were hardly known, the ventilation grossly inadequate, and 'drainage was often unprovided for'. He reserved special condemnation for Hartland with at least forty houses 'unfit for human habitation' and another twenty-three 'doubtful'. In parishes around Torrington – notably Alverdiscott, Ashreigney, Beaford, Merton, Shebbear, Sheepwash, Winkleigh and Yarnscombe – Carnwath inspected 185 houses, mostly cob, 'of which 93 were, in his opinion,

A tourist postcard of cottages at Hope, *c.* 1900. (Author's collection)

unfit for human habitation, and 73 doubtful'. Rather unfairly bearing in mind the longevity of sound cob, the *South Molton Gazette* condemned it as reminding 'one that even in England the age of the mud hut is not so long ago'.

Soon after Carnwath's report, Torrington Rural District Council contacted major landowners about building new houses but got short shrift. Sir Thomas Acland, Earl Fortescue and Lord Clinton said their properties were well maintained, they had no complaints from tenants and needed no more cottages. In February 1914 a conference in Torquay lamented the double failure of, first, private enterprise to create adequate new housing and, second, rural district councils to take responsibility for buying land, securing government loans and managing new 'council houses'. The financial risks, it concluded, were considered too great.

There were, though, a few modern 'model cottages' erected by landowners. In 1911 the Honourable Lionel Walrond built twenty-five new houses on the family estates at Willand, Cullompton, Kentisbeare and Uffculme. The *Tiverton Gazette* was lavish in its praise of Mrs Walrond's 'keen personal interest' and suggestions for improvements to the architect. Bearing in mind the criticisms of many workers' cottages it noted the large kitchens, sculleries and washhouses, the four separate bedrooms and the sound drainage of each property. The divining skills of the Reverend W. F. Newman, vicar of Hockworthy, had ensured the houses had pure water supplies from nearby springs.

Dangerous Lanes

In 1902 a well-publicised dispute broke out between the county council and district councils around South Molton and Tiverton regarding the inability of the packed earth and stone surfaces of most roads, outside a few tarred main routes, to withstand their increasing use by heavy traction engines and steam-powered goods lorries with their serrated and spiked metal wheels. Ian Heathcoat-Amory also waded in with a public letter condemning the district council's roads around Witheridge: 'Horses and carriages are knocked about, farmers have to send two horses where one should do … altogether one feels when driving over them as if one were being jolted back twenty years.' The district councils deeply resented the accusations that they were wasting the county grants by inadequately supervising the quarries and road packers, and asserted that the county council should consider undertaking the maintenance itself.

The county council's minutes for 1905 reveal that the mechanisms for monitoring, surveying, costing and improving roads were significantly tightened up, and succeeding years show the steady flow of grants for modest improvements to ancient bridges, dangerous corners and narrow roads, and for tar paving a few more miles of busy highways. Typically, in March 1910 it made grants towards improving the main road through Budleigh Salterton, widening Exeter Road in Exmouth, Torquay Road in Paignton, District Road in South Molton and Blacks Hill and Teignmouth Road in Torquay. In addition, Shutterton Bridge in Dawlish was rebuilt and Brixington Bridge in Exmouth widened. As these examples show, most road improvements were undertaken in or near towns; the majority of country roads retained their packed earth and crushed stone surfaces, rendering them obnoxiously dusty in summer and mud laden in winter.

Complaints continued to mount about the endless damage to lesser roads, including by the growing fleets of 'motor omnibuses' run by the two railway companies. Accusations flew around newspaper columns and correspondence that tourism might be badly affected if drivers, passengers and cyclists refused to be lurched and jolted along the dangerously pitted surfaces anymore. Besieged local councils were incensed at accusations that the new surfaces were too thin, too porous and poorly cambered.

Controversy reached a head in 1910 in a Plymouth conference called to discuss highways issues. The main speaker, Tiverton's borough surveyor, argued that stone packing was a waste of money; from now on roads must be solid, smooth and dust free. The only solution was a rolled surface of grit on top of 4in of gently sloping tar on top of firm foundations.

In seeming confirmation of the danger, on the main road just outside Cullompton in March 1912 a motor car sank about 2ft into the rain-softened surface and needed two horses to pull it out. Later that year the county council became far more proactive and agreed to the preparation of three-year rolling

The untarred main street in Cheriton Fitzpaine, *c.* 1905. (Beaford Arts)

programmes of recommended improvements based primarily upon its own survey-ors' reports. Anxieties expressed by several parsimonious councillors were brushed aside, and the recommendation was accepted. There was general agreement that heavy vehicles should be more heavily taxed.

Despite the Edwardian growth in motor vehicles, horses undertook most farm work and powered the majority of private and public conveyances. *Kelly's Directory* for 1914 noted that there were 33,000 horses working on Devon farms and other commercial concerns. Working animals could be unpredictable and dangerous, especially in the presence of noisy engines, and each year a number of tragedies occurred. In August 1901 horses pulling a carriage away from Lynton Station took fright and crashed into another carriage, crushing two ladies against a stone wall, injuring one but killing the other. In May 1903 a groom and his passenger were injured when their horse was frightened by a steamroller in Torquay and bolted into a furniture wagon. That June, two men were using two horses to pull a cart-load of barrels of lime from East Anstey Station when one patted the lead horse on the rump to encourage it uphill. Startled, the horse jumped forward, kicked out and struck the man, fatally staving in his ribcage.

In September 1904 a pony pulling a cart at Hatherleigh bolted, the wheels became caught in a deep rut and the carrier was thrown out of his seat and killed when his head struck a gatepost. In June 1906 a young worker was found dead in the yard at Sherwood Farm, Sidmouth, and the inquest concluded he had been kicked in the head by one of the horses he tended. In August 1907 horses pulling a charabanc at Bovey Tracey bolted and crashed into a bridge, hurling all seven occupants into a stream. No one was killed but all were badly hurt. And so the accidents went on. In August 1910 a Broadclyst butcher's man was thrown from his horse and killed.

Storms and floods periodically wreaked havoc across the countryside, making roads impassable, damaging property and decimating crops. In February 1900, for example, a great storm caused landslides to block the railway between Exeter and Teignmouth, and swollen rivers to flood parts of Ashburton, Exeter, Hatherleigh and Totnes and the lines between Exeter and Tiverton Junction, Tiverton Junction and Culmstock, Heathfield and Chudleigh, and South Brent and Kingsbridge. Hundreds of sheep were drowned and numerous hayricks washed away. Similar damage was wrought by another storm in October 1903 when road and railway connections between Newton Abbot and Moretonhampstead, Crediton and Exeter, and Braunton and Ilfracombe were severed, and parts of Plymouth and Exeter flooded. The whole of north Devon was 'sodden and cold', said *Trewman's Flying Post*, and crops of potatoes, cabbages, plums and strawberries failed disastrously. Shoppers hunted in vain for affordable supplies. Throughout the period, the logbooks of numerous schools, espe-cially in low-lying areas such as Pinhoe, Poltimore and Broadclyst in the farmland outside Exeter, record the roads made impassable by periodic floods. Those on the uplands circling Dartmoor cite the howling gales and violent snowstorms.

◌❧ *Fairs & Markets* ☙◌

Rural life in Devon was nothing if not resilient. Depopulation, insecurity and poverty were constant worries, but they had not adversely affected the agricultural recovery nor seriously eroded key aspects of rural life.

In July 1905 the *Western Times* published an evocative account of the annual St Peter's Fair in Holsworthy:

> It was a busy scene in Holsworthy on Tuesday which was regarded as the chief day for business; farmers and dealers were early in the town, and for miles round livestock had been sent in until the square and the streets, and the roads leading into the town, were filled up with horses and cattle, besides which, from the station end of the town to the Post Office, all the available space was occupied with shows, booths, shooting galleries, and Cheap Jacks. In front of the Stanhope Hotel was the imposing 'Anderson's Show', reminding one of the 'Richardson's Show' of former days, with its stage upon which a quartet of prettily dressed girls gracefully danced before each performance commenced, assisted by clowns and other players.

Since 1844 the Fair had included awarding a prize of £2 10*s* 0*d* in accordance with a rector's legacy to a spinster under 30 years of age 'generally esteemed as the most deserving and handsome, and the most noted for her quietness and attendance at church'. The rector's legacy, and the prize giving, remained popular.

Crowds, stalls and amusements at Barnstaple Fair, *c.* 1910. (Beaford Arts)

The fair was traditionally the time for the settlement of tradesmen's and merchants' bills by farmers, and of drapers', milliners' and dressmakers' bills by farmers' wives and daughters.

Families still traded at the great Devon fairs in Tavistock, Barnstaple and Bampton. October's 'Goosie' Fair in Tavistock abounded in farm products besides the traditional geese, but by Edwardian times the fair also attracted numerous professional entertainers – jugglers, singers, dancers, organ grinders, magicians, the proprietors of boxing booths, freak shows, swing boats, helter-skelters and hawkers of pies, ribbons, trinkets and feathers. They ensured, sneered the newspapers from time to time, that 'simple yokels' would be defrauded and robbed. The prevalence of card sharps, pickpockets and prostitutes, and the frequency of drunkenness and brawls, especially, it was alleged, when the railways brought in groups from Plymouth and Devonport, led to regular calls from affronted residents for greater policing and even the end of the fair itself. It was, though, too profitable to cancel, and so was the equally popular and ancient four-day Barnstaple Fair. By Edwardian times, the animal sales and auctions were held in a different part of Barnstaple to the professional fairground sideshows and entertainments – which included the awesome Edwardian novelty of a moving picture show.

Bampton Fair had been held each November for many centuries, and by 1901 its prosperity as a specialised pony fair had soared as the fortunes of Dulverton Fair and Tiverton Fair had faded. In 1903 a visitor arriving by train said the 'long straggling street is lined with booths on either side and we are pushed and jostled by women and girls in velvet gowns, fantastically adorned, and very much befeathered headgear.

Baskets of produce for sale at Barnstaple's pannier market, *c.* 1912. (Author's collection)

Cattle market in Crediton High Street, *c.* 1912. (Beaford Arts)

So decidedly brown are they that we know them at once as "fair" people.' The visitor noted the crowds of country folk gathered around the persuasive purveyors of cure-all medicines and the preachers 'shouting about cant and hypocrisy'. Onlookers bantered with the auctioneers in the pens in the side streets, groups of men were gathered around the chief inns, and women 'chatter gaily, as daintily they treat their way through the crowded street'. A newspaper the previous year was less flattering, highlighting the 'particularly thick and adhesive quality' of the mud, the life-threatening dash of uncontrolled ponies through the crowds, the notices warning of pickpockets and the unseemly rush for seats on the overcrowded trains at the end of the day. Many houses resorted to barricading their windows for the duration of the fair.

Every country town had its market; some several each week, as at Barnstaple where particular days were earmarked for particular produce. Tavistock's huge event was on Fridays and it attracted people from as far away as Calstock and Gunnislake. Countrywomen, often with a young child or two in tow, walked in with baskets of produce to sell or to seek out cheaper food than that sold locally. Live chickens were crammed into baskets. Wagons and carts lurched along laden with vegetables, fruit, flowers and others with domestic and farm utensils. Cattle, sheep, pigs and geese had been driven along the Tavistock road at dawn, and the town's great market square was adjacent to a weighing shed and slaughterhouse. Butchers' stalls were numerous and so were those selling ribbons, bonnets, shawls, trinkets and games of chance. The day was full of noisy bidding and bartering, eating and drinking and the killing and cutting up of animals.

◌ *Farms & Farmyards* ◌

As many guidebooks and historians such as Robin Stanes have noted, farmhouses were sited near good water supplies, and if possible in sheltered spots. In Devon they were usually built from local materials, notably ashlar stone from Dartmoor or cob – basically subsoil mixed with straw and water to a thick paste. Timber came from local woods and roofs were often thatched with rye or wheat straw rather than specially grown reeds.

By Edwardian times most open halls and lofts of ancient, but still sturdy, properties had been divided into more comfortable and certainly more useful parlours, sculleries and kitchens downstairs and small bedrooms for family members and servants and, perhaps, lodging workers upstairs.

Many farmhouses were equipped with the assorted pots, pans, jugs and crocks to make cheese, butter, clotted cream and honey to sell at local markets, alongside spare eggs, vegetables and poultry. Many, too, retained the vast open stone fireplace with its raised grate, hooks for boiling pots and spits for roasting meat. It was the warmest place in the house and around it was placed the high-backed draught-proof settles.

North Devon thatched farmhouse and yard with farmer and family in best clothes and servant.
(Beaford Arts)

By 1901 rye and barley bread had been discarded in favour of the loaves made from hard grain from North America and most village mills were reduced to grinding cattle feed. Beef, bacon, ham and mutton were eaten, although the better cuts remained costly, with salted fish, especially cod, being commonplace for poorer families. Most families grew a variety of vegetables, although potatoes, cabbages and peas predominated, and they strove to rear chickens and buy and fatten a pig. Sometimes poorer families would share the cost of a yearly piglet, and after it was killed in the autumn half of it would be sold to raise funds to purchase the next one. Cider making was universal, but especially productive in east and south Devon where most parishes and some individual farms had presses. Farm workers consumed vast quantities of 'rough' cider as part of their remuneration, but some was refined to sell commercially.

Assorted buildings usually surrounded the farmyard, including the 'shippon' where cows were stalled and fed, a calving shed, a stable and pigsties. The large dung heaps that often adorned the outside walls and yards of farmhouses were prized and far from shameful possessions, and comprised everything organic that would rot down, mixed carefully with straw.

Sale catalogues itemise the crops, animals and equipment that might make up an Edwardian Devon farm. Batthills Farm, a mile from Cullompton Station, was a typical modest-sized east Devon mixed holding. It was auctioned in March 1903. There were several cows and a dozen 'fat' pigs and breeding sows, sixty chickens, 'a set' of geese and four turkeys. The two cart mares – 'Dent' and 'Blossom' – along with a pony, were described as 'good and quiet in harness'. There was part of a rick of meadow hay, 35 acres of 'luxuriant' pasture and meadow, ¾ acre of fruit trees, and 74 acres of 'excellent game and rabbit shooting'. Among a vast array of machines, equipment and utensils were a dog cart with cushions and lamps, three goods wagons with sideboards, a mowing machine, self-binder, turnip and mangold drill and cutter, horse hoe, horse rake, iron harrow, stone roller, single-furrow plough, animal troughs, poultry coops, cider press and funnel, numerous buckets, knives, three shotguns and several hundred faggots of green and dry wood.

When Westbrook Farm near Bampton was auctioned in February 1905 it too possessed several powerful horses – 'Diamond', 'Poll', 'Boxer', 'Madam' – and the large wheeled wagons they pulled. Here, though, it was the 116 Devonshire Longwool ewes, the 'grand' ram, and the herd of Devon dairy cows that dominated the farm, along with twenty hogsheads of cider representing its subsidiary enterprise.

Despite the glowing accounts of picturesque farms in tourist books the look of the place was unimportant to the farmer, who usually had not got spare money or was disinclined to spend it on 'niceties'. In 1913 the *North Devon Journal* reproduced a pamphlet condemning the current habit of fitting cottages and farms with cheap and 'frankly, hideous' corrugated-iron roofs instead of traditional thatch. It took as one example 'the exquisitely beautiful villages' of Hennock and Ashton in the Teign Valley whose charms had been 'completely destroyed'.

❧ *Variety & Resilience: The Variety of Skills* ❧

Rural life still provided livelihoods, if varying widely in quality, for many families and most villages remained surprisingly self-sufficient despite all the criticisms. Between 1891 and 1901 there was a slight rise in those employed in specialist rural trades. In 1901 there were 118 agricultural machinery proprietors and their assistants, 339 shepherds, 256 woodsmen, 633 gamekeepers, and 4,177 male and 69 female commercial nursery and market gardeners. Numbers remained around these levels in 1911. In 1891 there were 489 thatchers, and although they were not categorised later, it is reasonable to suppose their numbers remained constant.

Other tradesmen with a significant but not exclusively rural clientele in 1901 were the 2,834 blacksmiths, 790 wheelwrights, 486 saddlers and harness makers, 735 sawyers, 139 slaughterers, 681 male and 17 female millers and cereal makers, and 340 male and 23 female corn, seed and flour dealers. And, of course, a significant proportion of the 2,434 domestic gardeners, 34,546 female and 1,164 male indoor domestic servants, 1,677 domestic grooms and coachmen, 5,916 non-domestic coachmen, carters and wagoners, 961 Anglican and 353 other clergymen, and 3,875 female and 1,491 male teachers were country dwellers, as were some miners, roadmen, railway workers and a host of other families engaged in the making and selling of clothes, furniture, tools, food and drink.

Denis Cluett was born in 1907. Between the ages of 2 and 11 he lived in Sampford Peverell, to the east of Tiverton, and his memoirs highlight the village's self-sufficiency. He recalled its two grocers' shops, two butchers, the baker, harness

Farrier's workshop near Plymouth with wheels and farm machinery awaiting attention, collection or sale, and a horse being shod, 1907. (Beaford Arts)

maker, blacksmith and cobbler, the newspaper and sweet shop, post office, school, Anglican church and Nonconformist chapel, at least two public houses and a dairy factory making clotted cream, butter and cheese for nationwide sale.

He remembered, too, watching the noisy and bloody business of slaughtering animals, the grocer weighing and packaging every item the customer wanted from large tins, boxes and barrels, and most men preferring a barber's shave on the way to or from work rather than doing it themselves.

Local hedgerows as well as vegetable plots provided food. Children went out picking blackberries, their mothers made as much jam as possible, and onions from the garden and nuts from the countryside helped with the chutney. When Alfred Abraham wrote about his childhood in Newton St Cyres at the turn of the century, he recalled the odours as often as the sights. Among them were the lighted candles and paraffin lamps, the baking bread, the salting of the family pig and the stables and yard where customers at his father's inn kept their horses.

Writing about Payhembury, Robin Stanes highlighted how endlessly busy it was with the butcher and baker at work from before dawn, the postmaster doubling up as a harness maker, the thatcher always somewhere around the parish, and the wheelwrights and carpenters making productive use of local timber.

Kelly's Directories show that many other villages possessed similar facilities. In 1902, for example, Harberton parish, a few miles south-west of Totnes, had a population of 678, but possessed a builder and threshing machine contractor, a general shopkeeper, tool maker, mason, thatcher, miller, lime merchant, two grocers, bakers and boot and shoe makers. The village had a public house, reading room, ten almshouses, a post office with two deliveries and collections a day, an Anglican church and school and a Wesleyan chapel – together with the clergy and teachers serving them.

Community Activities

Village sports days were common annual events. In July 1903, for example, Harbertonford ran ten events, including the high jump, obstacle race, handicap races of varying length, an open mile and a steeplechase. The money prizes donated by local dignitaries totalled an impressive £15. Totnes Borough Band played popular pieces from America – 'The Belle of New York' and 'Happy Days from Dixie' – along with items from Gilbert & Sullivan.

There were a number of locally organised annual horse races, usually held in farmers' fields. In September 1909, for example, Thorveton Races had pony, novel, open flat, ladies' plate and hurdle events, and at Cheriton Fitzpaine similar categories were complemented by other competitions including various adult and children's bicycle races. Prizes were attractive at around £5 for winners.

Many villages had football and cricket teams, and matches were reported in local newspapers, although far greater attention was paid to the more socially elevated game of cricket. In 1902 the *Torquay Times* noted that the cricketers from the village of Marldon were due to play teams as diverse as Brixham, Starcross, Montpelier School, Exeter Teachers' Training College, the Royal Naval College, Ivybridge, Ashburton, Paignton, Kingswear and Haytor. The men of Marldon were usually the victors.

Kingskerswell's cricket team was equally proud of its achievements; in 1909 it won twelve of the nineteen fixtures against opponents such as Buckfastleigh, Chudleigh and Moretonhampstead. Many teams were encouraged by local clergy and landowners, most of whom had attended public schools where the highly desirable qualities of perseverance, tolerance, integrity and selflessness were believed to be enhanced by competitive team games. However, as Prebendary Jackson asserted at a cricket club meeting in Kingsteignton in 1910, these qualities could never be associated with professional players, especially those engaged in football.

There were a host of local horticultural shows each year, and several major agricultural shows around the county, the biggest of which was the County Show in May that drew 28,000 people when it was held in Exeter in 1905. The large estates were usually well represented. In 1913 Lord Poltimore's horses won first prize at the Somerset County Show, and his horses and cattle won second and third prizes at both the Devon County and Bath & Wells shows. He did well again in 1914, and hosted the British Dairy Farmers' Association meeting at Poltimore that May – probably the last great event on the estate under his ownership.

Most local shows were not traditional events; many were recent creations, such as the Garden Show at Uffculme which celebrated its tenth anniversary in August 1904. The August Bank Holiday – the first Monday in that month – had existed only since 1871, but by Edwardian times it was a popular day for communal events. Typically, the Uffculme Show had three classes, clearly based on social class. There was the 'open', the 'amateur for those who do not employ a gardener', and the 'cottagers'. The newspaper report highlighted the glorious array of fruit and flowers, especially the sweet peas, geraniums and begonias, from the professional gardeners in the open section and the commendable size of the cottagers' onions and potatoes, although it did not think much of their peas and beans. There were few 'amateur' entries, perhaps because it was not a class inciting pride in membership. On 3 August 1914 the flower shows and sports at Alphington, Chagford, Drewsteignton, Exmouth, Huish, Lydford, Pinhoe & Poltimore, Shute and Whimple were among the final Edwardian summer days out before war was declared.

Autumnal ploughing matches remained popular and highly competitive. The one held at Thelbridge in October 1905 was typical. It embraced Witheridge and East and West Worlington, as well as Thelbridge, and had matches for farmers and farmers' sons, men over 20, boys under 20 and an open event. The matches were mid-Victorian in origin, but ploughing itself was in transition. By Edwardian times most, but not quite all, farmers were using horses rather than oxen to pull ploughs, and the ploughs themselves, although still single-furrow ones, had evolved to include moveable metal mould boards so that the soil could be turned to either the left or the right. This made it possible to plough down and then up the steeply sloped fields so common in the county. Seed was still sown by hand on many farms. Mechanical seed drills were expensive, but everyone now used drag harrows to minimise the loss of seed to birds.

The Thelbridge event included competitions for the 'best and cleanest' 2 acres of mangolds, 2 acres of swedes and 2 acres of turnips, and for hedging, thatching, and rope and spar making. A modest prize of 7s 6d was awarded to a man who had served on the same farm for thirty-one and a half years. The clergy had a high profile at the event as they formed part of the team of judges and, perhaps more unusually, the evening dinner included well-received speeches celebrating the absence of Romish practices in local parish churches. The evening dinner speeches after the Rackenford Ploughing Match in 1907 also turned to religion, and welcomed the apparent calming down of sectarian rancour among county councillors during their discussions on education. As we shall see in chapter five, it was a topical issue.

A Time of Rejoicing

Denis Cluett recalled how machines speeded up Edwardian corn harvesting. First, men scythed a path about 6ft wide around the field that allowed a self-binding mowing machine to start work without trampling down any corn. The machine delivered cut and bound sheaves which were manhandled into stooks – six to eight sheaves leaning against each other, with the ears upright. If rain threatened everyone worked fast and into dusk. When fully dry the sheaves were made into ricks and waited for the arrival of the hired threshing machine, traction engine and their operators. Arduous threshing with handheld flails in double door barns had long faded away.

Nevertheless, the ancient celebration of Harvest Home, marking the safe gathering in of the year's crops, was still common, although now usually shorn of some of its earlier pagan elements. At Butterleigh in 1911 it was held in a marquee in a farmer's field. Organised by a committee of farmers and the rector, seventy people enjoyed a midday dinner and toasted King George and Queen Mary. The Cullompton Territorial Band provided the music, the afternoon was devoted to children's and adults' sports, and in the evening there was dancing in the schoolroom.

By Edwardian times most churches held Harvest Festival services complete with decorations of flowers and gifts of produce for later distribution to the poor. In September 1901, the Harvest Festival and Harvest Home were combined in Stockland. The service took the form of a full choral evensong with relevant hymns and prayers, followed by tea and music for the congregation of over 300 people in

A group with a horse-drawn reaper binder and children with refreshments: High Bickington. (Beaford Arts)

A threshing machine powered by a traction engine at work on Horwood Farm, Torrington, with thatched rick in the background. (Beaford Arts)

the grounds of a local mansion decorated with fairy lights and Chinese lanterns. Celebrations with acts of Christian worship firmly at their centre became widespread. In 1912, 400 attended the harvest festival in North Molton parish church with tea afterwards in the schoolroom, while at Clayhidon everyone wandered across to the nearby Half Moon Inn for the post-service dinner.

Interestingly, Clayhidon's event was announced as the 41st festival. The overtly Christian bias had only taken hold in the later part of the nineteenth century, after the Reverend Robert Hawker introduced Harvest Festival services at Morwenstow in Cornwall in the 1840s, and a spate of newly composed harvest hymns had achieved popularity. Earnest Victorians sought to minimise the pagan legacy and tame the riotous drink-fuelled rites linked to ancient harvest celebrations, notably the traditional songs of fertility, the taming of mischievous spirits lurking in the final patch of corn to be cut and the belief in favourable spirits residing in corn dollies. By the time Queen Victoria died, they had been largely successful, and corn dollies were relegated to the status of local curios for tourists.

A few old customs were preserved whose origins were lost in the mists of time. Each Whitsun a procession of Kingsteignton villagers, maypole dancers, a local band and decorated carts accompanied the carcass of a ram to a local field where it was roasted and devoured amidst the election of a May Queen, various games and sports and a parade of local horses. Much cider and ale was drunk.

As court records of verbal abuse and physical violence show, drink retained its unsavoury side in rural communities despite the determined onslaughts of the temperance societies and Bands of Hope. Newspapers did not hesitate to name, and possibly shame, the offenders. Sometimes it was done humourously, as in July 1911 when an elderly haymaker at Halberton left work with £1 in his pocket and spent most of it on drink rather than the clothes he had said he needed. Sometimes, though, incidents were serious. In April 1910, for example, the drunken driver of a steam lorry from Lapford was pulled by passers-by from his 'rambling' vehicle in South Street, Exeter, after it careered into a wall.

Church and chapel congregations remained strong and often vied strenuously for worshippers within individual villages. The Bible Christians, an independent offshoot of the Methodists, were particularly strong in Devon's poorer rural communities, and especially so in the north of the county. They founded many simple chapels that were at the centre of vibrant local groups whose trenchant Sunday schools and Bands of Hope rivalled those of Anglicans and other Nonconformists. At High Bickington a typical Bible Christian Band of Hope meeting blended earnest talks and catchy songs with topical recitations, including 'The Publican's Family', 'Not Dead but Drunk', 'Norah and her licensing Father', 'Pat and the Whiskey' and 'A Speech on the Gallows'.

As both *Kelly's Directories* and Nikolaus Pevsner and Bridget Cherry reveal, numerous Anglican parish churches were substantially renovated in the second half of the nineteenth century, and, as Gerald Parsons and Nicholas Orme argue, this was the tangible sign of the massive resurgence of pastoral work by Church of England clergy and wealthy local laity who sought to make the churches, and not the rival Nonconformist chapels, the spiritual and social centre of local life. In 'Christianising' the harvest celebrations, and in encouraging and helping organise local shows and ploughing matches, the clergy were largely successful in raising the profile of themselves and their church.

Among literally hundreds of rebuilt towers, additional transepts, restored chancels, new stained-glass windows and cleaned interiors, the 1880s and 1890s witnessed a surge in activity with architects, builders and decorators at work across the county from Abbotskerswell, Blackawton, East Ogwell and Slapton in the south

THE SON OF MAN IS COME TO SEEK AND SAVE THE LOST — WE HAVE REDEMPTION THROUGH HIS BLOOD THE FORGIVENESS OF SINS — THE CHURCH ARM[Y] — EX...R DIOCESAN VAN No.

A Church Army van and travelling evangelists at High Bickington. (Beaford Arts)

to Ashreigney, Braunton, George Nympton, Horwood and Rose Ash in the north. The initiatives continued well into the Edwardian era, when parish churches at Bickington near Barnstaple, St Peters in Ilfracombe, Jacobstowe, Loxhore, Marwood, Rattery and Wembworthy were substantially restored. As we have seen, wealthy local families sometimes bore the whole cost, but usually there was a need for a determined rallying of communal effort. At High Bickington in July 1903 a typical Edwardian church restoration fete of sideshows and local produce was followed by a Cart Horse Parade and then a series of tableaux in the schoolroom portraying 'England', 'Scotland', 'Wales', 'Ireland', 'Britannia', 'A Gypsy Encampment' and 'Home they brought her warrior dead'.

The Church of England's home missionary branch – the Church Army – brought a new dimension to the Anglican gospel across rural Devon. Three Church Army officers lived in horse-drawn caravans and criss-crossed the county preaching to whomsoever they could attract. In March 1901, the *Devon & Exeter Gazette* interviewed one officer, Captain Narbeth, whose simply furnished van was covered in Biblical quotations. He acknowledged that he never knew how communities would receive him – some were welcoming, others merely curious and a few apathetic. It was the novelty of the van and the out-of-doors meetings, said the captain, which attracted his audience. In a telling comment on his view of the countryside, he added, 'It is the same old message that we bring; but a new voice. A new light on an old subject will often light a new life in a soul that has become deadened through the monotony of a rural life, and the indifference it often engenders.'

5

FIRMLY IN THEIR PLACE
Children, Schools & Welfare

❧ *The Controversies are Created* ❧

In 1810 and 1811 respectively the mutually hostile Nonconformists and Church of England (Anglicans) formed rival national societies to help local chapels and churches found schools to bring religious instruction and a modicum of literacy and numeracy to working-class children. From 1833 a hard-pressed government agreed to give both societies modest annual grants to promote their work. It was a decisive moment, and henceforth the vexed question of public funding of education became inextricably embroiled in Victorian and Edwardian issues of class distinction, social stability and religion. Very public controversies over the purpose of education, the curriculum, the length and cost of schooling and indeed the nature of childhood and parenthood, never went away, and they reached a climax in Edwardian England.

In 1861 a typically monumental report by a Victorian Royal Commission pin-pointed the chronically uneven and unco-ordinated spread of government-assisted schools across the country. Unless a locality desired such a school – and many did not – and was prepared to match one of the society's grants – and many could not – local children had no schooling at all, unless they attended a private one, if one was within reach, if it was affordable, and if parents thought the expense worthwhile. And even when grant-aided schools were established, they struggled with a variety of problems. Attendance was voluntary, but financial survival each year depended on the regularity of attendance, the 'pence' collected in weekly fees, the government inspector's report on the standard of work and the state of the building, and all too often on the continuing financial support of sympathetic squires and clergy.

In 1870 an Education Act filled the huge gaps left by the churches. It obliged every civil parish without a school aided by one of the religious societies, or with one that could not accommodate all the local children, to create a popularly elected school board which could then secure a government loan and levy a local rate to build and run a state-inspected school. The act, however, created as many problems as it solved, and encapsulated the chronic divisions within Victorian society that persisted well into the twentieth century.

The bill had been hotly contested as it progressed through Parliament. There were bitter arguments about the burden on tax and rate payers, about the real need for working-class children to have several years of schooling, about whether education should raise or control children's expectations of life, but most of all about the sort of religious education that might go on in board schools. A few argued that religious education should be banned in these schools, but to most people this was unthinkable. A compromise was reached that satisfied no one, whereby board schools were limited to 'undenominational religious teaching'. This was widely misunderstood, and often misinterpreted, by clergy and teachers, sometimes deliberately so, but fundamentally it barred any doctrine or formulary peculiar to a particular church. Bible stories could be taught, but not, for example, the Church of England's Catechism.

The School Board Era 1870–1903: A Curate's Egg

Between 1871 and 1903 129 board schools had to be created in Devon. During the same period many Church of England parishes roused themselves to hold school boards at bay, and they managed to build 146 new voluntary schools. The Nonconformists, although numerous, were less able to compete financially and added very few to their total – one at Lynton, another at Pancrasweek and a third at Kingsteignton. Many Nonconformists, however, were content with the relatively straightforward unsectarian syllabuses in the board schools. In practice, the 1870 Act ensured the rivalries between the churches, and between the Church of England and the board schools, for the hearts and minds of local children soured political, religious and social relationships within the county for many decades to come.

As late as the 1870s some Devon villagers were having their first sight of a purpose-built school and its structured routines. In a naturally conservative rural environment beginning to experience the horrors of a depression, it was hardly surprising that such strange and costly intrusions were not always as welcome as their instigators had expected. As school logbooks reveal, head teachers were quick to equate pupils' annoying absenteeism with working-class parents' general neglect of their children and abiding contempt of education.

Such sweeping judgements, though, ignored the priorities pressing upon many families. Poverty, and an unyielding hand-to-mouth existence, meant the extra pence children could earn instead of attending school were vital to the family income. Illness within families often meant children had to undertake more

The main room at the board (later county council) girls' school at Hatherleigh. (Beaford Arts)

domestic tasks – washing, shopping, preparing meals, nursing – than they usually did. Numerous logbooks record the foul state of Devon's roads in bad weather, the long distances children had to walk to and from school, their often leaking footwear and the inability of schools to dry their sodden clothes. No wonder absences plummeted at such times.

Many thought much the same as William White and Rider Haggard, that prolonged elementary education in rural areas was a waste of everyone's money and time. And conversely many proponents of extending elementary schooling had no wish to disturb the social order. They argued that if girls were given intensive training in sewing and needlework, cookery and housework, and boys more handicraft and gardening, and both had some rigorous physical drill as well as regular religious instruction, they would be better prepared to serve their employers as domestic servants, estate workers and artisans, and to care for their own families. Few saw any working-class children, other than the exceptionally talented ones, struggling through the educational and social barriers to earn a scholarship to one of the essentially middle-class fee-paying grammar schools.

After 1870 the fate of each Devon school depended greatly on the attitude of local managers if it was a 'voluntary' Anglican or Nonconformist one, and school board members if not. Not surprisingly, their fates varied widely. Robert Bovett's researches show that over 110 impoverished Church of England and Nonconformist schools agreed, with varying degrees of relief and reluctance, to be taken over by school boards who possessed the statutory means to renovate and redesignate them.

However, in some urban areas the battle for control was fierce. In Plymouth the Church of England fiercely rivalled the school board in building schools, and its clergy sought election to the board to influence its policy in their favour. In 1898 the partisan *Western Times* celebrated the triumph of the 'progressive' Liberals in Plymouth who would restrain the influence of the 'clerical and denominational party'. Here, as often elsewhere, the Anglicans accused board schools of neglecting religious instruction or rendering it incomprehensible to pupils, while their opponents decried Anglican and Roman Catholic schools as instruments of pernicious and superannuated indoctrination.

The Anglicans in Torquay had even greater success. The wealthy Palk family had been generous with gifts of land, and when the Nonconformists had to close their three schools in 1893–94 and petitioned for a school board the Anglicans leapt into action to fight off the proposal and build replacements themselves. Henceforth Nonconformist families – estimated at one-third of the borough's families – had no choice other than the Anglican schools (there was also a single Roman Catholic one). The bitterness lingered long into the new century.

Controversy was rife in many rural parishes too, as historian Roger Sellman has found out. Some communities, such as Chittlehampton, Ilfracombe, Landkey and Loddiswell, possessed both Anglican and Nonconformist schools which engaged in constant civil war. Parents could be adept at playing them off against each other. As their logbooks reveal, in 1901 and 1902 Ilfracombe Church of England School lost several children to the Nonconformists when the headmaster said some were backward and reprimanded others for unashamed truancy in order to sell newspapers or give donkey rides to holidaymakers. The two head teachers at Loddiswell also lost the children of aggrieved parents, however justified the teachers felt in their response to bad behaviour and poor work, and the two schools never arrived at a mutually satisfactory modus operandi. At the general election in January 1910 the village's Nonconformist children were granted a holiday and caused 'great annoyance' outside the Church of England School 'by their continual howling and singing the song for Fools that they had been taught for the Election'.

School boards themselves were of varying efficiency. Farmers were elected to some with the deliberate intention of keeping the education rate as low as possible. In the 1880s, for example, Hennock School fell into disrepair and the single teacher was obliged to teach seventy children of all ages. Clayhanger School was forced to close on several occasions as few teachers endured the dismal salary and decrepit building for long. In 1901 the local newspapers printed every detail of HMI's condemnation of Willand's failure to improve its impoverished buildings and lamentable educational record.

Exeter and Plymouth, on the other hand, built schools to a high standard and maintained them well. And among many examples, in 1901 His Majesty's Inspectors (HMI) deemed the children in all Tiverton's board schools – Bampton Street, Bolham, Chevithorne, Cove, Elmore and Withleigh – to be very well taught. In 1903 their religious instruction inspection confirmed that the six schools ranged from 'good' to 'excellent', and were far from being the 'Godless' board schools of their Anglican critics.

In both voluntary and board schools a minority of Devon teachers were found to be incompetent, as Roger Sellman has highlighted. But many, however inadequately qualified, did sterling work and impressed inspectors time after time, often while coping with freezing rooms and ill-tempered stoves, damp buildings and inadequate ventilation, primitive middens and no running water, dangerous gravel yards and, most worrying of all, a room of children many of whom were ill-kempt, ill-fed and often coughing and spluttering with incessant colds.

The Evolution of the Middle-Class Grammar Schools

Parents with incomes allowing them to avoid sending their children to local church or board schools – known collectively as elementary schools – generally did so. The Victorian obsession with social class, and ideally improving one's place on the ladder, meant that a wide variety of old established and new educational institutions, no doubt of widely varying quality, were available to suit every pocket.

At the summit were the renowned and expensive 'public' schools offering a hefty diet of classics interspersed with some mathematics and literature, a little science and a great deal of competitive sport. They provided the opportunity to forge advantageous friendships, opened the gates to universities and, if one had to earn a living, to professional careers. Beneath these, both in terms of costs and social status, were schools and academies more biased towards science, mathematics and commerce, and an array of modestly priced historic foundations, confusingly called grammar schools, which perpetuated the teaching of Latin but strove to ensure their survival by adding a chargeable selection of subjects such as French, mathematics and English literature. For girls, drawing and music were fashionable additions.

The style, atmosphere and aspirations of the hierarchy of greater and lesser fee-paying schools were well established by Edwardian times, and their advertisements and speech days, along with numerous newspaper articles, editorials and correspondence, made no secret of the fact that they reflected, refined and perpetuated the social divisions across the nation.

In 1901 Devon had a scattering of schools serving the middle classes, but overall they were failing dismally to provide enough easily accessible places. The sixteenth and seventeenth-century grammar schools founded in Ashburton, Bideford, Crediton, Dartmouth, Honiton (Allhallows), Kingsbridge, Okehampton, Ottery St Mary (King's School), Tavistock, Tiverton (Blundell's), Torrington and Totnes had shaken themselves out of their eighteenth and early nineteenth-century lethargy, and very often their trustees' corrupt use of endowments, to offer families better value for money. Most had needed the shock of the 1868 Schools Enquiry Commission, another massive Victorian investigation, and the ensuing legislation to set about modernising their trust deeds, syllabuses and facilities and expand their staff.

In line with the commissioners' perception of national needs, three distinct grades of boys' school were envisaged, depending on whether students stayed until 18/19, 16/17 or 14/15 years of age, whether they were taught Latin and Greek or just Latin, and whether their wider courses aimed at sending boys to university, straight to the professions and the higher branches of commerce, or into farming and the lower branches of trade. Fee levels varied appropriately.

Most medieval founders of grammar schools had thought bright but poor local children would be the main beneficiaries of their legacies, but often the Victorian legislators thought otherwise. Tavistock and Crediton grammar schools continued to serve their local communities well with the benefit of enhanced funds, in Tavistock's case from the Duke of Bedford. Both took local pupils as well as boarders, and both gave prominence to mathematics, science and commerce as well as the humanities and a respectful nod to the classics.

The Episcopal Middle (Class) School for Girls, Exeter, *c.* 1900. (Author's collection)

In contrast, Mike Sampson highlights Blundell's School's ambitious rise to 'public school' heights and its increasingly tenuous links with Tiverton itself. Other than Blundell's tercentenary procession through the town in 1904, his chapters devoted to the twentieth century rarely mention Tiverton itself. A crucial moment reported in the *Devon & Somerset Weekly News* in January 1903 was the Mayor of Tiverton's disgust that Blundell's had rejected the county council's grant because it would oblige them to take scholarship boys from local elementary schools. Allhallows in Honiton did much the same, and eventually took over the Peek family's mansion in Rousdon.

In Exeter the diocesan bishop, the Rt Revd Frederick Temple, a former Schools Enquiry Commissioner, was instrumental in securing the revision of local educational endowments and other charities, despite the objections of descendants of some of the donors, to place four middle-class schools on firm foundations. In 1878 the ancient St John's Hospital Trust was reconstituted as Exeter Grammar School in a grandiose William Butterfield building. In 1870 the ancient Bishop Blackall School was revitalised and split into two new schools – the explicitly named Episcopal Middle Class School for Girls and the more socially elevated Maynard School for Girls, pointedly named after an historic benefactor. The fourth institution to profit was the seventeenth-century Hele's Grammar School for Boys that had struggled financially for many years.

In 1903 the ancient Plympton Grammar School finally closed, primarily, said the *Western Evening Herald*, because 'pupils have been abandoning it for the more up-to-date scholastic advantages of its big neighbour, Plymouth'. In 1874 Frederick Temple helped found Devonport High School for Girls, in 1892 Devonport Technical School opened, followed by Devonport Boys' High School in 1896 and the Girls' High School fifteen years later. They were small but housed in purpose-built premises and possessed syllabuses biased towards the area's commercial needs.

In 1901 there were other options available to parents seeking schools outside the elementary sector. A few tiny 'parish grammar schools' offering some Latin, French, mathematics and commerce to local boys and a few boarders lingered on into Edwardian times, such as those at Bovey Tracey and Colyton – the former to shrivel and die, the latter to grow and prosper.

In the 1860s the Devon Bible Christians established a college at Shebbear, initially to train the sect's ministers and teachers and to educate their sons. In 1884 they opened a similar 'middle-class' girls' boarding school at Edgehill, and soon both schools opened their doors to all-comers who could pay the fees. Both prospered under the authority of the enthusiastic breakaway Wesleyan movement, even after it merged into the United Methodist Church in 1907, not least because they offered various sciences, foreign languages, commerce and art alongside English, mathematics, history, geography, physical education and moral and religious instruction. Edgehill, the girls' school, was especially successful as it had far fewer rivals than Shebbear, but both benefitted from the attraction of their

Bovey Tracey Grammar School, *c.* 1907. (Devon & Exeter Institution)

sympathetic undenominational approach to religious education. Not surprisingly it was this quality that attracted the financial support of the county council early in the twentieth century.

A host of small private schools, often ephemeral and frequently run in family homes, advertised in local papers. In January 1901, for example, the *Devon & Exeter Gazette* advertised Heavitree College and St Hilda's, Dixfield, Haldon View, Mount Radford, Regent's Park, Southernhay and the Misses Trobridges' Schools in Exeter, Summerland College in Honiton, Southlands School in Exmouth, and Wallingbrook School in Chulmleigh. They were all for the sons or daughters of gentlemen, and kept them well away from working-class children. Several other advertisements promoted schools specialising in music and dancing for girls. Miss Hickey in Exeter offered additional 'Court Presentation Lessons'.

A New Elementary School Era Approaches: The Prelude to the 1902 Act

In 1901 universal, free and compulsory elementary education was a very recent phenomenon. In 1876 an act placed parents under a legal obligation to ensure their children received a basic education in literacy, numeracy and Christianity, barred paid employment to children under the age of 10, and established local attendance committees to persuade, shame and coerce recalcitrant families. Further education acts in 1880, 1893 and 1899 made full-time attendance compulsory up to the age of 10, 11 and then 12, and another in 1891 finally made elementary education free of all charges. Until then many schools had charged a few pence each week. In 1899 the government finally created its own Board of Education.

Despite all this legislation, in 1901 the system was in financial and administrative disarray. Attacked on all sides, the school boards' days were numbered. Their critics damned many rural ones for being parsimonious and many urban ones for extending courses dangerously, and some thought illegally, close to the more elevated fee-paying schools. Meanwhile, though, many politicians, businessmen and humanitarians thought the maintenance of British industrial, commercial and imperial supremacy demanded the creation of a far fitter and better trained workforce. However, the decisive argument came from the Church of England which loudly complained that its schools were being penalised unfairly because they relied on voluntary giving as well as their government grants whereas school boards possessed the legal right to draw freely on the rates. It was this that persuaded the deeply Anglican Conservative Prime Minister, Lord Salisbury, to take drastic action. The solution – another education act in 1902 – split the country apart.

Certainly Devon's elementary schools had their vociferous critics in 1901. Head teachers highlighted in particular the minimal enforcement of the attendance regulations and the lack of qualified staff. The magistrates pay more attention to 'dog muzzling cases' than children's education, lamented one head teacher at a conference in Exeter in 1899, and he read out government figures showing Devon was a lowly thirty-fourth on the list of English counties for attendance, averaging just 81.8 per cent. Exeter was thirty-seventh, Devonport fortieth and Plymouth forty-seventh on the list of county boroughs.

Visiting Exeter that same year, Dr Thomas Macnamara, president of the National Union of Teachers (NUT), condemned the abysmally low standards required by most of Devon's school boards and attendance committees for early leaving certificates for older pupils. None required the highest seventh standard, and half of them only the lowly third or fourth. In addition, he noted, whereas 81 per cent of London teachers were fully qualified adults, Devon's figure was 43 per cent. Twenty-two percent were 'Article 68s' – women whose qualifications were limited to being over 18 years of age and vaccinated – the rest were young apprentice teachers or ex-pupil teachers learning on the job with some help from head teachers or through training at pupil-teacher centres. Sensing the growing tension, local newspapers delighted in the diatribes – as they did when Macnamara repeated his speech in Torquay in July 1901 – and highlighted the pitifully small amounts schools were allowed to spend on books, stationery and furniture.

⟨ℛ *Polarisation & the 1902 Act* ℬ⟩

The 1902 Education Act achieved all of the government's objectives, except peace. County and borough councils replaced school boards as local education authorities (LEAs). Significantly, they could spend up to a *2d* rate promoting schools 'other than elementary', 'as seemed to them desirable'. These schools were increasingly termed 'secondary', although they were relatively exclusive fee-paying institutions running parallel to the elementary sector (rather than universal, free and following on from the primary stage as today). Larger borough and urban district councils could opt to become education authorities in their own right, but only for elementary education. Barnstaple, Tiverton and Torquay chose to do so.

Voluntary schools got their much-desired rate support, and in return for only a third of their managers being local authority nominees. The majority remained church appointments. The LEAs, though, would control their curriculum, with the important exception of religious instruction which would stay denominational. Dr Archibald Robertson, the Bishop of Exeter, was delighted and he admitted that the voluntary schools had been saved from ruin. He ignored the key fact that most Nonconformist schools had failed to survive into the new century, which went a long way to explaining the president of Exeter's Free Church Council's announcement that its hostility to this 'crime against common sense' was nothing less than 'a sacred crusade'.

The national outcry was loud and persistent. Devon's strong Liberal associations and Nonconformist congregations denounced the Education Act at public meetings,

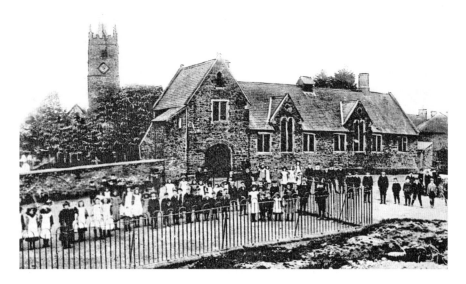

The parish church, Church of England School, pupils and teachers at High Bickington.
(Beaford Arts)

in the press and by the refusal of many otherwise well-respected law-abiding citizens to pay the proportion of their rates they had calculated would go to the local voluntary schools. 'We must obey God, rather than man,' stated an impassioned speaker at the formation of Plymouth's Citizens' League of Passive Resistance in May 1903, and seek 'to follow those who through hardship and suffering, even to death itself, won for us the liberty now so ruthlessly taken from us'. This was 'a priest-framed and not a people-framed law', thundered a correspondent in the Liberal *Ilfracombe Chronicle* in February 1904, while a vitriolic speaker at the launch of Crediton's Citizens' League warned against Roman Catholicism and its 'fearful doctrines' reasserting its authoritarian grip on the country despite that church's mere handful of schools. In more measured tones, Ashburton's Liberal MP Charles Seale-Hayne denounced the act for denying ratepayers a genuine say in local educational affairs.

The act took effect in October 1903. A confused and divided County Education Committee incurred immediate Nonconformist odium when it ruled that the vicar of Salcombe could give religious instruction in the Anglican school despite the opposition of Nonconformists who had no other choice of school, and again in 1905 when it allowed the vicar of Shobrooke, who was a school manager of the council school, to take scripture lessons there.

Across Devon Nonconformist clergy and determined members of their congregations – farmers, shopkeepers, tradesmen and artisans – withheld part of the rates, and in due course received the inevitable summons. Exact numbers of these 'passive resisters' are hard to identify, but possibly 1,000 or so were involved. In Torquay, where all the schools were Anglican, Nonconformists were quick to register their protests through the courts. After due warning, two dozen ended up before the magistrates in September 1903. One resister proved to be an overseer whose official duties included seizing goods from those who had not paid their rates. When his colleagues visited the passive resisters everyone was courteous, and the overseers made a point of accepting what was offered, provided it was of appropriate value, rather than push in and take whatever they chose.

One hundred and twelve appeared in court in Plymouth in October. Among them was the chairman of Plymouth Education Committee, along with fourteen Nonconformist ministers and 'several ladies'. Some resisters, such as John Dennis in Tavistock and George Prestige in Paignton, were also magistrates. Newspaper reports made much of the general embarrassment caused by the unusual court proceedings. Some resisters in Paignton, Torquay and Tavistock attempted to read statements in court justifying their actions but the chairmen either denied the request or halted any defence when it became a political diatribe rather than a legal argument.

Similar non-confrontational 'seizures' occurred the following year across the county. In Cullompton one resister handed over a marble clock, another a set of silver mounted carvers, a third a gold chain and seal, a fourth a set of plated knives and forks and a fifth a gold watch. At the subsequent auctions passive resisters rarely faced any rival bidders if they wanted to buy their goods back at the reserve prices. They had achieved the publicity they sought. In a rare act, though, in February 1905 the Reverend W.Veale, a Bible Christian minister in Chulmleigh, was sent to prison for three days as he had made over all his effects to his wife in his determination not to pay the education rate in any form. For several years more convictions and seizures occurred across the county, and embraced rural communities such as Bovey Tracey, Chudleigh, Kingsteignton, Lapford and Winkleigh as much as towns such as Newton Abbot, Plymouth, Teignmouth and Torquay.

Anti-Education Act rallies continued unabated across Devon in 1904 and 1905. They were characterised by a hatred of the Anglican clergy's influence in local communities, and a mounting suspicion that the local aristocracy, like the House of Lords generally, was loaded heavily against the Liberals and Nonconformists. One speaker acidly asserted that one peer exercised as much influence as 100,000 Nonconformist voters.

In 1905 Sir George Kekewich, soon to be Exeter's Liberal MP, gloated that a new Liberal government would soon take away the Church of England's 'ill-gotten grabbed money'. In this atmosphere of simmering rage, in April 1905 a class of children from St John's School in Plymouth witnessed their vicar and a local councillor angrily laying hands on each other in the parish church when the latter shouted out that the former was lying when he told the pupils, 'This is the only House of God in the parish'.

The vicar of Seaton regularly used the parish magazine to defend the 1902 Act against local critics. In January 1904, for example, he compared the vast sums – £22 million, he claimed – that the Church of England had spent on building schools with the £5 million from all the other denominations combined. That October he sought to confound critics of Anglican 'favouritism' by explaining that parishes remained responsible for their school building repairs, that teaching appointments were subject to the approval of the local education authority, that only one specialist Anglican religious instruction teacher was legally 'reserved' for each school and that parents could remove their children from denominational lessons.

In 1906 the Liberals triumphantly returned to power only to see their bill to place all schools under state control and make denominational teaching the exception not the general rule wrecked and rejected by the Lords. The government tried twice more in 1908, with complex contracting-out clauses for voluntary schools, but to no avail.

Not surprisingly, the bills accentuated local controversies. The Anglican clergy roused their congregations once again, this time in opposition to government bills. In Newton Abbot, the town's clergy compared the Church of England's 14,000 schools and thirty-one training colleges with the Nonconformists' surviving 1,400 schools and three colleges, and asked disingenuously, 'Why don't you build some yourselves?' They damned the Nonconformists as mean-spirited, jealous and dog-in-the-manger. In Torquay, Brixham and Okehampton, and no doubt elsewhere,

Church of England protagonists promoted their partisan views in public meetings, sermons and parish magazines, and friendly newspapers were on hand to ensure the widest possible readership.

The interminable wrangles persisted until 1914 – and indeed afterwards. The Edwardian County Education Committee expended a vast amount of time compiling a religious instruction syllabus and service book deemed acceptable to all denominations, but no one other than the Nonconformists really liked it.

In 1912, the Bishop of Exeter was delighted that Goodleigh had saved its Anglican school as now its pupils would continue to be 'brought up not only with some religious knowledge but also with some religious belief'. In that year the vicar of Seaton was heavily criticised when the Boy Scout troop attended a parade at his church. He was unrepentant, arguing that thirty-two of the thirty-eight Scouts were 'Church boys'. In Torquay, incessant arguments on the Town Council and Education Committee, and between them and the Board of Education, delayed hopes of at least one new council school until March 1913 when Homelands opened.

Children & 'Treats'

Comfortably or uncomfortably, schools were integral parts of the community. They were expected to prosper academically and to promote good causes. In Seaton, for example, the vicar and Lady Peek encouraged the pupils' membership of the Band of Hope with its vow of abstinence from alcohol. Baden-Powell's post-Boer War creation of the Boy Scouts, with its emphasis upon obedience, duty and service within an all-embracing Christian context, was avidly promoted here and in many other parishes. Boys were encouraged to join church choirs, and to enjoy their outings. In 1901 Ipplepen's choristers went on a Tamar River steamer to Calstock for a strawberry and cream tea. In July 1902 St George's Choir in Tiverton took a train to Minehead, then charabancs to Porlock Weir for lunch and to Lynton for an afternoon walk through the Valley of the Rock. In 1912 Seaton's choir went by train to Torquay and then by ferry to Brixham to see the trawlers and colliers and visit the Seamen's Orphans' Home.

Schools enjoyed a surprising number of interruptions. In a not unusual list, between July 1899 and February 1901 the children of St George's Church of England School in East Stonehouse enjoyed holidays for the arrival procession of Barnum & Bailey's Show, the parish bazaar raising funds for the school, the annual steamer trip up the Tamar, the surrender of the Boer General Cronje, the Relief of Mafeking and the Fall of Pretoria. In addition there were several Sunday school 'treats'.

It was customary for rival Church of England, Methodist, Bible Christian, Congregational and Baptist Sunday schools to reward regular members with an annual 'treat', usually an outing involving assorted team games, tea, songs, hymns and an uplifting talk. Invariably they were on a school day to add to the children's fun and to head teachers' frustrations if, as frequently happened, the rival churches could not arrange them on the same day.

Numbers could be large. During July 1902 special trains took 240 teachers and children from Tiverton Congregational Sunday school to Teignmouth, 180 from the Baptist Sunday school to Teignmouth too, and 170 from the Bible Christian Sunday school to Dulverton. The following year, 350 members of Tiverton's Church of England Sunday school went by rail to Exmouth, and 370 from Paignton's two parish churches to Moretonhampstead and the moors.

The outings were colourful affairs, and as much concerned with publicity and recruitment as enjoyment. Sunday schools were influential enough to be immune from criticisms by any head teachers who suddenly found themselves with very poor attendance figures. Insufficient notice, though, meant school managers were unable to use one of the 'spare holidays' they kept in reserve for such emergencies. As grants were linked to attendance percentages this was no minor matter.

As we have seen, in some villages there were other treats. Each August the children of Jacobstowe and their mothers enjoyed games, tea and presents at Broomford Manor, the home of Sir Robert and Lady White-Thomson. Mrs Pine-Coffin did the same at Kenwith for the local schools. Not far away, the local landowners, clergy and traders of Halwill and Morleigh combined to give the school children an afternoon of races finished off with cake, buns and ginger beer to encourage, the *Western Guardian* said in 1903, 'regular attendance'.

Petrockstowe Wesleyan Sunday school outing in horse brakes and carriages to Westward Ho!, 20 July 1909. (Beaford Arts)

A school treat at Fort Hill, Barnstaple. (Author's collection)

In 1902 and 1911 many school children attended tea parties to mark the corona-
tions of Edward VII and George V and were given decorated mugs or medals and
brooches by local dignitaries. Some elementary schools copied the grammar school
practice of prize days, with parents and managers watching musical or dramatic
performances and applauding the prizes for good work, for perfect or almost
perfect attendance, and for commendation by the religious instruction inspector.

In 1913 Exeter City Council itself provided a treat when it voted to hold a
summer holiday school to 'take some of the children out of the miserable squalid
surroundings of a poor district into a playground or fields where organised games
and organised occupations could be arranged'. It was at a time when much publicity had been given to the West Quarter's slums and to a worrying level of juvenile
delinquency. That August, 160 children enjoyed several days of singing, storytelling,
acting, reading, dancing, drill, flower pressing, doll dressing, cardboard modelling
and walks centred upon the County Showground in St Thomas. Many others,
Trewman's Flying Post reported, looked on enviously through the railings. It was
repeated in 1914, a few days before war broke out.

The Cult of Imperialism

Empire Day on 24 May became a particularly special day in schools during the
Edwardian era, and must have seemed exciting and mystifying in about equal measure.
It aimed to instil in the rising generation not only pride in being British when the
country commanded the largest empire the world had ever seen, but also a sense of

Christian service towards the subordinate nations and tribes within it. The Earl of
Meath promoted the idea in 1904, and the chosen date was the birthday of Queen
Victoria, during whose lengthy reign so many territories had been acquired.

Initially a patriotic song or two followed by buns, orange squash and a half-
holiday were the order of the day, but within a few years formal ceremonies took
over, venerating the Union Jack and past imperial heroes and embracing lessons, hymns and prayers on the Empire Day 'watchwords' of 'Responsibility, Duty,
Sympathy, Self-sacrifice'.

In 1908 the vicar of Ilsham ensured that pupils were suitably awed by the fact
that 400 million people around the world were 'controlled by a little island in the
North Sea' and 'the strains of the National Anthem were circulating the Globe in
one unending, universal song of praise and loyalty'. The preservation of the empire
became inextricably tied to the children's moral conduct. At Great Torrington in
1909 pupils were told its future well-being meant they should never be 'slaves to
drink, gambling, laziness and bad language'. In 1913 the Mayor of Exeter urged the
pupils of Episcopal Boys' School to pledge themselves 'that under Providence we
will … strive to the uttermost to make our country stronger, better, juster, holier'.

Managers and squires gave many schools flagpoles and Union Jacks, and from
then on Empire Day included formal marches with the children giving smart
salutes to the national flag. Sometimes pupils were dressed in allegorical costumes – such as Justice, Liberty, Peace and Plenty – as at Silverton in 1913. Urban
celebrations often involved massed ranks of school children. In 1911, 3,000 Exeter
school children assembled at the County Showground in St Thomas and whole
classes resplendent in traditional costumes of the dominions and colonies paraded

Merton School after the songs, marching and salutes on Empire Day, *c.* 1910. (Beaford Arts)

before the mayor, education committee and assembled crowd. In the same year 2,000 Barnstaple school children marched to Rock Park to sing the empire hymn 'Unfurl the Empire's Flag' and hear the mayor equate the Union Jack with the 'justice and truth and honesty' that shone over the empire, and henceforth should guide their own lives.

In 1913 all 1,350 school children in Tiverton were taken in two parties to the picture theatre to see a 'cinematograph' of the king's coronation procession, the career of Cecil Rhodes, pictures of the Delhi Durbar and 'a moving representation' of the Naval Review. Afterwards the mayor told the children that India and Africa would never have enjoyed peace and stability but for the law and order brought to them by the British. Teachers were expected to inculcate patriotism, and in 1911 the headmaster at Pinhoe, near Exeter, received the unwelcome attention of his managers, the County Education Committee and the local newspapers when he was accused of instilling 'disloyal ideas in the minds of the school children' and showing 'a reluctance to national songs being taught'.

The Battle for Attendance

After the 1902 Act all of Devon's education authorities battled to raise attendance rates against the counter-attractions of local fetes, fairs, point-to-point races, fox, otter, hare and stag hunts, weekly markets, seasonal circuses, summer regattas, offers of casual work by rural and urban employers and the demands of family life with its frequent crises, including sickness, births and deaths. Schools rarely competed successfully with the annual tours of Devon by Messrs Bostock & Wombwell's Menagerie with its captive vultures, chimpanzees, gorillas, kangaroos, lions, leopards, elephants, camels and polar bears. And the lure of short-lived seasonal work such as haymaking and soft fruit picking, potato planting and digging and poultry plucking was hard to combat when children, parents and employers often acted in concert, and were prepared to risk the threat of summonses and fines.

Most head teachers were obsessed with attendance figures, although logbooks, letters and reports reveal that some were as sympathetic to the needs of local employers as many of the magistrates who were supposed to wage war alongside the attendance officers against families of regular absentees. In September 1902 Stoodleigh's head teacher accepted local priorities, writing, 'This has proved to be one of the finest weeks of the year, with Harvest, which was sadly interrupted last week, being in full swing and completed on many farms. The attendances have consequently suffered, many boys assisting, and carrying their parents' meals.' Similar entries appeared each succeeding year. In 1909 a discussion at Tiverton's Education Committee revealed that members had long accepted that a number of girls were kept home on Mondays to help with the washing.

Nevertheless, the attendance war was slowly won. In 1903 Devonport's Education Committee agreed that the town's 80 per cent attendance rate was unacceptable. It meant that 2,000 children 'were running about the streets', and each one lost rate-payers £1 7s a year in grants. Fines were doubled to 10s and even £1 in some cases. In 1905 the South Devon School Attendance Officers' Association was formed to share experiences, raise their public and professional profile and act corporately to encourage and coerce parental responsibility, not least by bringing more cases to court.

In March 1901 the average attendance for Tiverton's six board schools was 81 per cent, although sickness caused individual schools to vary from 62 per cent to 90 per cent. By 1910 the twenty-four schools in and around Tiverton averaged 92.1 per cent, despite illness reducing Oakford and Bickleigh to 74–75 per cent. It was a significant improvement, and was happening elsewhere. As the chairman of Exeter Education Committee remarked after laying the foundation stone of the new St James' School in 1907, just one generation ago, in 1870, 5,000 of the city's 7,000 children did not attend school at all.

The Epidemics

Sickness was ever present, and epidemics of measles, mumps, whooping cough and chicken pox were common, always alarming, and frequently long lasting. Honiton Council School was not unusual in experiencing all three between September 1913 and April 1914. Deaths were common. Whooping cough killed several children in Holsworthy in 1900, fourteen children died from measles in Northam in 1906 and fifty-seven in Exeter in 1911.

Diphtheria was ever present. In 1900 it was endemic in Thornbury, and the district medical officer of health blamed the deaths of twenty-six babies there on the district's polluted water supplies. When several deaths occurred in Bampton that year a frantic public meeting railed at the 'evil-smelling slaughterhouses, unclean yards and piggeries causing nuisances in the midst of dwelling houses'.

Throughout 1905 and 1906 outbreaks of diphtheria ravaged Bradninch, frightening residents, closing the school and puzzling doctors. Antitoxin injections, gargles and throat washes were given free of charge, the school's books, stationery and pictures were burned and walls scraped and repainted, but, the medical officer of health admitted, to little effect. Ninety days of schooling were lost in 1906. The contagion spread to Silverton and Cullompton, where ninety-five cases were reported, and Tiverton's new isolation hospital became overcrowded. Once again, the erratic water supply and poor sewage system were heavily criticised, and the district council promised remedial action. A further thirty-five cases were reported around Barnstaple, and for years afterwards diphtheria struck down other families across north Devon. In the south, Kingsteignton endured a nightmare succession of cases from October 1912 until early 1914.

In 1909–10 twenty-one schools closed due to outbreaks of poliomyelitis, which terrified families, mystified doctors and had an alarming death rate. There were eighty cases: sixteen children died and 'a great many' were left paralysed. During the second half of 1911 another 130 children contracted the disease, mainly in and around Bideford, and twenty-two died. Thirty-eight schools closed for at least four weeks. Needless hardship and suffering were caused, the local government board inspector stated, by the absence of isolation hospitals in many districts.

Scarlet fever was feared too, and in 1902 136 cases were reported in Ashburton when it returned after an outbreak the previous year. In February 1906 it broke out in and around Crediton, and returned in the summer and autumn closing several schools for weeks at a time. The medical officer bemoaned the defective drains and sewers and 'offensive pig-styes', and once again, the lack of an isolation hospital. The disease was ever present in the county; head teachers gloomily recorded its return to Okehampton in 1910, Barnstaple in 1912 and Ilfracombe during the Great War.

Contaminated milk accounted for periodic outbreaks of tuberculosis (TB). Medical officers of health urged a range of public health reforms – purer water, efficient sewers and eradication of rubbish heaps – but, above all, the education of mothers in the virtues of hygiene and baby care. Dr Slade-King in north Devon made his views clear, asserting, 'The large majority of children are born sound in wind and limb … but ignorance, dirt, prejudice, poverty, and difficulty of obtaining and storing milk too often baffle even a mother's love.'

By 1914, though, there were three main hospitals and 'working colonies' in Devon treating TB patients. In 1903 the Devon & Cornwall Sanatorium at Didworthy, near South Brent, and in 1913 the County Sanatorium at Hawkmoor, near Bovey Tracey, had joined the Western Hospital for Incipient Consumptives in Torquay founded in 1850.

The long, hard battle for state-supported maternity and childcare support was getting under way, but it would take the appalling slaughter of the Great War to make it a reality. 'Lectures on child-rearing have been tried,' lamented Dr Slade-King, in 1907, 'but only the better class woman attends them.' Others, such as Dr Jackson in Barnstaple, blamed the widespread farming out of babies 'to persons indifferent to their welfare' by mothers compelled to go out to work.

Infant mortality remained stubbornly high in Devon, and rarely fell below the national average. In the borough of Torquay 14 per cent of infants under 1 year of age died in 1908, 12½ per cent across Barnstaple Rural District in 1910, and 12½ per cent in Exeter in 1911. It remained a dangerous time to be a baby. One advance was the introduction of hygiene into the school curriculum, with Dr Dunlop, Torquay's medical officer, taking a lead in 1906. The syllabus was wide ranging, and touched upon knowledge of healthy hair, teeth, breathing, diets and habits, personal hygiene, and, for girls, good baby care.

❧ *The Battle for the School Medical Service* ❧

The publicity given to the alarming news that a third of army recruits during the Boer War were rejected as falling below the basic physical requirements led to the impressively titled 1904 Inter-Departmental Committee on Physical Deterioration. As expected, it confirmed the army's findings.

Widespread cries of 'racial degeneracy' helped create the momentum for the growth of healthy outdoor movements such as the Boy Scouts. They were popular across Devon. In March 1910 Lieutenant General Sir Robert Baden-Powell him-self inspected the 400 Boy Scouts gathered smartly before him in Plymouth. Three years later, 150 Scouts from north Devon paraded before General Sir Richard Harrison and heard him say that such a magnificently disciplined turnout gave the lie to the tales of national degeneracy. As always on such occasions the boys were urged to even greater heights of moral probity and public service.

The well-publicised 1904 inquiry generated enough political will to create the Medical Branch of the Board of Education and from 1908 local authorities were obliged to appoint school medical officers and inspect all elementary school children. Any treatment, though, would be the parents' responsibility.

Dr Adkins was Devon's first county medical officer for schools and he brought a vast array of statistics and accompanying conclusions to the County Education Committee's sometimes shocked and bewildered attention. Each year, thousands of school children were examined, their 'defects' recorded and their parents instructed to secure the necessary treatment. And the medical staff experienced at first hand the same bleak, cramped, dusty buildings and primitive sanitary arrangements as many of the teachers and pupils. Some parents, perhaps fearing the cost of any treatment or seeing the inspection as an insult or embarrassment, refused to attend, or kept their children away on the day. As late as May 1910 the nurse in Brixham received threatening letters, and the one in Paignton had to be escorted to and from some homes by the police.

Dr Adkins and his team quickly uncovered an array of 'defects'. In the first year, 1,800 Exeter children were examined and 17.6 per cent found to have defective eyesight, 12 per cent poor hearing, 6 per cent enlarged tonsils and adenoids, 3.5 per cent rickets, 2.3 per cent lung diseases, 2.3 per cent heart problems, and 35 per cent of girls and 7 per cent of boys had verminous heads, the former mainly because of their long but unkempt hair. One hundred and forty-four children – 6 per cent – were deemed 'mentally weak'. The Torquay oculist examined 511 children's eyes and found 369 suffering from untreated problems, but the only way poor families could obtain spectacles was through a local charity hurriedly set up for the purpose. And Dr Slade-King, in north Devon, was horrified at the potential illnesses and deformities facing the large number of children still attending school in ill-fitting and leaking boots, often hand-downs. Footwear was expensive, and there was no solution other than charitable aid.

Across the county early inspections revealed that 90 per cent of children had defective teeth, and, said one Devon medical officer, the vast majority had never seen a dentist. Ten per cent of children were deemed to be seriously malnourished, but no local council offered a solution beyond asserting that charitable effort had always sufficed – and certainly various charities did provide hundreds of Exeter and Plymouth families with free or farthing meals in recessions and hard winters.

One long-standing problem was tackled in a typically Edwardian manner. The incidence of body and head lice was high. In September 1909 Burlescombe's headmistress was disgusted that some children's heads were so filthy that the 'parasites' fell onto their desks. In July 1910 Dr Adkins reported that 475 out of 900 children inspected in and around Kingsbridge were infested, and his colleagues confirmed that lice were everywhere, in large quantities.

The County Education Committee agreed that verminous children should be barred from school until they were cleansed, and if the parents neglected to achieve this in a reasonable time they could be prosecuted for failing to ensure their children were educated. As Adkins possessed a low view of working-class mothers' childcare skills, he heartily agreed. To assist in the campaign, 'cleansing stations' with disinfecting baths were established in Exeter, Plymouth and Torquay by 1912. Nevertheless, victory was a long way off – during the last three months of 1913 Devon's nurses issued 1,351 'verminous notices'.

Throughout the later Edwardian period tensions existed between doctors and teachers and school managers over the merits of attendance prizes when the pressure for the highest possible grant so obviously conflicted with the argument that some sick children were lured into school to the peril of themselves and others when they should have stayed in bed at home. The prizes won the day.

This was just one instance when the County Education Committee felt besieged by its critics, especially as the medical officers' professional status and battery of figures ensured their recommendations had to be heard, if not necessarily acted upon. The newspaper reports revealed that some members thought the replacement of odious middens and earth closets, the provision of piped drinking water, wash basins and clean towels, the tarring of dangerous and filthy gravel yards, the replacement of flickering oil lamps by gas or electric light, the fitting of more windows that opened, the installation of stoves that warmed the children as well as the teacher and did not fill the room with smoke and fumes, and the regular disinfection of buildings were not only prohibitively expensive but also represented unnecessary luxuries – especially as it was hinted that these things, although no doubt desirable in an ideal world, were largely absent in the children's homes.

Adkins' criticisms hit an all-time low in 1913 when his list included the need for proper toilet paper at East Budleigh and Dittisham. HMI added their own criticisms of many buildings, and from time to time the Board of Education issued warnings – as at East Worlington, Farway and Holsworthy – that grants would be withheld if particular rebuilding or refurbishments were not carried out. As the headmistress at Westwood, near Broadclyst, noted in February 1911, even on ordinary days her primitive school buildings presented problems – 'The rooms are already looking rather dirty, through muddy roads; the coal makes a great quantity of ash; and the stove chimney is inclined to smoke, badly.'

It was not so much that the committee as a whole was parsimonious per se, as its minutes regularly list a number of maintenance and modernisation projects, such as the new drains, water closets and basins provided at Elmscott, Meldon, Oveston, Sherford, Shute, Welcombe and Werrington in the summer of 1907. However, the backlog of inadequate school board and transferred voluntary schools was substantial, and all the while the Board of Education's standards for space and facilities continually rose and, as committee members frequently remarked, the ratepayers who bore much of the cost got as angry as those demanding better schools. In January 1914, though, Dr Adkins told the committee that whereas twenty-four Anglican and Roman Catholic schools were still very seriously sub-standard, only the four council ones at Washford Pyne, Cheriton Bishop, Haccombe and Dartmouth remained in that utterly degrading category. The committee, no doubt relieved, voted to bring discrete but firm pressure on the voluntary schools to take action.

Child Labour

The county council was certainly resistant to one reform. In 1909 the Children's Act took effect, and substantially extended and strengthened the half-hearted earlier restrictions on children begging and selling in the street and consuming alcohol, and also working in dangerous and inappropriate environments, including 'places of ill-repute'. New juvenile courts were established, and the disciplined routines and training of industrial schools and reformatories replaced incarceration in prisons.

The act revealed the horrors to which children had been exposed until then, but one of them was well known and it remained protected at a high level. For decades teachers, managers, magistrates, clergy, parents and, of course, numerous rural and urban employers knew that many children worked long hours outside those they spent in school.

At Pinhoe, near Exeter, the logbook records children in 1907 working up to five hours before and after school and in between morning and afternoon lessons. As late as 1913, eighty-two out of the 332 boys aged 10–14 at Bideford Boys' School were employed for an average of four and a half hours a day, plus all day Saturday. Forty of these, recorded the headmaster, were late to school nearly every day.

Yet in August 1912, Exeter magistrates found a woman who employed a child at midday most weekdays, and also for seven hours on Saturdays, not guilty of acting illegally; she claimed she did so partly out of pity for the child's large family. The chief constable said he had issued the summons as an example of 'some hundreds of children so employed in the city'.

Typically, Exeter's bylaws looked strict but possessed plenty of loopholes. In 1907 it had banned boys under 12 and girls under 16 from street trading. It also stopped children doing 'industrial work at home' on schooldays, except between 5 p.m. and 7 p.m., to limit, but certainly not stop, the intensive piecework schedules governing tailoring and millinery. Effective inspection would have been difficult, as no doubt everyone knew.

The county council itself only considered firm action in 1913. Its new bylaw proposed that 'no child liable to attend school full time shall be employed on school days at any time between 8.15 a.m. and 4.30 p.m.' The Home Office was astounded to receive 170 formal objections, and it mounted a series of district inquiries. Some clergy held strong views. The rural dean of Cullompton asserted 'that in 99 cases out of 100 we were over-educating boys'; the rector of Kentisbeare called the proposal 'vexatious and meddling', as school hours left plenty of time for work; the vicar of Appledore argued that ships docking or departing at midday needed plenty of assistance; the vicar of Offwell asserted that 'hardly one teacher was able to say that a child came to school the worse for work'; the vicar of Stoke Fleming agreed with him and the vicar of Kingsbridge believed that working children were acquiring invaluable habits and skills for later life.

Not surprisingly, the Devon Farmers' Union was firmly opposed, claiming it 'would be an interference with the private rights of parents and employers'. Other employers feared that fathers would be denied their lunches if children could not bring them at midday, that the London newspapers could be delayed interminably, or milk deliveries would not be completed, essential deliveries of groceries would be delayed until the evening and many families would be impoverished without the extra pennies the children earned. If the bylaw was adopted, one rural head teacher claimed, children would be forced to get up even earlier than usual to milk cows and clean their stalls.

The Home Office had some sympathy with employers and parents, and said driving cattle to and from pasture, leading horses to and from farriers, undertaking domestic errands and carrying water and meals could be exempted from the definition of 'employment' at these times. Otherwise, no child could work within thirty minutes of the start and end of each school day, or at midday. Arguments were still raging early in 1914 when Dr Adkins claimed 210 out of 265 children specifically examined because they were employed out of school were suffering as a result of their employment. He called it 'white slavery'.

❦ Stimulating the Children ❧

At a Devon NUT conference in 1902 HMI Mr Cowie elaborated on the essential truth that it was futile to treat children as 'passive receptacles into which information is pumped'. He urged stimulating pupils by varying the teaching approaches throughout each day to embrace silent reading, oral discussions, practical work and enjoyable physical exercise.

Not surprisingly, local practices varied widely. HMI reports reveal the approaches they considered superannuated. From many examples, the adverse comments made around 1910 to Culmstock School, Salisbury Road Girls' School in Plymouth and the Blue Coat School in Barnstaple show that some children still endured a monotonous and increasingly unacceptable diet of dull history and geography readers, inappropriate military drill, interminable singing exercises, memorising lengthy poems they did not comprehend, the rote learning of tables without understanding, copying drawings without adequate training, copying down isolated facts told to them in 'object lessons' and undertaking ill-digested dictation and grammar exercises and excessive copy writing.

In marked contrast, some lessons were far more stimulating as teachers responded to new ideas. In 1907 classes at Holy Trinity in Barnstaple grew flowers, kept pets and studied the local environment at first hand, and during that year, Freidrich Froebal's 'Learning by Doing' theories prompted clay and paper modelling, the creation of a museum and visits to the lace factory by Heathcoat School in Tiverton.

Logbook entries and HMI reports towards the end of the era record an increasing number of innovations. In 1911 Westwood School was one of several recording new mental arithmetic, original composition, drawing from life and observation lessons. In Moretonhampstead mathematics included practical measuring and calculating household bills, while English lessons here and at Cadbury and Crediton included access to library books donated by well-wishers. Buckfastleigh children visited a local textile factory, those at St Philip & St James in Ilfracombe toured the recently established gas, electricity and water works and watched demonstration lessons in science.

Boys at Ashleigh Road, St Mary Magdalene and Holy Trinity schools in Barnstaple, Abbotsham, and Haywards School in Crediton and Abbotsham were among those who undertook practical gardening projects. Girls in Plymouth visited the new day nursery for instruction in baby care. A field club at St Thomas' School in Exeter engaged in after-school nature rambles. Games of football, if schools were lucky enough to secure pitches, balls and boots, and district swimming galas (invariably in unheated outdoor pools) became more widespread. Highly competitive head teachers such as at St Philip & St James in Ilfracombe proudly recorded their annual swimming trophies. St Sidwell's School in Exeter became famous for its football team; indeed its Old Boys' team became Exeter Football Club.

Gardening class at Abbotsham School, 1912. (Beaford Arts)

Schools were even occasionally taken to a picture house. In 1913, 1,400 children in schools across Torquay were taken to see *From Manger to Cross* in the Picturedrome. The tickets were offered free of charge by the shrewd owner at a time when gangster films were being blamed for an alleged rise in juvenile crime. In March 1914 *Trewman's Flying Post* thought *Sixty Years A Queen* was entirely suitable for children with its uplifting survey of Victoria's reign, notably regarding the successful expansion of the empire.

In 1914 Tiverton's newspaper carried an interview with an 'old boy' of Heathcoat Boys' School who had high praise for the advances since his time there in the 1890s. Its recently opened new building was far better heated, ventilated and equipped, and the old 'simple theory' instruction had been replaced with more stimulating practical approaches. Nature study and botany in the classroom were connected to work in the school garden and mathematics and drawing were linked to three-dimensional model making. Music had blossomed through the formation of a band and physical exercise was enlivened by team games and athletics.

Parallel Systems

Despite such progress the educational opportunities for older, elementary school children were essentially training programmes for skilled working-class occupations. In May 1904 *Trewman's Flying Post* praised the range of tools in Exeter's Manual Instruction Centre, together with the complicated joints and inlays its reporter had seen there. The emphasis, though, was upon achieving the highest standards of technical proficiency, with little room for creativity. Artisans, not artists, were the aim.

In 1907 Tiverton's education committee expressed itself very satisfied with its vocationally biased syllabuses in handicraft, gardening and cookery. A few years later two wealthy sisters, Miss Lazenby and Mrs White, provided the borough with a manual instruction centre for boys and a domestic subjects centre for girls to consolidate the good work.

In 1912 the *Flying Post* praised Exeter's plans to add laundry work and household management to its cookery classes for older girls. 'It would fit the girls for domestic service,' said Miss Montgomery, a member of the education committee, 'and also prove of incalculable benefit to them in their homes later in life.' The chairman asserted that no one could complain this vocational initiative was a waste of money.

The 'working-class' elementary and 'middle-class' grammar schools (increasingly, and confusingly, also termed 'secondary' or 'high schools') were advancing in very different directions. Late in 1904 Devon County Council voted through its long-term secondary school development scheme. It did not amount to much. From 1905 it grant-aided the secondary/grammar schools in Ashburton, Bideford, Bovey Tracey, Braunton, Crediton, West Buckland, Edgehill, Kingsbridge, Shebbear, Tavistock and Totnes. It also proposed new county secondary schools in Barnstaple, Newton Abbot and Torquay at some unspecified time in the future on cost sharing agreements with their borough councils. With pupil rolls of around 300, by 1914 these modest undertakings had been, or were about to be, fulfilled. Amidst some controversy, in 1911 King's School in Ottery St Mary was rebuilt as the county's first mixed secondary school, largely because the district could not support two single-sex ones. In 1913 the education committee was less than pleased when Dr Adkins condemned mixed secondary schools as 'morally, intellectually and physically' detrimental to children over the age of 11, and 'ruinous' to 'the souls and bodies' of girls exposed to competition with boys.

Newton Abbot, Tiverton and Torquay epitomised the trend at this time for major towns to equip themselves with a range of educational facilities for older pupils carefully tailored to meet the needs of local employers. A substantial number of courses within the small science, art and technical schools in all three towns – Torquay's had just 294 students in 1905 – had acquired the enhanced secondary school grants offered after the 1902 Act, and a new equally small secondary school was perceived as completing the spectrum of their educational provision. In Tiverton the Technical, Art & Science School was scattered in four ancient buildings but finally amalgamated with the Middle (Class) School in 1906 and a new pupil-teacher training centre was created – a sure sign of 'secondary' status and grants. Four years later members of the Heathcoat-Amory, Walrond and Northcote families graced the opening of an impressive new building housing these various programmes, a good proportion of which possessed a distinctive vocational bias.

Newton Abbot's hopes finally blossomed when the county council eventually opened the new secondary school premises in 1915. Even relatively small communities such as South Molton possessed similar ambitions, and in 1909 proudly added a technical and art extension to its main elementary school.

The county council's 1904–05 scheme looked generous, but as local newspapers were quick to point out, the investment represented just a halfpenny county rate, nowhere near the 2*d* permitted by the 1902 Act. During the debate the education committee noted that in Devon just '2.3 boys per 1,000 of the population' attended secondary schools. In Wales and the West Riding the figures were twice as high, members were informed, but they merely voted that Devon's modest ambition should be to raise the figure to between two and a half and three per 1,000 for both boys and girls. They just about achieved it by 1914.

In 1905 the renowned educationalist, Michael Sadler, published a thorough survey of Exeter's 'Secondary and Higher Education' and pinpointed its strengths and weaknesses. The 'first grade' Boys' Grammar School and Girls' High School received high praise for their range of subjects, and, less enthusiastically, Sadler judged the Episcopal Middle School for Girls and Hele's School for Boys to be as successful as they could be with the limited facilities and few teachers at their disposal due to their small size and inadequate financial resources. The city took note. In 1909, Lord and Lady Northcote, accompanied by the Bishop of Exeter, opened an extension to the Episcopal Middle School for Girls. Several new classrooms, science laboratories and a library enabled the school to double in size to 300 students.

Countess Fortescue laying the foundation stone of the technical and art extension to South Molton's Church of England United Schools, 12 February 1909. (Beaford Arts)

A major issue pinpointed by Sadler, especially regarding the girls' schools, was that too little time was spent in them by too many students to benefit fully from the courses, either because they were admitted late or left early, or both. Overall, a minority of men went on to university; most went into the middle tiers of trade, commerce or engineering. Few girls took up careers. Given the high quality of Sadler's report it is reasonable to suppose the situation was similar in other Devon towns.

The institution most impressing Sadler was the Royal Albert Memorial College, whose practical and theoretical courses covering a range of levels up to university standard in the arts, humanities, sciences, commerce, technology and teacher training, currently attracted over 900 day and evening students. In 1911 John Stocker, chairman of Exeter's Education Committee, 'hailed with delight the fact that any poor boy could now work his way from the elementary schools to the great Universities'. He was overstating the case; it was not quite that simple for most working-class families.

Edwardian logbooks refer in glowing terms, and sometimes in red ink, to pupils gaining a rare scholarship to secondary schools. Speakers at numerous NUT meetings urged the prohibition of coaching children for these scholarships – a sure sign that it was thought to be widespread. No head teacher ever admitted to coaching, but invariably basked in the lustre a winner bestowed upon the school. Ironically, leaving an elementary school as a scholarship holder was the best thing a child could do for its reputation.

The Children in Institutions

Few children with what contemporaries termed 'physical or mental defects' received specialist care. Most did not, and endured life in ordinary schools or, with the tacit agreement of all concerned, never went to school at all.

Plymouth had had a special school in Salisbury Road since 1898 for physically healthy, 'feeble-minded' children capable of simple training. In 1910 Dr Rosa Bale told the *Western Evening Herald* that its children were regularly tested, and those who progressed well were sent back to normal schools and those who did not were excluded – she did not say where they went, although she, and most other pioneering experts, firmly believed that residential institutions protected society from 'mental defectives' as much as they protected the patients themselves.

At Starcross, between Exeter and Dawlish, a grimmer-looking Victorian charitable institution housed children termed 'feeble-minded', but physically healthy and capable of learning simple tasks. Financed through fees levied on boards of guardians and voluntary subscriptions and donations, it aimed to train its residents through strict domestic routines, a variety of manual tasks and regular moral and religious instruction. A visit by a *Devon & Exeter Gazette* reporter in 1903 revealed

R.W.C. Institution, Starcross.

The Royal Western Counties Institution, Starcross, known as the Western Counties Idiot Asylum until 1914. (Author's collection)

a calm, clean and very well-ordered environment. The children were trained to make shoes, clothing, baskets, mats, hats, brushes and lace, grow vegetables and flowers, tend a variety of farm animals and undertake all the domestic chores. As in all schools, physical exercises were imbued with strong moral overtones.

A few years later the HMI for special schools rated Starcross highly, citing the sophisticated practical skills the children were acquiring. One cannot help suspecting the accuracy of the initial judgements made about some of these children on the evidence of the complex tasks these reports said the young inmates mastered. However, the records of those discharged intimate that only a small minority could look after themselves independently, and the fate of many others as they grew into adults was probably alarming. The Charity Organisation Society was less than solicitous regarding their well-being, with a speaker at Torquay in 1911 asserting, 'At present released from control at the age of 16, the majority become drunkards, criminals, paupers, and they were left to marry and propagate their kind, to be, in turn, supported by the rates'. These people, she said, must remain under permanent control in residential institutions.

6

PAINFUL ADJUSTMENTS
The Poor, Charities & Workhouses

⟡ *The Genesis of the 1834 Poor Law* ⟡

For centuries, those who possessed nothing relied entirely on the willingness of the wealthy to take pity on them. Numerous gifts and legacies led to the foundation of hospitals, almshouses and other charities offering food, fuel, clothing and money to the needy of the locality. Many survived into the Edwardian era and beyond. They stemmed from natural generosity and the understandable desire to be recalled favourably in this world, and possibly treated mercifully in the next. Their proliferation across Devon was evidence of the widespread poverty the benefactors had witnessed and, indeed, possibly feared for themselves in a society offering little alternative protection from dislocations in the economy, natural disasters and the ravages of disease. And those fortunate to possess property and incomes were well aware that the poor presented a constant threat, not least because their soaring numbers in times of high inflation and economic depression frequently led to riots and acts of violence against those they held responsible for their hunger and homelessness – primarily employers, landlords and magistrates.

Workhouses providing shelter and work for the abject poor were established in the sixteenth century, and so was 'outdoor relief', whereby food, fuel and clothing were given to the aged and infirm as needs arose, and perhaps a few families received a little money to supplement their low income. A rate to help the poor was levied on every household in the parish. Practices varied widely, but by the beginning of the nineteenth century Poor Rates were soaring alarmingly – many quadrupling between 1780 and 1820.

The national economy had fluctuated wildly during and after the Napoleonic Wars; the Industrial Revolution had mechanised the means of production and

The drive and main entrance to Exeter Workhouse from an eighteenth-century drawing.
Notwithstanding extended wings, the frontage was much the same in 1901.
(Devon & Exeter Institution)

destroyed many cottage industries, notably the home-based spinners and weavers;
threshing machines threatened the livelihood of many rural workers and land
enclosures had taken away the rights of common grazing and foraging long held
by poor country folk. Violent protests targeted not only the new machines but also
those who owned them.

A frightened government took action, and the Poor Law Amendment Act of
1834 did just what its title said. The existing system whereby low wages were sup-
plemented by 'outdoor relief' payments was abolished, primarily because it was
perceived as encouraging employers to pay grossly inadequate wages knowing
the Poor Rate would make them up. A new type of workhouse replaced the wide
variety of small local institutions and their varying customs and practices. The act
was based on the premise that life in workhouses should be sufficiently basic and
humiliating to ensure only the genuinely needy sought admission to them. It introduced a standardised system based on four principles close to Victorian legislators'
hearts – it reduced costs, it identified genuine need, it placed the decision to enter
the workhouse in the hands of the applicant and it ensured the idle and degenerate
element in the population did not profit from it.

By separating men, women and children once they were inside the workhouse,
it was hoped that the strictly disciplined regime and Christian tone would restore
some moral worth to the inmates and perhaps equip them to return to the outside
world. And if the unemployed preferred to move away, or even emigrate, to seek
work elsewhere, so much the better for them and for the locality. There was the
vague hope that the act would oblige local employers to raise wages to a living
standard, and the equally vague belief that there was enough work available, especially in the towns, for those who actively sought it.

❦ *Flaws & Effects* ❧

The new system was not intentionally inhumane but, in common with most national systems involving numerous large institutions, the people that ran them varied widely in industry, imagination and integrity. Most corrosive of all was the lasting impact of the four principles buttressing the new Poor Law. They undermined it from the outset because it was impossible to apply them sensibly when the economy, right through to the reign of Edward VII, was so volatile and prone to what contemporaries called 'flushes and crashes'. The assumption that most poor people had somehow chosen to be destitute through their own fecklessness and debauchery, and therefore deserved minimal sympathy and care, was proved false but unfortunately only a few vociferous critics of the workhouses wanted to believe it, and nobody came up with a better system.

The country was quickly covered with vast workhouses, each one housing many hundreds of inmates and supervised by a board of guardians drawn from the dozen or more parishes in the 'union' that funded it according to the new criteria. In due course, the monolithic and unyielding system developed a momentum of its own that rendered fundamental changes extremely difficult to implement. As early as 1869, though, George Goschen, president of the Poor Law Board, tacitly admitted its main flaw – that destitution could be the result of fluctuations in the economy as well as individual weaknesses – in a memorandum requiring the guardians who had reintroduced 'outdoor relief' to stop it and asserting that every union should discriminate between 'deserving' and 'undeserving' applicants seeking admission to its workhouse.

The 1834 Act had three key results. Deeply satisfying to some, there was a massive decrease in admissions alongside a mounting horror of the taint of 'pauperisation' among the 'respectable' working classes. There was also a surge in the activities of charities striving to identify 'deserving' cases with the aim of keeping them out of the workhouse, and 'tiding them over' until health was restored or re-employment secured. Most left the 'undeserving' cases to the bleak comforts of the workhouses. The late Victorian perception of charity as Christian aid to support the respectable poor to get over a temporary dilemma, probably outside their control, was far removed from the guardians' duty to act as the final safety net for the locality's most destitute people, especially when many were suspected of being personally responsible for their plight.

Public attention began to be drawn to specific groups of 'deserving' workhouse inmates – the deserted, orphaned and vulnerable children, the physically and mentally sick, and the elderly and infirm. The monthly meetings of boards of guardians were public occasions, and the vast range of opinions freely voiced created endless 'copy' for reporters. Long reports appeared on the frequently heated discussions, generally centred on the costs of staff, food and equipment, the need for repairs

Inmates, staff and visitors in front of Newton Abbot Workhouse, *c.* 1910.
(Peter & Aileen Carrett)

and improvements, the accuracy of assessments of new admissions and how to deal with troublesome inmates. Editors welcomed the subsequent flow of letters from readers sympathising with or complaining about the inmates or the guardians. Everyone, it seems, had a view.

Not surprisingly, the incessant rows, the periodic scandals about cruelty and starvation, the uncertain relationship between public aid and private charity and indeed the emotionally laden stories of Charles Dickens, George Elliot and Thomas Hardy, stimulated endless public debate about the cause of poverty, its possible eradication and, more immediately pressing, its effective relief. The debate was still raging in 1901.

By then, Devon possessed a formidable array of twenty extremely solid brick and stone workhouses still publicly proclaiming their original purpose as grim deterrents. Exeter, Plymouth, Devonport and East Stonehouse had had their own unions and central workhouses before 1834, but elsewhere, in accordance with the act, parishes grouped themselves around large new institutions in Bideford, Barnstaple, Holsworthy, Torrington, South Molton, Okehampton, Crediton, Tiverton, Tavistock, Plympton, Kingsbridge, Totnes, Newton Abbot, St Thomas (circling Exeter), Honiton and Axminster. A couple of western parishes and half a dozen eastern ones joined unions in Cornwall, Dorset or Somerset.

Tiverton Workhouse was typical. Like most large, purpose-built Victorian institutions – be they hospitals, prisons or asylums – it looked overbearing and dehumanising, and indeed that was its original purpose. Built in 1837–38, its square figure-of-eight format followed a standard pattern adopted by George Scott and William Moffatt, the architects of more than forty post-1834 workhouses. Most original plans have been lost, but a detailed archaeological excavation at Tiverton in 2010 suggested that the chosen design met its original purpose very satisfactorily. It seems to have been built to house around 300 people, the average size in Devon, although Exeter and Plymouth workhouses were far larger.

In Tiverton, as at Axminster, Newton Abbot, Tavistock and Totnes, the front was a long single-storey range housing the porter's lodge, guardians' boardroom, receiving wards and a chapel. The male and female dormitories and day rooms formed the lengthy two-storied sides of the workhouse extending at right angles from the corners of the frontage. A central archway in the frontage led through to an inner courtyard with the boys' walled yard on one side and girls' on the others. A three-storied central range with an awesome four storey-high tower in the middle stretched across the middle of the building. This housed the master's offices and lodgings, and further wards, dormitories, day rooms and workshops. They looked over the segregated open exercise courtyards for the men and women. The range at the back of the workhouse contained the service quarters – the dining rooms, stores, kitchens, bake house, scullery and laundry. A lying-in room and infirmary would be included somewhere in the buildings.

✺ *The Mid-1890s: Scandals & Their Aftermath*

The Edwardian era was a period of marked reform in the accommodation and care offered in most workhouses. A key factor had been a hard-hitting series of surveys of their medical and nursing facilities in 1894–95 by the influential *British Medical Journal* (*BMJ*). Several workhouses in Devon were visited, and most found wanting.

In 1895 Tiverton's infirmary was condemned by the *BMJ* 'as unfit for human habitation … The wards are overcrowded, insanitary, so insufficiently warmed that the old women must stay in bed to keep themselves warm.' The *BMJ* welcomed the *Devon & Exeter Gazette*'s conclusion 'that the criminals in the County Gaol live in what is a palace compared with the ward for the sick women in the Tiverton Workhouse'. Similar denunciations of the absence of baths and hot water, the verminous partitions and clothing, and the use of paupers as ward assistants, occurred at Holsworthy and the surly response of the guardians that 'what was sufficient in the past is good enough for the present', was heartily condemned by the *BMJ*. With an ill grace, in late 1898 the guardians eventually agreed to build a new infirmary – but it was a long time coming.

In 1895, revelations at Okehampton about the conduct between the porter and cook, the intoxication of the matron and the frequent absences of the master and matron until the early hours of the morning led to their hurried departure. It was a low point in the guardians' reputation, but worse was yet to come. The *BMJ* described the workhouse as comfortless, with 'nothing to relieve the dreary monotony of its bare whitewashed walls'. The female ward had 'an open stove which smoked persistently', the nursery cradles 'were antiquated wooden boxes on rockers', and the scantily equipped kitchen could boil but not roast food. In 1898 Okehampton's parsimonious guardians were shamed again by the adverse publicity following a pauper's funeral in a crudely constructed coffin without the benefit of pall-bearers. It took several more years, though, to shake this union out of its apathy and neglect.

A year earlier, Newton Abbot had provided a greater scandal. Here, one determined guardian, Dr John Ley, publicised the sworn statement of Nurse Hinton, the workhouse nurse, regarding the abuses inflicted upon the physically sick and mentally confused. The laundrywomen would only wash their clothes and towels if paid in food or money by the inmates; many inmates were covered in lice; the inmates were allowed to fight among themselves; elderly inmates were stripped naked and thrust into 'jumpers' with ties to secure them in bed all night; an inmate who soiled herself at night died after a ward assistant thrust excrement into her mouth; a young girl was placed with three women of immoral character, and, said the *BMJ*, 'then came various details about immorality into which we will not enter'. It expressed disbelief that, thirty years after the negligence and gratuitous cruelty exposed by Louisa Twining in several London workhouses, similar scandals were still going on unchecked in Devon.

Soon afterwards well-wishers presented Nurse Hinton with an inscribed watch in recognition of her courage in the face of hostile questioning, when 'the counsel for the defence endeavoured to bring discredit to the witness'. The beleaguered guardians were forced into action. More nurses were employed and with carefully defined duties, and the workhouse medical officer was given a more intervention-ist role. In January 1898 due ceremony attended the opening of a new infirmary comprising three wards complete with modern bedsteads, armchairs, circulating air heating, hot and cold water, a laundry and nurses' quarters. It was enlarged in 1903 and again in 1910 to care for the 'imbeciles'.

Meanwhile at Totnes, the *BMJ* reported, 'we found idiots all over the place: there was no classification' and, although efforts had been made to make the rooms cheerful with fires and flowers, 'the usual group of listless old men were seated on benches round the fire', the closets were primitive, the urinals foul, the baths hardly used, the nurses not hospital trained and too much care entrusted to ill-trained paupers acting as ward orderlies. It took a dozen years for the reluctant guardians to act but, in February 1909, amidst both self-congratulation and grumbling that the debt would take thirty years to repay, 400 guests attended a luncheon at the

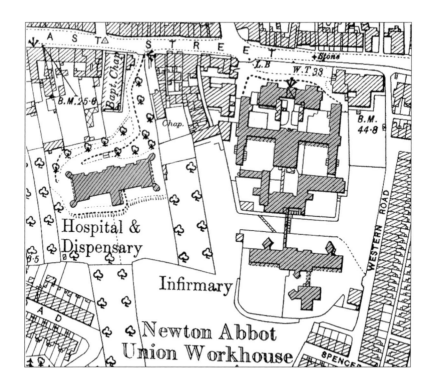

OS plan of Newton Abbot Workhouse and Infirmary, 1906 and a photograph of the infirmary
c. 1911. (Devon & Exeter Institution and Newton Abbot Town & GWR Museum)

opening of the new infirmary. It had cost £8,500 – four times as much as the town's voluntary cottage hospital, but it was four times as large.

Exeter had made greater efforts. Most 'sick and infirm' inmates were in wards in a separate building. The walls were painted in colour, not whitewashed, and the wards decorated with pictures and plants. Each ward had an open stove with a fenced stove pipe allowing clothes to be hung and aired, and both hot and cold water were freely available. There were separate wards for imbeciles and violent inmates. The nursery was 'bright and cheerful' and complete with a rocking horse. However, the *BMJ* condemned the thin straw bedding, the lack of ventilation and the mixing of children with adults, and Exeter was yet another workhouse castigated for its nurses' lack of hospital training, the reliance on inmates to give much of the care and the absence of night-time supervision. The city took action, and in 1905 a new infirmary was opened at the rear of the workhouse site, with well heated and ventilated single-sex wards containing a total of ninety-two beds. They were linked to each other and the main workhouse by wide corridors, and contained nurses' quarters, consulting rooms, dispensary, patients' sitting rooms, fully flushing toilets and baths and basins with hot and cold running water. Within a few years it would become a city hospital.

Plymouth Workhouse housed 600 paupers. In 1894 the *BMJ* acknowledged its 'imbeciles and feeble-minded' received excellent care under 'skilled attendants', but added, 'like many others in this county' the sick wards were dark, cramped and

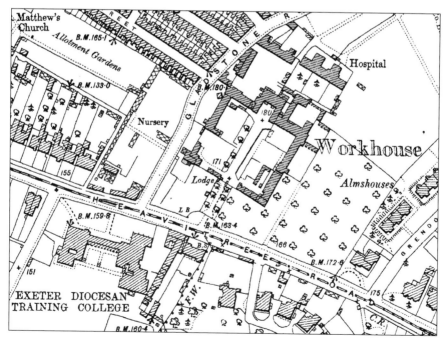

Exeter Workhouse and Infirmary from the 1906 OS map. (Devon & Exeter Institution)

insanitary. Hot water had to be carried to each ward in buckets. There were too few nurses and too many pauper assistants, and no nurse was on night duty. The lying-in ward offered no privacy and little comfort, and 'we saw a poor woman who had had a severe time – indeed her face told the tale – seated on an upright hard settle, eating some unappetising gruel'.

When nothing had been done by 1905 the local government board inspector, Mr Preston Thomas, vented his frustration on Plymouth guardians, saying their dismal insanitary infirmary was 'discreditable to the town' and plans to merely patch it up were unacceptable. Eventually isolation and maternity units were added, but it took until 1910 for new and well-equipped hospital blocks and a nurses' home to be completed. A fire in July 1907 gutted much of the workhouse without, fortunately, injuring any inmates, and prompted most of the major works. Soon after its restoration and expansion an enthusiastic reporter claimed the workhouse now resembled a village with its avenue of tall trees, large vegetable plots, numerous flower beds – 'promising a good show of roses' – and its separate areas for babies, children, old women, younger women, old men, younger men, sick men, sick women, 'imbecile' men, 'imbecile' women and tramps.

Other workhouses were also cajoled into action at this time. In 1895 Bideford Union's advertisement for a nurse who not only understood midwifery but also would 'make herself generally useful' invoked a *BMJ* diatribe against the tendency of many unions to employ 'a modern Sarah Gamp' and then turn her 'into a serving maid'. Nevertheless, the guardians roused themselves sufficiently to open a new infirmary amidst great ceremony in June 1903. Preston Thomas hoped the well-serviced wards would become 'a harbour of refuge and a home of healing'.

St Thomas' Workhouse was in the shape of a letter 'Y' enclosed in a hexagon, a form favoured as an alternative to the squared '8' and sometimes used for prisons. The *BMJ* found much to praise. The infirmary was spacious, with fireplaces, armchairs, night commodes and individual towels, brushes and combs at the end of each bed. The toilets and baths were modern, hot and cold water was freely available and the meals wholesome. 'The bread is baked in the house, and it tasted good.' Only the lying-in ward, with its evidence of punitive attitudes, troubled the *BMJ*, but for financial rather than humanitarian reasons:

> The poor weakly creatures were seated on ordinary chairs by the fire. We understand the feeling that prompts the hard measure so often dealt out to these women who make such a shameless use of the shelter which they can claim; but surely it is good policy to accelerate as far as possible their recovery and so discharge them the sooner.

In May 1910 *Trewman's Flying Post* described a tour of Exeter Workhouse, and in doing so summed up the dramatic changes that had taken place since the mid-1890s.

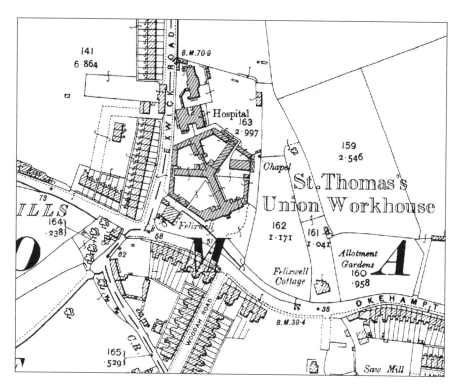

St Thomas Union Workhouse from the 1906 OS map. (Devon & Exeter Institution)

On the ground floor, the newly decorated chapel was a highlight, followed by the bedrooms for the 'infirm old women, but who are not sick'. Their day room was 'a cheerful hall, not unlike a farmhouse kitchen, with two corner fireplaces, a long dresser with crockery, &etc, and high-backed basket chairs for the ancient guests'. The able-bodied women had a separate day room with stairs leading upstairs to their dormitory. A separate block housed the 'female imbeciles' with their own 'trained attendants'. Children under 4 had their own 'cosy nursery'. The older children had a quad for a playground, they attended local schools and now had no distinctive uniform. The steam laundry possessed a modern washing machine 'consisting of a perforated cylinder revolving a few turns one way and then another'. A Cornish boiler powered an 18hp engine.

There were plentiful baths, basins and toilets in each section. The bakery and cookhouse had huge cauldrons to make soup, and the visitors observed inmates preparing onions dug from the garden for the next day's meal. All the bread was made in-house 'from stone-milled flour'. Other departments included the important wood chopping shed, where able-bodied inmates were kept busy, and the 'casual section' where tramps were kept away from everyone else. On the upper floor was the old board room, complete with the president's high chair and coat of arms, but now reduced to a committee room as the new board room was in Castle Street. The reporter said the 'showpiece' was the new infirmary – 'a tribute to Hygeia' – that superseded the block built in 1821.

Edwardian tenders reveal the range of items some Devon guardians were ordering, although some purchases were for the staff as well as, or maybe rather than, the inmates. There were no obvious shortages of items to keep the workhouses clean, reasonably warm and as free from infection as possible. Coal and coke, soap and washing powder, soda, starch and blue bags, fly papers, 'sanitary oil' and various disinfectants, and wood polish and black lead were regularly listed. Newton Abbot's clothing tenders included men's and boys' cord suits, men's hats, braces and trousers and rolls of white calico, aprons and handkerchiefs. Crediton's dietary tenders included beef, mutton, pork and bacon, bread, flour and barley meal, new and skimmed milk and other unspecified 'groceries'.

The 1895 *BMJ* report on Okehampton provides a rare example of the weekly rations. Each male pauper was allocated 6lb bread, ¾lb boiled meat, 1lb 'pudding' (rice or suet), 6oz cheese, 3lb potatoes, 10½ pints of gruel, 3 pints of soup, 1lb stew, 6 pints of broth and a ¾ pint of milk. In 1901 complaints about the inadequate quality and quantity of food surfaced in both South Molton and Barnstaple. On Mondays, said the *North Devon Journal*, Barnstaple paupers received just 1 pint of broth (meat boiled with some lentils or beans), 4oz bread, 2oz cheese and 8oz dumplings. A guardian admitted the dough dumplings were 'like lead' and indigestible, and said suet should be substituted. However, in 1908 Totnes guardians were ordering tea, cocoa, coffee, sugar, jam, butter and mustard alongside the usual meat, potatoes, treacle, sago, flour and cheese. In 1913 a Newton Abbot clergyman objected to the emphasis upon *British* butter and *new laid* eggs in the tenders, complaining 'People are fed better here than in palaces'.

◈ Children ◈

Children entered the workhouse for a variety of reasons other than the abject poverty of their parents. Neglect and abuse were common causes. Some babies were quietly left at workhouse doors to be found by the staff; many more had to be taken away from parents who were sent to prison for their ill treatment. In 1901 the NSPCC, Barnstaple police and magistrates combined to remove five verminous, rag-dressed children, thin to the point of deformity, from their feeble-minded mother and frequently drunk father, a farmer in Rose Ash. One girl was covered in blood from her incessant scratching.

In 1905 young George Winston was seen crying in a street in Ivybridge and the police found his father drunk, the home filthy and several other children starving. There was no mother around and, with the father's history of violence, the children were sent to the workhouse, although a neighbour took in George himself. In 1906 William and Mary Berry, aged 11 and 9, frightened, cold, dressed in rags and unwashed, were taken to Barnstaple Workhouse from their filthy and evil-smelling home. Their parents told the NSPCC inspector that they did not care what he did with them. In September 1908 a young mother living on the streets of Barnstaple was admitted to a charitable house of refuge in the hope, the magistrates said, that she would acquire the attitude and skills necessary to become a good domestic servant. Her two badly neglected children were taken to the workhouse for future adoption. There were many cases each year.

Each year, too, lengthy reports in the local newspapers revealed the unhappy lives of single, young women who sought to conceal the birth of their babies or, worse, were suspected of infanticide. Among many examples, in 1905 a dead baby girl was found in a tin chest in South Molton and in 1907 a newborn baby's body was found hidden under brushwood in Abbotsham. In 1908 one was discovered among refuse in Barnstaple, in 1909 another was left wrapped in brown paper on a train at Chapelton, in 1911 a railway worker found one in a shed at St David's Station, and in 1912 a gardener came across one in a shrubbery in Torquay and a single mother from Holsworthy hid hers in a dress box.

Due to medical doubts about the nature of such births, the courts mercifully decided that the children had been stillborn and most of the mothers brought to trial escaped imprisonment, even on the lesser charge of concealment. Although the local newspapers named the women, the courts did display a degree of concern and the mothers were usually directed to workhouse infirmaries to recover from their ordeals and then offered places in homes of refuge on condition of good behaviour.

In 1899 Preston Thomas, the inspector, said that Tiverton was the only union in Devon still educating its children in a workhouse school, and its guardians duly agreed that the hurly-burly of mixing with other elementary school children would be beneficial. As one enthusiastic member said, 'With the exception of a few treats given them by kind friends the children had few bright hours and it was the Guardians duty to march with the times and let the children see more of the world than the Workhouse walls.'

The inspector was not alone in fearing the adverse influence of some adult inmates on children. In 1901, for example, Totnes School Board refused to exempt some older workhouse girls from school attendance, even though the law allowed it if they had reached a certain standard of attainment, when it learned that the guardians wanted them to work in the kitchen alongside, it believed, 'women of bad character'.

There were accusations, probably justified, that workhouse children were 'taunted' by other pupils, but the guardians at both Tiverton and Totnes seemed to accept this as a sad but inevitable aspect of pauper life.

Corporal punishment was routine in schools, and no doubt in workhouses too, and sometimes it was excessive. In 1909 the master of South Molton Workhouse was publicly cautioned by the guardians for his excessive caning of thirteen boys for 'playing outside his office, [and] making a dreadful noise'. Some townsfolk heard about the incident, and perhaps seeing the wheals on the boys' legs, reported it to the police. In future, the porter had to witness any corporal punishment.

Sometimes of their own volition, but sometimes under pressure from Preston Thomas, an increasing number of guardians housed children away from the workhouses. In 1900, all seventy-eight children aged between 3 and 14 in Plymouth Workhouse were grouped in six small 'scattered homes' across the borough. The aim was to imitate family life, albeit on a large scale, under trained and trusted 'house mothers'. In 1910, Mr E. D. Court, a local government board inspector, confirmed the efficacy of Plymouth's approach, asserting, 'nobody seeing the children in the streets in Plymouth would know where they had come from'. Polite and well trained, many were found jobs as domestic servants, or on ships or farms. 'Very few dropped into casual employment.' It did not last. In March 1914 the clearly negligent Plymouth guardians had to dismiss their scattered homes superintendent and matron after a disastrous inspection report on the poor diet, inadequate facilities, lack of medical care and the 'unsatisfactory condition' of many children.

In 1901 Barnstaple guardians opened three scattered homes for their thirty children, but other unions were more cautious or penny-pinching. After several years of internal wrangling, Newton Abbot guardians followed suit and removed the children from their unpleasantly overcrowded workhouse. In 1901 the *Torquay Times* had berated the union's ultra-conservative rural members 'with their muddy boots, old-fashioned gaiters, and ruddy complexions', grunting out phrases like 'us won't have it' whenever a reform was mooted. It condemned the female guardians for vacillation – voting for change at one meeting and against it at another. Only Dr Ley and a few other 'progressives' were praised, and clearly this board, like many others, was finely divided during this crucial era in Poor Law history.

Conflicts were so frequent, so public and often so petty that in May 1902 Preston Thomas himself told Newton Abbot guardians that they had become a laughing stock and lectured them on the merits of diplomacy, courtesy and clear agendas. However, when the union's 'scattered homes' in Greenaway Villas, St Leonards and Prospect Terrace were inspected in 1906 and 1908 they were deemed very satisfactory, although a little overcrowded. The interminable rows continued, though, whether it was over which children were Anglican, Nonconformist or Roman Catholic, which priests could minister to them, and which schools they should attend, or the allegedly fearsome cost of the guardians' decision in 1906 to give the pauper children free dental treatment when ordinary school children were not similarly 'pampered'.

Workhouse children photographed pre-1913 in uniform outside the
main entrance to Tiverton Workhouse. (Tiverton Museum)

In 1906 nobody challenged a vituperative female Tiverton guardian who
asserted, 'In the Tiverton Union most of the children were illegitimate, and their
parents in many cases vicious people, and under these circumstances they had very
few children suitable to board out in cottages'. It was agreed that they were best
kept incarcerated. As a result, it was only in 1913 that the guardians succumbed to
official pressure and the children were moved to Shillingford House, a couple of
miles outside Bampton. It was hoped, said Mayor Gregory at its opening, that the
children would learn useful rural skills and gain purposeful employment.

Exeter, too, steadfastly kept its pauper children within the workhouse. In 1908 a
report by the 'lady Guardians' advocated detailed training of girls aged 13 and over
'in cooking, washing, dusting, sweeping and in cutting out and making their own
clothes; the elder girls to learn how to manage babies in the children's nursery'.
The tasks were just those calculated to reduce the running costs of the workhouse
as well as reinforcing habits of obedience and humility, and fitting the girls for paid
employment. When Exeter's Children's Home was built alongside the workhouse
complex in 1913–14 the guardians intended most of the household chores to be
undertaken by the girls. The home accommodated seventy-four children and came
complete with electric power, day rooms, bathrooms, several dormitories, a sick
bay, a dining room and kitchen. The guardians saw their initiative as less costly and
troublesome than creating scattered homes or 'boarding out'.

'Boarding out', or fostering, was an option taken up by a few Devon unions who believed the children would receive better practical training because ordinary families such as farmers and small tradesmen would have just one or two pauper children in their care. At a conference in Plymouth in 1905 Dr Ley expressed confidence that many 'thoroughly good homes' could be found where children could be brought up to 'learn self-reliance and be capable of fighting against the hard knocks of life in a way those who were brought up more or less cribbed or cabined in an institution would never be able to'.

Nevertheless, he recognised the dangers. Some foster parents merely wanted the money, others just a cheap servant, or a 'toy' or 'pet companion'. He urged the need for the careful selection and matching of families and children, and very careful supervision afterwards. The idea was not new, but it caught on during the Edwardian period. Inevitably perhaps, there was a scattering of complaints by foster children, and by foster parents themselves, and perhaps inevitably too, guardians found it almost impossible to unravel them. An exception was the Plymouth foster mother who was dismissed in 1910 for locking her charges in the coalhouse and cupboards. Such incidents proved the soundness of Ley's cautionary advice.

Tramps & Vagabonds

Able-bodied men who had to be admitted on their plea of unemployment and homelessness incurred the greatest condemnation, especially if laziness was suspected. In 1904 a hairdresser who haughtily refused work as a mere barber filled Newton Abbot's newspaper with contempt for 'drones of this class'. They 'deserve no pity,' it thundered, 'and should be compelled to perform some sort of labour, or starve'.

Throughout the period exasperated boards vainly urged the idea of labour colonies on the government, where, argued one Newton Abbot guardian in 1905, 'worthless vagabonds could be compelled to work' until they seized 'the chance to start in life again'. The following year, Preston Thomas himself suggested that Newton Abbot's guardians reduce the food allowance to the able-bodied 'loafer class', and in 1912 Exeter's guardians limited their visitors from once a week to once a month. As the city's guardians disliked many of the female visitors who associated with the pregnant women, the restriction was applied to them too.

Large number of tramps sought overnight board and lodgings. Most were men, but not all. In 1904 Plympton workhouse took in sixty-four female and thirty-three child vagrants as well as 1,067 men. Tramps irritated all boards, not least because many of them made every excuse to avoid undertaking work to earn their overnight stay. In 1903 Newton Abbot guardians only decided against reducing the bread and gruel meal to the barest minimum allowed by the local government board because several members believed some of the tramps were ex-servicemen from the Boer War, and genuinely seeking work. A year earlier, Devon's chief constable thought the unusually high number of tramps staying in workhouses overnight included many 'travelling navvies' attracted by the building of Keyham Docks, Dartmouth Naval College, the Holme Waterworks and the Lyme Regis, Teign Valley and Budleigh Salterton railways.

Many boards remained unsympathetic. On several occasions the Barnstaple, South Molton, Tiverton and Totnes guardians secured fourteen days' imprisonment with hard labour for young able-bodied tramps refusing to undertake the required daily task of breaking 2cwt of stones into gravel or sawing 300lb of wood. Tramps who were truculent in court, especially if they criticised the workhouse, risked their sentences being doubled.

House to house begging was common throughout the period, but as two tramps in Bampton found out in 1910, being caught red-handed usually incurred at least fourteen days' imprisonment with hard labour. The general feeling was summed up that year when Crediton's guardians bowed to local pressure not to release tramps on Sundays as churchgoers complained about the 'ragged, worthless looking itinerants' pestering them for alms.

Inmates' Complaints

In 1912 the *South Molton Gazette* secured a tramp's caustic view of the workhouse. He said tramps were stripped, ordered to wash, given a slice of bread and boiled meat broth, issued old nightshirts and told to sleep in hammocks in a cold ward with just a dirty worn out blanket. In the morning they were given 'skilly' – thin oatmeal porridge – and ordered to work until midday. His story was confirmed that year by the experiences of a *Western Times* reporter who disguised himself as a tramp and wandered across Devon.

Other inmates were not averse to complaining, and it is impossible to judge the truth behind the allegations. In April 1904 a pauper employed in the Newton Abbot Workhouse dining room refused to work when the master failed to investigate his complaints about the 'wretched bathing accommodation, the bad condition of the vegetables served, and the potatoes which were allowed to soak in water for 24 hours before cooking'. When he protested further he was put on the tramps' diet and ordered to break stones. When further protests were ignored, he wrote to the local government board. The subsequent investigation led him to court where he was sentenced to fourteen days' imprisonment with hard labour on the grounds that he was lying, although his claims were not formally examined during the trial. In 1907 a pauper known as 'Gentleman John' sent a series of postcards to various Newton Abbot guardians asserting the master was a liar, a thief and detested by staff and inmates alike. As he failed to provide any supporting evidence he received forty-two days' imprisonment, also with hard labour.

In 1910 Thomas Gregson, an inmate at Newton Abbot, spoke at a Mid Devon Labour Club debate on 'Poor-law Administration, good and evil', but the report in the *Mid Devon Advertiser* suggests his talk was more an emotional rant than reasoned argument. He asserted that the 'most intolerant and unsympathetic' guardians were the clergy and women, and added:

> It made one's heart ache to see the poor creatures confined as they were in Newton Workhouse, like wild beasts within iron railings, objectless and hopeless. Anyone who entered the Workhouse with his mental balance slightly upset, grew worse and worse, until confirmed lunacy and death overtook him.

Whether true or false, the diatribe had little effect as Gregson was already labelled a troublemaker. In 1907 he had led a strike when dinner was late and the inmates had been ordered back to work until it could be served. When summonsed he had sought a warrant against the master for acting illegally. In 1908 he had served fourteen days with hard labour for visiting the infirmary without permission and refusing to pick oakum as a punishment.

Plymouth was probably the most genuinely troubled workhouse, especially after 1910 when it seems the master's authority was breaking down. Despite the much admired new buildings, low morale led to staff quarrels and very public complaints by the inmates about the appalling food, the dirty linen, the nurse's cruelty and the doctor's lack of care. By the summer of 1912 the beleaguered guardians had to agree that more, and better qualified, staff were essential, irrespective of what ratepayers thought of the cost.

✎ *Treats* ✎

In a rare act of generosity, in 1902 the local government board allowed guardians to provide extra refreshments to workhouse inmates to celebrate the coronation. At South Molton this included roast pork and mutton followed by fruit and cream, with a pint of beer for the men. Those in receipt of outdoor relief received an extra shilling.

Local well-wishers, though, provided most other treats. Since the 1860s a group of Torquay families had provided their union's workhouse in Newton Abbot with a New Year's treat. In January 1909 the tea consisted of 'cream and jam, three different kinds of cakes, brown and white bread and butter', and each woman received half a pound of tea and a pound of sugar, each man a quarter pound of tobacco and each child a toy.

At Christmas 1911 Newton Abbot's staff and inmates decorated the workhouse with imitation flowers, fairies and teddy bears, and also banners with various seasonal mottoes, including one that rather bizarrely read, 'May you live as long as you want and never want as long as you live'. As a result of all the gifts, the 460 inmates enjoyed a meal of beef and pork with potatoes, parsnips and cabbage, followed by Christmas pudding. After tea, staff and visitors toured the wards to sing songs with the inmates, and to distribute gifts. The guardians and local families ensured that those children boarded out and in the scattered homes had a similar dinner, along with teatime jellies, buns, cakes and presents. Other localities did much the same for their workhouses, and no doubt the speeches everywhere ended with the thought, as expressed by the Mayor of Barnstaple in 1913, that the inmates 'should feel very thankful for the good things that had been provided for them, and for the careful manner in which they were looked after'.

Publicity conscious local politicians were often benefactors. In June 1912, for example, Captain Ernest Morrison-Bell, the local MP, and his wife invited all ninety-eight Newton Abbot Union children along with their foster mothers and nurses to Pitt House for games, tea and presents. On occasions, military bands provided workhouse inmates with entertainment. Popular marches and songs such as 'Sour Apple Tree', 'He's Going There Every Night', Oh! The Khaki', 'Flight of Ages', 'For Britain's Glory' and 'For Old Time's Sake' were enjoyed in Barnstaple in May 1901. Sometimes groups of inmates went on escorted walks. According to the *North Devon Journal* they did so twice a week in Barnstaple in the summer of 1902.

Numbers & the Tightening of Criteria

Despite Goschen's 1869 ban, out-relief in the form of money or goods was common-place again by the end of the century. Several Devon unions also gave small grants to encourage surplus men and families to emigrate rather than remain long-term burdens on the unions. However, Preston Thomas believed that many boards of guardians were practising false economy when they refused to employ enough relieving officers to investigate applicants' claims with sufficient thoroughness. In 1901 he did not hesitate to say this to the Crediton guardians when their union pauper rate topped forty-six per 1,000 of the population. In that year the national average was twenty-five, but across Devon only Devonport (twenty-two) and East Stonehouse (twenty-three) were below this, while Axminster (fifty-six), Honiton (forty-eight), Torrington (forty-five), Kingsbridge (forty-three) Barnstaple (forty-three) and Okehampton (forty-two) joined Crediton at the bottom of the county league. The South West, Preston Thomas stated in his annual report, was 'more than a quarter of a century behind the rest of England'.

Urban Devonport and East Stonehouse remained high in Preston Thomas's favour at this time, largely because their low unemployment rates meant the guardians were not overburdened with applicants. Although several rural unions retaliated angrily by informing Preston Thomas that their largely agricul-tural districts had low wages and desperately uncertain employment prospects, the indefatigable inspector remained unimpressed and undaunted. For several more years he repeated his criticisms, arguing that the economy had recovered, and stricter inquiries would have the twin benefits of easing ratepayers' pockets and encouraging thrift in the poor. In 1905 and 1906 Torrington and Barnstaple Unions were deemed particularly culpable in refusing to employ more staff.

Gradually things changed. By 1913 the numbers of paupers receiving indoor and outdoor relief in Cornwall, Devon and Dorset had fallen from 49,600 in the late 1890s to 31,000, or from thirty-eight per thousand to twenty. Detailed figures for Devon survive for 1913, showing 3,945 indoor and 10,532 outdoor paupers. The highest numbers were the 945 indoor and 1,970 outdoor cases in Plymouth, followed by Newton Abbot with 581 and 1,075, Devonport with 297 and 892, Exeter with 258 and 322, St Thomas with 220 and 735, Totnes with 217 and 817 and Barnstaple with 191 indoor and 732 outdoor paupers. None of these figures, though, included the sick, the infirm elderly or the 'imbeciles', who between them kept the workhouse infirmaries almost full. There were also the 'temporary' and 'professional' tramps who made a total of 54,660 visits across the county.

But for the 'annoying' tramps, speakers at the 1913 South Western Poor Law Conference were satisfied with these statistics. They believed the Poor Law had successfully reinvented itself over the last couple of decades, and workhouses largely contained those that could not be cared for in any other way. Any further reforms, it was asserted, lay in upgrading medical facilities.

The rules for out-relief were complex, and no doubt difficult to implement accurately and evenly within and across unions. The local government board said it was reserved for those who had been residents in a union for at least two years. It was barred to able-bodied men; it was limited to four weeks, after which the relieving officer had to reassess the case; it was dependent on a medical officer's report and the results of an interview with the board of guardians, and it would be refused if relief was also offered by a charity. The maximum amount was 3/- a week if rent was paid, with 1/- a week added for each child living with a widowed mother. It was impossible for a sick man to keep a family on this amount and yet it would be denied him if he drew any money from a friendly society to which he had contributed.

A couple of incidents reveal the vagaries of the system. In the winter of 1904–05 the drift net and seine fishermen of Torbay caught very little, and were reduced to earnings of 15/- a month. Nevertheless, as able-bodied men they were refused outdoor relief and utterly rejected thoughts of admission to the workhouse. The Fishermen's Shelter fed up to thirty men a day, and a special charity was launched with local clergymen verifying the dire need for contributions. Its publicity promised that all donations would be 'judiciously applied to deserving cases'.

In Newton Abbot, a female inmate faced mockery by the guardians when she sought 2/- a week outdoor relief to pay her rent so that she could leave the workhouse. The newspaper reported the brief interview:

Mr Webber: She wants it for drink.

Mary: I don't drink now, sir. (Loud laughter)

Mr Webber: Then you have altered since last week.

Mr Lee: She is a drunken nuisance and a pest to Society.

Colonel Walcott moved that the application be refused. This was carried.

Troubled Relationships: Charities & the Poor Law

In 1908 Preston Thomas welcomed Exeter's decline in outdoor relief from 1,179 cases in 1897 to 452 a decade later. He welcomed, too, the guardians' justification of their tougher stance whereby they gave greater amounts to fewer, very carefully selected cases to ensure they lived sufficiently above the level of destitution to avoid degradation. The guardians were convinced the city's charities had the necessary funds and volunteers to investigate and support all the other cases. The weakness lay in the guardians' admission of the lack of co-operation between them and the charities.

The alleged indiscriminate nature of local charitable support worried many social commentators and boards of guardians. They strongly suspected that money, meals and goods were given to many plausible 'undeserving' cases by well-meaning but duped benefactors, thereby encouraging the idle and probably immoral lives of the recipients. Newton Abbot's board was just one that sought the channelling of all largesse from local charities through a single organisation well-versed in identifying genuine need and the correct amount of aid to be granted. The trouble was that few could agree on what these criteria should be, and many charities did not wish to be associated with the Poor Law. Nevertheless, when Sir William Chance, a northern businessman and Liberal MP, addressed a Devon Poor Law Conference in 1910 he saw Poor Law unions as bulwarks of effective relief only if they persuaded local charities to co-operate with them, thereby enabling more people to be supported without raising the rates.

The Charity Organisation Society (COS) was a powerful national organisation dedicated to persuading other charities to accept its strictures on the discriminating use of their funds. It sought the membership of clergy, influential local families, everyone concerned with the Poor Law and key members of independent local charities. In 1901 Torquay's COS annual report stated, 'The careful and intelligent organisation of a system of relief based on full inquiry into the character and circumstances of applicants was a very important and necessary branch of the work of the society.' The report fretted that the borough's numerous charities were overlapping and unco-ordinated and, worst of all, wasteful. They were accentuating the 'moral degradation of the recipients', many of whom were assumed to be unworthy, and causing hardship to the genuine cases who were less forthcoming and probably missed.

In 1905, another COS speaker in Torquay pursued the degenerative effect that thoughtless giving was having on working-class families. He cited in particular the fashionable habit of donating money to hospitals so that poor, but far from necessitous, families need not pay. As a result, such recipients were fast losing their self-respect, sturdy independence and integrity. Everyone should pay something for medical treatment, however small, or accept pauperisation and its attendant penalties. The speaker was heartily cheered, and so was Father Morton at the 1907 COS conference, who argued, 'The poor were not so lovable in reality as they were made out to be in story books', and urged those with charitable dispositions not to be taken in by unctuous approaches, sad tales and false humility. Giving money on a whim 'was the last thing to be done', and public attention should be focused on promoting friendly societies and thrift clubs.

At this time friendly societies were firmly established as popular self-help community institutions regularly engaging in social and sporting activities. Among many examples, in June 1901 Buckfastleigh's twin societies – the Oddfellows and Rationals – got large teams together for a well-attended sports day complete with prizes, side shows and refreshments. During the summer of 1904 the friendly societies in Chulmleigh and Kingsnympton organised club walks and sports days, all of them interspersed with hymns, prayers and sermons in church – fitting activities for the Edwardian adaptation of the Greek ideal of a healthy mind in a healthy body. And as we have seen, the grounds of local mansions were often offered as venues for these highly respectable and largely working-class events.

Perhaps the very vehemence of the COS's repeated assertions suggest it was not having the effect it wished on local charities. In December 1908 the annual meeting of Torquay's branch of the National Union of Women Workers highlighted the numerous charities supported by its members, and the never-ending need for them. They included the Women's Employment Bureau; a new Laundry Girls' Club complete with its savings club; the charity supplying groceries and clothing to the aged poor; the Church of England Temperance Society and its Temple Lodge Home; the always full St Faith's Home for Women and Girls in St Marychurch Street; the flourishing Girls' Friendly Society with its 374 contributing members; the Mildmay Consumptive Home; the Women's Total Abstinence Union; the Band of Hope with 140 members; the vibrant Young Women's Christian Association and the local nursing association with its nursing home and clinic. The Women's Total Abstinence Union also ran the Ellacombe Terrace Home for 'women in distress or unable to avoid temptation', arranged regular mothers' meetings and supervised the sewing, coal and clothing clubs. The COS was mentioned solely as running a new advice centre for pensioners.

Tellingly, in 1909 Torquay's assistant town clerk acknowledged that, beneath the veneer of Torbay's wealth and respectability, drink, gambling and the depressing effect of pitifully low wages were destroying the physical and moral health of many families.

⌒ *The Temperance Movement* ⌒

Torbay's relentless campaigns against drink were mirrored everywhere else. Typically, in August 1900 Hartland Band of Hope's Annual Festival captured a large audience through its fife and drum band, games with prizes, and gifts of sweets and tea party, to hear its speakers describe the frightening diseases brought about by drink, including 'Consumption, Chronic Inflammation of the liver, Gout, Delirium Tremens, Cerosis [*sic*] of the Liver'. As speakers were quick to note, the plethora of court cases involving drunks using obscene language, picking fights in the streets, causing disturbances at fairs and markets and beating their wives or children, provided copious evidence of its dire effects.

Plymouth and Exeter had active Church Army contingents and their Labour Homes were at the core of their evangelical mission. They took in destitute young men, often addicted to drink, and as long as they signed a pledge to try to lead a Christian life, they taught them the Bible, how to work hard and earn a reasonable wage, and then helped find them a permanent job, often in Canada or Australia.

A meeting of the Church of England Band of Hope, Hatherleigh. (Beaford Arts)

The causes of drunkenness were more contentious, though, and identified less frequently. Speaking in Exeter in 1905 a doctor argued that bad housing, bad feeding, poor health and long hours of work created a depressing atmosphere which induced a craving for drink. Drink, in turn, 'wore out the human machine' and rendered it incapable of renovation. Drink, he argued, was a primary contributor to national degeneration, and this was a theme central to many campaigners' speeches in the decade after the Boer War during which so many recruits had been rejected as unfit. When a speaker in Newton Abbot in October 1901 cried out, 'John Bull must wake up if he is going to maintain his place in the world … and he must wake up sober', he was following this lead. Many Bands of Hope had uniformed junior sections, with healthy recreational activities interspersed with uplifting meetings and services to ensure the virtues of abstinence were instilled at an early age. In May 1901 the Diocese of Exeter said 10,218 children were members.

The temperance societies often worked hand-in-hand with friendly societies. Ilfracombe was just one town where the strictly teetotal Rechabites ran both societies. Nonconformist and Church of England temperance societies existed side by side in many towns, although often uneasily. Perhaps it was the sense of individual inadequacy in the face of the much feared tide of national degeneracy that led them to co-operate in the massive temperance demonstrations that took place each year in Exeter, Plymouth, Tiverton and Tavistock.

In *Tavistock's Yesterdays* (No.14, 2006) Gerry Woodcock described the noisy and colourful procession through the market town in 1906 by 1,000 members of twenty-three local Bible Christian, Church of England, Congregational, Salvation Army, United Methodist and Wesleyan Methodist congregations.

In Tiverton, too, every church and chapel possessed a temperance club complete with its array of social and religious activities. Here, as everywhere else, they existed alongside local breweries and public houses. The violence stirred up in Tiverton in March 1908, when Mr Tennyson Smith, a notoriously provocative abolitionist, called the traffic in liquor, 'a mean, vile, despicable, diabolical, devilish, damnable trade', was testimony to the potentially lethal atmosphere. The *Crediton Chronicle* strongly hinted that notice of Tennyson Smith's arrival had been enough to attract as many opponents of temperance as supporters.

Supporting the Hospitals

All hospitals relied on voluntary contributions far more than on the fees they charged. In 1912 Torbay Hospital ran with a permanent overdraft, but survived thanks to outright gifts, a few legacies, the 582 subscribers and the money and goods donated by the King Edward Cot League, the Vegetable & Fruit League, the Ladies' Needlework Association, and the Ladies' Collecting Guild. Paignton's

An Edwardian ward at the Royal Devon & Exeter Hospital, 1907. (Devon & Exeter Institution)

cottage hospital was fortunate that the Singer family founded it in 1890 and supported events to ensure its financial security. And as we have seen, the Fortescues, Heathcoat-Amorys and the Churstons were among the other wealthy families actively supporting their local hospitals. Most towns also held annual Hospital Days with their crowd-pulling carnival processions made up of tableaux on wagons and carts created by local shops, schools, businesses and clubs; the accompanying street collections were vitally important in helping make ends meet.

Costs, though, continually outstripped income. In 1901 the new East Wing of the West of England Eye Hospital in Exeter was opened. It cost £18,000. Of this, £8,000 had been donated already, another £4,000 was a bequest from the late Mr West of Streatham Hall, leaving £6,000 still outstanding. By 1908 its mounting debts included an annual deficit of £3,988 for the previous year, and the hospital had to resort to pleas – ultimately successful – to local factories and businesses as its loyal subscribers and fundraising groups were overwhelmed.

In 1901 the opening of the new Totnes Cottage Hospital exemplified the efforts needed to supply localities with in- and out-patient care. Built on land donated by the Duke of Somerset, over half of the £2,222 cost had been given by three wealthy local families with subscribers and numerous fetes and sales raising most of the rest. Nevertheless, as several speakers noted, not all the building costs had been covered, the 'old' hospital had residual debts of £1,566, and no one knew where all the running costs of the new one would come from. As everywhere else, the nursing association serving Totnes depended far more on voluntary support than on fees. In 1902 it needed a combination of its 'members' pence', well-wishers' donations, local church offertories, the Borough Dramatic Society's entertainments and collections at Totnes Races to enable its work to continue.

There was a perennial shortage of trained nurses and midwives. The Devon Nursing Association welcomed the implementation of the Midwives Act in 1910, but while it appreciated the enforced departure of the large corps of untrained midwives with their variety of practices – some useful, but some dangerous – it failed to see how each rural parish could be provided with a fully trained one. The fees they earned would not remotely provide a living wage, and once again voluntary support was deemed essential until local councils and the Exchequer thought fit to increase their grants. Again, as we have seen, Earl and Countess Fortescue and several other influential families came to the rescue and ensured this charity maintained a very high profile and secured a steadily increasing income. In due course, the county council, no doubt under influential pressure, created six scholarships for trainee midwives. It was a start but it needed the slaughter of the Great War to shock the nation into bringing their work to fruition in a well-co-ordinated county scheme of state- and rate-subsidised maternity care.

Homes, Institutions & Asylums

In 1902 the Church of England's Women's Home of Refuge in Holloway Street, Exeter, was facing a financial crisis due to badly needed repairs and the deaths of several subscribers. The city's mayor and cathedral dean highlighted the importance of its work in providing refuge for women in grave moral danger through unwholesome adult influences, drink or prostitution, and also those unsupported in pregnancy, and trusted that funds would be forthcoming as, sadly, the home would always be needed. Their trust was rewarded. Within a few years the charity expanded into larger premises in Bartholomew Street East (known as St Olave's) and also Friars Walk. It remained full, but always perilously short of money.

The home, along with magistrates and parish clergy, sent some women who they thought 'redeemable' as 'penitents' to the House of Mercy in Bovey Tracey run by the Anglican Sisters of Mercy. Founded in 1863 through the religious convictions, humanitarian zeal and extensive social contacts of Canon Charles Courtenay, fourth son of the 10th Earl of Devon, the house sought to transform the lives of young women through prayer, Bible study, regular routines, hard work and training as future domestic servants. Reliant on charity, the sisters held fundraising events in association with the town, and also regular sales of the produce and clothing made by the eighty or so 'penitents'. In 1914 Lady Fortescue chaired a well-supported meeting in Barnstaple where she regretted there was no similar home nearby, and launched a campaign to raise funds for the employment of a trained rescue worker to assist local churches and charities in preventing the spread of immorality.

Some children were accepted, often from magistrates' courts, into the four Church of England Waifs & Strays Homes in Exeter, Torquay, Newton Abbot (St Michael's, Highweek) and Sampford Peverell (St Boniface's). They all relied upon voluntary support for funds, and for gifts of essentials, such as vegetables and fruit, and extras such as toys and day trips. Taking around thirty children each, they provided vulnerable children with highly disciplined routines, plenty of physical activities, attendance at local schools, regular worship in church and training for jobs such as domestic servants, soldiers and sailors, and farm workers at home and in the dominions. When the founder of the Waifs & Strays Society, the Reverend Edward Rudolf, visited St Boniface's in 1911 he was pleased to note, 'there was no crushing of their boyish spirits'. In Torquay, the Roman Catholic order of the Sisters of Charity of St Vincent de Paul cared for 160 boys, and the annual May Fair run by parishioners was crucial to its survival.

Several large institutions for 'mental defectives' were clustered around Exeter. Wonford House, originally founded in 1801 at Bowhill, was built in 1869 and cared for fee-paying patients. The Exeter Lunatic Asylum opened at Digby in 1886 for adult patients as the existing County Lunatic Asylum at Exminster was full and the city felt its charges were too high. Extensive grounds surrounded each of the vast institutions, perhaps to keep it hidden, perhaps to create an air of tranquillity, or perhaps both.

The Exeter Asylum's Edwardian visitors' book and inspectors' reports have survived, and suggest it was competently run with some trained nurses, the inmates received sufficient, if dull, meals and where possible were kept busy, but like most Edwardian institutions epidemics spread quickly. Deaths were frequent. Nevertheless, the historian of the Exminster Asylum has recorded the never-ending demand for places and its constant expansion, until by 1906 1,352 inmates were accommodated – many from far afield.

Their diet was little different to those in the workhouses. Breakfast and tea comprised bread and porridge, and dinner was boiled meat and vegetables, or vegetable pie, plus half a pint of beer. The various unions across the county had financial responsibility for patients sent to these asylums, and the typical charge of 14/- per week was more than twice the cost of a place in a workhouse. Those sent from local authorities, guardians or families from outside the county were charged even more.

✿ *New Laws & Missed Opportunities* ✿

In 1908 the introduction of modest non-contributory old age pensions stirred up many articles and letters praising its freedom – because it was an entitlement – from any taint of the Poor Law or charity. Although the idea had been discussed for decades, the act was innovative but far from free of typically Edwardian restrictions. Some commentators expressed anxiety about the ability of those over the age of 70 to live on 5/- a week, or 7*s* 6*d* for a couple, if they had no other means. However, these critics missed the Liberal government's point. The low level was a deliberate decision taken to avoid criticisms of pandering to fecklessness, and also to encourage people to save for their old age in friendly societies and savings banks. And the pensions were limited to those of proven good character earning less than £31 10*s* 0*d* a year who were also long-term British residents, had worked all their lives, and were not in receipt of poor relief. Notwithstanding all the limitations, in January 1914 Bideford's Liberal Association celebrated the fifth anniversary of the 'grand and glorious Act' that kept many old people out of the workhouse.

The bitter Edwardian arguments regarding identifying an effective working relationship between charitable and state intervention in people's lives when misfortunes struck failed to result in a solution. Indeed, the various welfare acts the Liberals introduced after coming to power in 1905 show how sensitive ministers were to the strength of public opinion, and in 1909 the divergent majority and minority reports emanating from the Royal Commission on the Poor Law and the Relief of Distress that had spent four years deliberating revealed all too clearly the divisions within that public opinion.

The majority and minority reports were distinguished by the ideological gulf between them rather than the actual recommendation they made, many of which they held in common. They recognised that 64 per cent of the 234,792 children receiving relief lived outside workhouses, and they aimed at reducing the overall numbers and ensuring those within the Poor Law – or, they preferred to say, those receiving 'public assistance' – re-entered society 'without disadvantages, mental, moral, or physical, and equipped for self-support'. The boards of guardians would be swept away and 'public assistance' would become the responsibility of county and borough councils. Workhouses, as currently constituted, would be abolished and replaced by specialised institutions for the sick, aged and mentally feeble. With regard to children, boarding out was preferred to 'scattered homes' as, with careful selection, good foster mothers would be next best to good mothers themselves. Both reports supported labour exchanges to help identify and smooth out irregularities in the labour market, labour colonies to absorb and usefully employ surplus workers, and detention centres for the 'work shy and vagrants'. Both advocated enhanced insurance schemes to cater for a range of family misfortunes.

Unfortunately it was the differences between the majority and minority reports that led to the contemporary patchwork of provision lingering on without a comprehensive overhaul. Asquith and Lloyd George decided to avoid becoming trapped between the majority report's emphasis upon a partnership of voluntary and public bodies organising a wide variety of relief and care (biased heavily towards the COS's principles), and the minority report's more socialist-inclined ideas on substantially increasing state intervention and control, irrespective of the views of morally charged charities.

In the South West, Sir Thomas Acland addressed the region's Poor Law Conference just after the reports were published. He assumed correctly that his audience thought the minority report's ideals should 'remain where they are at present, amongst the clouds', and that even the majority report failed to appreciate that 'flotsam and jetsam' would always exist and needed something like workhouses as alternatives to hospitals or asylums. For the time being views such as those of Sir Thomas held sway.

A couple of years later, though, the death knell sounded for the Poor Law. It started with the new labour exchanges in 1910. Barnstaple, Exeter and Plymouth were the first to have them in Devon. They noted the names of those seeking work and of employers offering it, and tried to match the two through advertisements and interviews. The only exception, said the caustic *North Devon Journal*, was domestic service, owing to 'the notorious fact that mistresses were more in want of maids than maids of mistresses'.

Labour exchanges were put to further use in 1911 when the National Insurance Act provided wage earners between 16 and 70 years of age earning under £160 a year with a contributory system of state-subsidised insurance against illness and unemployment. Workers paid 4*d* a week, their employers 3*d* and the State 2*d*, and when workers were sick they received 'free' medical treatment and 10/- a week for thirteen weeks and 5/- for another thirteen weeks. By 1913, nearly 15 million workers, although not their dependents, were insured.

Based upon additional payments by employees, firms and the State, the act also provided unemployment benefits for up to fifteen weeks a year to workers in engineering, shipbuilding and construction industries – and of course, some Devon families benefitted from this too. Asquith and Lloyd George were successfully sidetracking the Poor Law and starting to render the workhouses redundant – although not the work of their new infirmaries, which in due course were to transform themselves into public hospitals.

7

SOCIETY RENT ASUNDER
Devon & the Great National Crises — Female Suffrage, Irish Home Rule, Free Trade & the House of Lords

∾ *The Fight for Women's Right to Vote: The Beginning* ∾

All politicians in the Edwardian era had to come to terms with the enlarged electorate in their constituencies as a result of the 1884 Franchise Act. Henceforth, 60 per cent of men possessed the vote, but no women, even though they could vote in school board and board of guardian elections and indeed become members of them. Nevertheless, by 1901 some politically active women had become well-established members of the Conservative Primrose League and the Women's Liberal Association, and the suffragists among them had found a number of MPs, especially among the Liberals, sympathetic to their cause. Some small pioneering suffragist groups across the country had come together as early as 1868 to form the National Society for Women's Suffrage (NSWS) but other than a few abortive private members' bills the pressure for change was negligible.

Then, in 1897 Millicent Fawcett, the widow of Henry Fawcett, Gladstone's postmaster general, founded the National Union of Women's Suffrage Societies (NUWSS) linking together numerous local groups and absorbing the NSWS into a powerful national body devoted to peaceful methods of persuasion. A number of influential men joined and the NUWSS supported a wide range of welfare campaigns and those politicians interested in them, whatever their party. The ultimate aim, though, was to widen support for female suffrage.

Emmeline Pankhurst came from an altogether more radical Independent Labour Party background and by 1903 she was convinced that that only high-profile arguments and publicity concentrating solely upon female suffrage would arouse sufficient interest to secure a parliamentary majority. In that year, she founded the Women's Social and Political Union (WSPU) with her daughters, Christabel, Sylvia and Adela. They kept tight control of its affairs, even to the point of ejecting members, even old friends, who disagreed with their ever-increasing militancy when party leaders failed to embrace their cause. Colourful and fiery parades and rallies attracted tens of thousands of supporters from across the country, and a never-ending array of leaflets and pamphlets poured off WSPU presses. The rallies also attracted numerous opponents, both men and women, and WSPU activists endured considerable verbal abuse and, on occasions, physical violence.

The Leaders Scorned

Public attention did not mean political support. Many trades unionists feared that enfranchising property-owning women would, on balance, work against working-class interests. In 1907 the Labour Conference rejected outright a motion calling for female suffrage. Undoubtedly some members, including Arthur Henderson, the party leader, thoroughly disapproved of the Pankhursts' aggressive approach. When Emmeline had touted Conservative support some months earlier Arthur Balfour, the party leader then in opposition, expressed some sympathy but was careful to promise nothing, and must have known that his key supporters, Lord Curzon and Austen Chamberlain, had been instrumental in establishing the League Opposing Women's Suffrage.

From December 1905 the Liberals became entrenched in power and were effectively the suffragists' only hope. Working against the suffragists, however, was the conviction of many Liberals that extending the 1884 Act to women would strengthen the Conservative vote. Sir Arthur Campbell-Bannerman, the prime minister, expressed his personal conversion to their cause, but very carefully, not that of his party, and this bitter disappointment incited violent feminine protests in and around Whitehall. The WSPU delighted in the *Daily Mail's* mocking term 'suffragettes' with its suggestion of menacing feminine aggression, and when the openly hostile Herbert Henry Asquith succeeded Campbell-Bannerman in April 1908 all-out war was declared by the WSPU – although not the NUWSS. Ignoring all its critics, the WSPU intensified its destructive attacks on the property of its key political opponents, on empty churches and country mansions, and on major exhibits in museums and art galleries.

In Devon, as elsewhere, people were divided on the merits of female suffrage, let alone the means of achieving it. The NUWSS was active, and its meetings well supported and peaceful. Early in the new century Miss Ethel Phear, from an influential Liberal family in Exmouth, was among several local NUWSS speakers who were convinced that peaceful persuasion would achieve their aim. In 1909 Tavistock hosted two largely supportive meetings when NUWSS speakers limited their ambitions to women getting the vote but not becoming MPs.

But far more newsworthy across the county were the reports that summer of the raid by militant suffragettes on the House of Commons. Starting off as an apparently peaceful deputation waiting on the prime minister, it took on a far more fearsome aspect when a police inspector handed Mrs Pankhurst a letter saying no meeting would take place. When ordered to leave, she smacked the inspector's face, a fracas broke out and all members of the deputation were arrested. Outside in Parliament Square thousands of jeering and cheering suffragettes surged forward, stones were thrown, windows smashed and numerous fights and several injuries incurred as police barred entry to the Houses of Parliament. The women went on to hurl stones through the windows of the Home Office, Treasury and Privy Council buildings. One hundred and sixteen arrests were made, and this was just one of numerous high-profile, carefully choreographed and deliberately provocative rallies. The catalogue of violence, arrests, trials, imprisonment, hunger strikes and forced feeding ensured the WSPU pushed the NUWSS off centre stage.

A WSPU postcard
featuring Mrs Pankhurst.
(Author's collection)

Suffragette Violence in Devon

By 1909 many Devon towns, including Barnstaple, Bideford, Crediton, Exeter, Ilfracombe, Plymouth, Sidmouth, Tavistock, Teignmouth, Tiverton and Torquay, possessed active pro-suffrage societies linked to either the WSPU or the NUWSS. The leaders of both branches of the suffrage movement were often in the West Country to encourage and inform members, but the national outrages and the sharp criticisms of male-dominated institutions, notably businesses and Parliament, ensured the WSPU received greater local attention. In October 1909, for example, the renowned pionering doctor, Elizabeth Garrett-Anderson, now 73 years of age, highlighted the evils of women's sweated labour to keep Crediton's already vibrant WSPU membership in tune with the national campaign. In Ilfracombe in November 1910 Lady Isabel Margesson of the WSPU asserted the supreme importance of women finding a voice that would ensure the nation's physical and moral regeneration now that the evils of desperately poor homes and the chronic lack of effective childcare were so well known.

The violence, though, came to Devon. The WSPU targeted as many by-elections as possible. The women expected to be shouted down and perhaps physically jostled and bruised, but in the hard-fought Mid Devon (technically Ashburton) by-election in December 1908 Mrs Pankhurst found her own life in danger.

In late Victorian times several Devon MPs had been returned unopposed, but during the Edwardian era the array of bitter national controversies ensured every

A typically hard-hitting WSPU postcard. (Author's collection)

seat was hotly contested, with candidates obliged to weather as best they could not only the verbal assaults of opposing candidates and their supporters but also from time to time the very real threat of physical assault. There was an alarming return to the volatile temper of the hustings so common half a century earlier. In 1908 the Conservative Captain Ernest Morrison-Bell sought to capture the Mid Devon seat from the Liberals in a by-election just at the time social reform, import taxes and naval expenditure, as well as female suffrage, were dividing the nation. Devon's chief constable grew alarmed at the extent of the vicious heckling and scuffling at several village meetings addressed by the candidates, not least because of the presence of suffragettes.

Neither the Liberal or Conservative candidate had any interest in female suffrage, but the suffragettes' primary interest was in defeating any supporter of Asquith's Liberal government. To Liberal astonishment and fury, Morrison-Bell triumphed, and angry Liberal crowds who turned up in Newton Abbot hoping to greet their successful candidate stormed the Conservative Club, smashing most of its windows. Mrs Pankhurst and a colleague, Mrs Nellie Martell, were recognised by a gang of young men, instantly blamed for the Liberal defeat and pelted with eggs, chased through the streets and into a grocer's shop. Emmeline escaped out the back but was seen, caught and flung to the muddy ground, injuring her ankle. Just as the men were deciding what to do with her, the police arrived.

In June 1908 violence erupted in Torquay when Mrs Montagu tried to introduce Miss Annie Kenney, the militant WSPU activist. Sixty young men and several 'shrill-voiced young women' repeatedly shouted out, 'Rot', 'You're fighting for the Tories', and 'Go and get married'. Hand bells added to the din, and soon the men surged forward to the platform, forcing the speakers to retreat to back rooms until the police arrived.

At a local meeting the following day, Annie Kenney reused a common insult of the militants that revealed the gender hostility lying just beneath the surface of some WSPU activists. 'You men,' she cried, 'did not have the vote given to you because of your intelligence. It does not matter how stupid a man is, if he can make a cross on a paper he is all right.'

Lady Frances Balfour of the NUWSS preferred laughter to venom, and put it a little differently in Torquay in 1913 when she said, 'You cannot class women with the felons and feeble-minded and then tell her she is on so high a pedestal that she must not be brought down to the level of politics'.

In August 1909 suffragettes planned to ambush the Liberal minister, Earl Carrington, on his way from the Rougemont Hotel in Exeter to speak on the Budget at Victoria Hall. Forewarned, however, he avoided them only to have a crowd of women rush at the doors of the hall and almost, but not quite, overwhelm the police cordon. Three women were arrested and spent a week in Exeter Prison where they smashed the windows of their cells and went on hunger strike until they were granted 'political prisoner' status and a less draconian regime.

The Non-Violent Suffragists in Devon

Although NUWSS meetings created fewer dramatic headlines, their meetings attracted large audiences, their lack of deliberate provocation led to calmer tempers and less heckling and sometimes they received detailed reporting. Early in 1912 the sympathetic *Mid Devon Advertiser* printed Mrs Bruce Knight's speech at Newton Abbot town hall. She made the same points as any WSPU activist; the difference probably lay in style not substance. As women paid taxes and were subject to the laws of the land, she argued they should have a voice in decisions about them. She added that 5 million of the 14 million wage earners in the land were women, and many of them, notably widows, were the breadwinners putting up with wages no man would tolerate. Women remained severely disadvantaged in other ways – indeed, Mrs Knight asserted, 'the mother does not exist in English law'. She 'cannot legally say anything'. A wife could not stop her husband taking their children away, and she had no legal access to any poor law relief he was given. She scorned the counter argument that it was 'a man's job to govern', saying the government's concern for human life, even after its 'darker side' had been so clearly revealed, was risible.

That November the Countess of Selborne, along with Admiral Sir William and Lady Acland, spoke at another NUWSS meeting in the town. She mocked the vote being barred to women but allowed to tramps and drunks. She reiterated Mrs Bruce Knight's argument that men had manifestly failed to adhere to their claim that women were better off being 'protected' by men. Lady Selborne and Sir William took the argument further when they returned to Torbay in January 1914 to condemn both Houses of Parliament for allowing one baby in five to die before its first birthday.

Many similar meetings pervaded the county. All of them struck at the alleged inadequacies of a male dominated society and Parliament's pusillanimity in refusing to grant women the vote. Not surprisingly, when suffragists raised thoughts of women becoming MPs and agitating for costly social and employment reforms, and interfering in government policies generally, the fundamental aim of securing the vote became obscured in a fog of male fears and opposition hardened.

The Young Men's Christian Association Debates

Many men across Devon supported female suffrage – but many did not. Two well-reported YMCA debates highlight both the great interest and the great divide.

In Newton Abbot, a YMCA debate in November 1913 ended with the defeat of the pro-suffrage motion. The opposing speaker, the Reverend A. E. Hill, developed the commonly used points that women were 'constitutionally and temperamentally different to men' and unable thereby to determine policies concerned with 'national security, the provision of the army and navy, and the carrying on of all the administrative functions of the government'. Like many other critics, he doubted if many women were interested in such matters or, for that matter, issues of social reform as, he asserted, 232 boards of guardians had no women members. He poured scorn on any political action ever eradicating poverty, and rested his case on the rigours of the law of supply and demand. Finally, he joined the crowd of opponents who claimed that denying women the vote would protect them from the nastiness of political life and allow them to preserve 'the courtesy and chivalry for which they looked to those who regarded themselves as their natural protectors'. The Reverend T. James in Torquay was equally sure that the feminine virtues – he left them unspecified – he valued so highly, rendered women 'a thousand times' unsuitable to the political arena.

A Barnstaple YMCA debate in 1913 produced the opposite result. Here, the common arguments that the vote should be denied women because they could not take up arms to defend the country, and their families would suffer if they became MPs, were soundly beaten by ones asserting that women were well regarded members of the Primrose League and Liberal Women's Association and were 'no longer men's chattels' but their equals as 'helpmates, companions and friends'. Several years earlier, in 1907 in Exeter, Mrs Pankhurst had confounded the military service argument by saying that the vast majority of soldiers and sailors did not qualify for the vote themselves. She had added that the respect men claimed they owed women should include trust with the vote. In a speech in April 1913 H. E. Duke, Exeter's Conservative MP, represented the moderately progressive view that women should have the vote despite the appalling behaviour of some of them.

The Anti-Suffrage Meetings

WSPU violence permanently alienated some influential families in Devon – although probably it merely confirmed their initial prejudices. Soon after the assault on Parliament in 1909, Sir Thomas Acland chaired a meeting of the Women's National Anti-Suffrage League at Exeter, and read out pointed letters from Countess Fortescue and Lady Audrey Buller saying that such vitriolic out-bursts confirmed their feelings that women as a whole were totally unfit to have the vote. Bizarrely, Sir Thomas himself asserted that most women themselves had little interest in securing the vote and claimed never to have heard of any woman being oppressed at work during a decade (1882–92) as a Liberal MP.

His wife was equally hostile. She lamented that suffragettes were doing women a great deal of harm by undermining 'the chivalrous nature' which young men were taught to express towards them. The WSPU agitation was completely unneces-sary as there were 'women inspectors, women guardians, co-opted members of Education Committees, and they had votes for County and Borough Councils'. Thereby, she argued, women's influences were already wide ranging and leading to reforms. It was the key argument of the Anti-Suffrage League.

George Lambert, the Liberal MP for South Molton, was equally hostile. When Mrs Montagu, the suffragist leader in Crediton, wrote a public letter urging his support for the suffragettes enduring forced feeding in Winson Green Prison in

1909, his scornful reply merely stated that they had broken the law and their lives were being saved from their own foolish actions. Lady Fortescue, Lady Audrey Buller, Sir Thomas and Lady Acland, and George Lambert were conspicuous figures on Devon's anti-suffrage platforms. Most were there when Mrs Greatbatch, a noted national speaker, claimed her long experience in an industrial town had convinced her 'that the women there did not want the vote and would not know what to do with it'.

Not surprisingly, throughout 1913 and 1914 news of the slashing of pictures in the Dore Gallery, including one of the Grand Canal by the Devon artist, John Shapland, the incessant breaking of windows in London, Edinburgh and Belfast, the verbal and physical assaults on unsympathetic newspaper editors and politicians, and the arson attacks on golf clubhouses, post offices, Kew Gardens' refreshment pavilion, churches in Wargrave and Breadsall and empty houses such as Sir George Newnes' mansion in Lynton, polarised local opinion. Typically, in June 1914 the unsympathetic *Trewman's Flying Post* declared the women who stalked and attacked Holloway Prison's medical officer with whips 'behaved like mad persons in Court, and it took a dozen constables to get them into the dock'.

Mrs Pankhurst in Exeter Gaol

In December 1913 upwards of 200 suffragettes, some from as far afield as London and Plymouth, gathered in front of Exeter Prison when they heard Mrs Pankhurst had been taken there after being arrested on the liner *Majestic* when it arrived in Plymouth from New York after a successful fundraising campaign. The police had invoked the terms of the so-called 'Cat & Mouse Act', that permitted the release of convicted women weakened by hunger strike but allowed them to be reincarcerated when they recovered. The police had difficulty controlling the crowd, and the situation almost got out of hand when groups of men charged the pickets and jostled the women. One woman was nearly thrown over the nearby railway bridge.

The rough handling of the women and confused scuffles between the men and women and the police went on throughout the night. To ecstatic cheers, Mrs Pankhurst was released after a few days, on licence, and went straight to London and Paris, ignoring the order to return to prison in a fortnight. At Exeter Cathedral, the dean acceded to requests to offer prayers for her safety.

By the summer of 1914 the suffragettes seemed no nearer their objective; certainly Asquith had not changed his mind. In Devon there was just one poll attempting to identify local opinion. It was carried out in November 1911 by Torquay's branch of the Women's National Anti-Suffrage League. One can wonder why only 720 of the 1,640 forms were returned; of these, 468 (about 65 per cent) said 'No'.

Mrs Pankhurst's next visit to Exeter was in November 1914, and it was to urge women to encourage their menfolk to enlist in the armed forces. She did not mention the vote.

Multiple Crises:
The Background to the Tariff Reform Controversy

In 1901 Great Britain was the most powerful nation in the world. Its empire was the largest, its trade was the greatest, its navy ruled the oceans and its capital city dominated global finance. The empire bolstered British internal pride and international prestige, and perhaps as a result of the shock of the Boer War and Germany's delight in Britain's embarrassment an aggressive patriotism crept across the nation. Imperialism penetrated more deeply than ever before into major areas of British life, notably the army and public schools but also trading companies, missionary societies and all those who thought the British had a moral, even divine, right to control the destinies of other races. All this came just at the time that British military capabilities and coal and steel production were being overtaken by the United States of America and Germany. Great Britain was paying the price of being the first country to experience mass industrialisation, and perceptive contemporaries such as the renowned American economist Thorstein Veblin criticised British factories for failing to modernise and their wealthy owners for their commercial inertia and enervating obsession with the pursuits of country gentlemen.

It was in the anxiety-ridden aftermath of the Boer War that Joseph Chamberlain, the maverick Secretary of State for the Colonies in Lord Salisbury's government (1895–1902), began to promote the idea of tariff reform. He sought the end of Victorian free trade, that is, trade without import duties, and urged their imposition on selected goods coming from countries outside the empire, notably the United States, France and Germany, who already taxed some British exports. This would bind the empire closer together, he asserted, and raise funds for new battleships and welfare reforms.

Chamberlain managed to split the Cabinet, then the Conservative Party and finally the country. Arthur Balfour succeeded Salisbury as Conservative Prime Minister in 1903, but Cabinet resignations, the defections of ardent free trade Conservatives to the Liberals, and controversies over indentured Chinese labour in South Africa, eroded Balfour's credibility and his majority. He resigned in December 1905, to be replaced by Campbell-Bannerman whose Liberal Party secured a massive 132 majority in the January 1906 election.

Tariff reform, though, had not gone away. Indeed it cut across party loyalties; some Liberals professed sympathy for tariff reform, as did many Conservatives, while others in both parties stayed committed to free trade. The possibility of new import tariffs forcing up the price of food, especially bread due to the massive grain imports from outside the empire, became a hot political issue. Free traders seized every opportunity to arouse working-class hostility to the 'dear loaf'. Tariff reformers, though, shrewdly played the patriotic card, portraying gloating foreigners, especially Germans, offloading their surplus products cheaply on Great Britain while slapping duties on British imports.

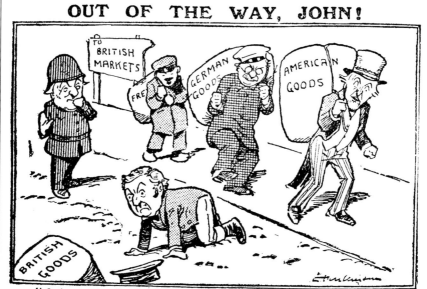

Pro-tariff reform cartoon. (*Trewman's Exeter Flying Post*, 16 March 1912)

The wild accusations made by both sides, that their opponents' views would do irreparable harm to the nation's prosperity and every voter's pocket, complicated and inflamed Edwardian elections. Devon's voters not only had to consider election candidates as Liberal or Conservative (there were no Labour ones in the county during this period) but also identify whether they were free traders or tariff reformers, and in favour of or opposed to female suffrage.

❦ *Multiple Crises:* ❧
The House of Lords & Irish Home Rule Controversies

Voters also needed to find out whether candidates favoured or opposed Irish Home Rule, and favoured or opposed limiting the political power of the aristocracy.

Long before the Act of Union in 1800 many Irishmen had sought independence from Great Britain, by force if necessary, but always unsuccessfully. And since that act episodic violence by the Irish Republican Brotherhood, or 'Fenians', had been accompanied by a growth of political pressure by an ever-increasing number of Irish MPs committed to self-government – or Home Rule – within the United Kingdom. In the 1885 election they captured eighty-five of the 103 Irish seats, and the following year the Liberal Prime Minister William Gladstone tried, but failed to pass a Home Rule Bill. He succeeded, though, in splitting his party as many Liberal 'Unionists' joined with the Conservatives to oppose future bills. And all the time the Fenian attacks against English landowners, property agents and their sympathisers continued unabated in Ireland.

In 1893 Gladstone tried again, and once again the Lords rejected his bill. Between 1895 and 1905 Home Rule was never part of the Conservative government's agenda, and the Liberals displayed little interest when they first returned to power. However, the situation changed dramatically in 1910 when two elections reduced the Liberals to reliance on Irish Nationalist MPs to achieve a working majority. Asquith did a dramatic deal with them; if they supported his Parliament Bill to reduce the power of the House of Lords he would support a Home Rule Bill.

In 1909, a lengthy trial of strength between the House of Lords and the Liberal government had caused yet another national crisis. The largely Conservative Lords had wrecked a succession of Liberal bills, but in that year Lloyd George, the Chancellor of the Exchequer, who hated the aristocracy as much as, or maybe more than, he advocated social reform, submitted a Budget containing a massive investment in his striking National and Unemployment Insurance schemes and in naval expansion. He intended to raise the money through increasing inheritance tax and higher rates of income tax, and introducing a land transfer tax and higher duties on liquor licences, spirits, tobacco and petrol.

The Lords chose to reject it, thereby causing a major constitutional crisis and bringing down upon their heads a storm of invective from Lloyd George and other radicals. After two bitterly contested elections in January and December 1910, centred upon the relative merits of aristocratic and popular rule, the combined Liberals and Irish Nationalists maintained a slender majority. The Lords finally caved in when Asquith announced that the new king, George V, would create, if necessary, 400 new Liberal peers to ensure the passage of a Parliament Bill severely reducing the power of the so-called Upper House. The threat was enough; henceforth the Lords could only delay a bill for two years, and could not interfere at all in purely financial legislation. The aristocracy had been made to look selfish, reactionary and foolish.

As Asquith promised, the Parliament Act in 1911 was followed by an Irish Home Rule Bill in 1912. This was duly delayed by the Lords for two years, but became law in 1914 with implementation planned for the autumn. In the intervening period recruits flooded into two large and well-equipped paramilitary forces – the Ulster Volunteers, determined to keep the Protestant north free from 'Popish' Dublin's control, and the Irish Volunteers, dedicated to enforcing the act across the whole country. Both sides smuggled in thousands of guns, often from Germany. Talks failed, and civil war looked inevitable.

❧ *Devon's Violent Elections* ❧

Mid Devon/Ashburton

The swirling currents of these controversial cross party issues meant that parliamentary elections were hard fought, incited high emotions and attracted very high turnouts – exceeding 80 per cent and sometimes 90 per cent in Devon. Indeed, it did not require party meetings to be held at election time for hostile crowds to amass. In 1904, for example, a mob claiming to be Liberal free traders invaded a Tariff Reform League meeting about to be addressed by Rear Admiral Sir John Hext, a local dignitary, and Sir John Cockburn, the ex-premier of South Australia, in Newton Abbot's vegetable market. The intruders reached the platform, overturned tables and chairs, caused several injuries, ejected the speakers and announced a Liberal meeting instead.

After the sudden death of Charles Seale-Hayne, Harry Trelawney Eve, a south Devon lawyer, easily held Mid Devon for the Liberals at the 1904 by-election against General Sir Richard Harrison and again in the 1906 general election against Captain Ernest Morrison-Bell.

As we have seen, the 1908 by-election held there after Eve was appointed a judge was a very different affair. After his victory, Morrison-Bell lost no opportunity at numerous local rallies to chastise the Liberal government for encouraging Germany to start a naval race by neglecting the Royal Navy, and he could not resist mocking Lloyd George's pacifism during the Boer War. Not surprisingly the local Liberals, already enraged by their surprise defeat, ensured he had a rough ride during the January 1910 campaign. After one meeting in Newton Abbot, the Conservative *Mid Devon Advertiser* claimed that 'the gallant Captain appeared to be simply revelling in the questioning', although much of the meeting and its aftermath consisted of rival groups striving to outdo each other with songs, shouts, cheers and insults.

His Liberal opponent, Charles Roden Buxton, played successfully on a vote for the Conservatives being a vote for dearer food, the end of social reform and the perpetuation of the self-centred House of Lords. He played heavily, too, on Morrison-Bell's investment in the Teign Valley quarries and his alleged pressure on the manager to tell the sturdily Liberal workers to vote Conservative or place their jobs in peril. The candidates criss-crossed the constituency, abusing each other at four or five meetings a day. At Chudleigh, local children divided into partisan groups and rivalled each other with politically loaded songs and catchphrases as they stormed around the village.

After Buxton's victory the *Mid Devon Advertiser* repeatedly tarred him and all Liberals as troublemakers bent on 'inspiring the working classes with feelings of hatred and malice towards their own countrymen, whose interests are in all essentials bound up with their own'. This remained a key Conservative argument when Asquith called another election in December 1910 to bring the House of Lords

Ernest Morrison-Bell. (Devon & Exeter Institution)

crisis to a head. Buxton chose to smear Morrison-Bell and the Conservatives with deflecting attention away from their lack of interest in social reform with a panic-mongering obsession with building costly battleships to counter the ridiculous threat of a German invasion.

Across Devon, as across the nation, each party condemned the other as unpatriotic, ignorant of economics, uncaring of ordinary families and claimed to have the solution to hunger and unemployment. Voters heard that both free trade and tariff reform would raise the price of bread, and both parties cited convenient statistics 'proving' workers in tariff-protected countries such as Germany, France and the United States were either better or worse off than British families. In the end, Mid Devon preferred Morrison-Bell's emphasis on social stability and national defence, and he retook the seat with a modest majority of 354. It was one of several Devon seats turning Conservative in 1910.

In Tavistock, Sir John Spear, an ex-Liberal turned Conservative Unionist, also broke a long-standing Liberal stranglehold on a Devon seat. A gentleman farmer, a highly respected county councillor and chairman of Tavistock Rural District Council, he won the seat by just fifteen votes from a Liberal in 1900, lost it by 1,209 in the landslide Liberal triumph in 1906, lost it again by 227 in January 1910, but recaptured it by 390 in December.

Barnstaple & South Molton

In 1906, and again in January and December 1910, Ernest Soares easily maintained the long-standing Liberal domination of the Barnstaple constituency with his staunch defence of free trade, enduring opposition to the 1902 Education Act, bitter condemnation of the House of Lords and his commitment to a revision of the rural rating system. His opponents' attempts to label him a dangerous Socialist, to deny that the 'People's Budget' would help working-class families, and to sow fears that the Parliament Bill would free the Commons 'to pass into law any measure, however unwise', carried little weight.

The 1906 election was particularly violent across north Devon, with the *Western Times* and *Western Morning News* describing two frightening attempts to overturn Soares' carriage as Liberal supporters drew it into Barnstaple, several angry attacks on Conservative sandwich-board men in Bideford, and the foulmouthed abuse hurled by Conservatives when men from Shapland & Petter's Cabinet Works marched in formation to record and loudly proclaim their votes for Soares. Soares was at great pains to visit this and other factories – including Barnstaple's Derby Lace Mill and Pilton's Glove Works – to highlight the threat of retaliatory tariffs on British goods. Typically, though, the rival *North Devon Herald* and *Journal* reported different views of his reception, especially at the Derby Lace Mill where deep political divisions between the staff, managers and owners had soured working relationships.

When Soares' victory was declared several violent incidents occurred as crowds roamed the streets – it was 'strongly reminiscent of Barnstaple Fair', commented the *Western Morning News*. There were several summonses for assault, although perhaps with some deference to tradition, the presiding magistrate imposed minimal fines, 'making allowance for the fact that it was election day'. Earl Fortescue, originally a Liberal but now increasingly moving towards the Conservatives as a Unionist, joined in the 1910 north Devon campaigns with speeches defending the House of Lords. They were, he argued, the champions of the people against

Sir Ernest Soares from 1911. (Devon & Exeter Institution)

foolhardy legislation and Devon had benefitted for generations from the public services undertaken by the local aristocracy. Possibly he made a little difference, but it was far from enough. Although his majorities were eroded, Soares won easily on both occasions.

In neighbouring South Molton the local gentleman farmer, George (later 1st Viscount) Lambert, had held the seat for the Liberals since 1891 and continued to do so with a sizeable majority throughout the Edwardian era. Indeed, in 1900 and 1906 he was unopposed; but not so in 1910. However, the perils of impending

George (later 1st Viscount) Lambert. (Devon & Exeter Institution)

Socialism and the folly of emasculating the House of Lords, the 'people's protec-
tor', paraded by his Conservative opponent, Lieutenant Colonel John Woolrych
Perowne, made no inroads against the popular Lambert. He ensured his largely
rural audiences always joined him in mocking Perowne's claims that food would
get cheaper, not dearer, with tariff reform. When Perowne argued that the poor
would have to eat fatally adulterated bread if free trade persisted unchecked, his
words merely became part of an insulting song:

> Donkey bones and gee-gee
> Add acids of great power,
> Perowne's latest recipe
> For good old English flour

Lambert could even invoke approval and applause for his support of Irish Home
Rule on the grounds that Australia, Canada and New Zealand possessed it.

So great were the tensions in this constituency at this time that political rallies
addressed by Perowne well outside the elections themselves attracted enough rowdy
opponents to disrupt the event and sometimes force its closure. In March 1908,
for example, a torch lit procession accompanying the carriages taking Perowne
and Sir John Shelley from a meeting in Crediton to the latter's house at nearby
Shobrooke Park was accosted by a gang of political opponents. Stones and abuse
were hurled and ill-tempered fights broke out with the torchbearers.

Tiverton

Conversely, in 1906 and 1910 neighbouring Tiverton returned Conservative MPs
with safe, if not huge, majorities. The two major families – the Liberal Heathcoat-
Amorys and Conservative Walronds – remained socially close but deeply divided
politically. Sir William Walrond had held the East Devonshire seat and then
the reorganised Tiverton seat since 1880 and he had been unopposed in 1886,
1895, 1900 and 1902, although not in 1892. In 1906, however, Sir John and Ian
Heathcoat-Amory actively supported W. H. Reed's free trade arguments in a vigorous Liberal attempt to unseat Sir William. Free trade, asserted Sir John in a public
letter, had been responsible for the prosperity of the nation and especially the
working classes; tariffs would 'hamper our trade, and increase the number of our
unemployed'.

Despite Sir John speaking as a major employer with many overseas connections, the constituency remained unconvinced and returned the Honourable
Lionel Walrond, the young son of the recently ennobled Lord Waleran. However,
the Conservative majority was halved. Walrond himself argued that trade, not senti-
ment, must hold the empire together, with the empire's primary function being to
supply the raw materials such as cotton and tobacco for British factories to turn
into manufactured goods which they later sold back to the colonies.

In January 1910 Ian Heathcoat-Amory himself stood against Lionel Walrond,
but to no avail, and in December Walrond significantly increased his majority
against an outsider, A. E. Y. Trestail. Here, too, violence was never far from the surface. In January, 2,000 people from both political parties gathered in Tiverton along
the route taken by Walrond and his wife and Lord Clinton to address a rally in the
Drill Hall. The cars and accompanying mounted police were greeted with mixed
cheers and boos and the derisive popular song, 'The only horse I think that I can

manage is the one the missus dries the clothes on'. The police saved the Drill Hall from invasion but afterwards they had great difficulty in protecting the Walronds, Clinton and the Conservative agent from a determined and hostile charge as they entered their cars. A door was ripped off one car, several people narrowly escaped being pushed under horses, stewards were kicked, and, said the *South Molton Gazette*, 'one young hooligan was heard to make an offensive remark ("you're a b—dy suffragette") at a lady who was quietly leaving; and then he struck her in the breast with his clenched fist. Other ladies have since complained that they were struck.'

The Hon. Lionel Walrond. (Devon & Exeter Institution)

Ironically, Lord Clinton was no diehard defender of the House of Lords. Although he argued the need for an independent Second Chamber, he thought a better set of reforms would be to limit its numbers and subject its aristocratic membership to periodic election.

Devon's Liberals in Retreat : Totnes, Torquay, Honiton, Exeter & Plymouth

Totnes was even firmer Conservative territory. Francis Mildmay (later 1st Baron Mildmay of Flete) had been elected Liberal MP for Totnes in 1885, but a year later split with Gladstone over Irish Home Rule. Like Sir John Spear in Tavistock, Mildmay remained a Liberal Unionist in name but largely Conservative in views, and he defeated a succession of Liberal opponents from 1886 onwards by 2,000 votes or more – the most consistently high majority across the county. Repeated attempts to smear him as 'neither fish nor fowl' proved futile, not least because he proved adroit at using his 'transitional' status to advocate welfare reforms, such as curbing liquor licenses and modifying the 1902 Education Act, alongside promoting a stronger navy, defending the House of Lords and opposing Irish Home Rule.

In 1910 his majority was unharmed by his conversion from free trader to tariff reformer and ardent imperialist. An added bonus was the highly partisan *Totnes Times*, which consistently praised Mildmay's eloquence and sincerity while his

GENERAL ELECTION,
1906.

HONITON DIVISION.

Sir John Kennaway,

Your old and trusted friend for 35 years, asks for your

VOTE AND INTEREST.

Printed & Published by E. Dimond, Honiton.

Sir John Kennaway's publicity postcard for the 1906 election. (Author's collection)

opponents resorted to degrading personal attacks and remained nonplussed by questions. Honiton also remained steadfastly Conservative in the hands of the impressively bearded Sir John Kennaway until he retired as 'Father of the House' in 1910 and handed the constituency over to Arthur Morrison-Bell, the brother of Captain Ernest, who maintained the comfortable majority.

Torquay changed its colours twice during the Edwardian era. The Conservatives had narrow majorities of eighty, 394 and 175 in 1886, 1892 and 1895 respectively. In 1900 the Liberal Francis (later Sir) Layland-Barratt took the seat with a majority of just 129. He held onto it comfortably in 1906 but only narrowly in January 1910 against Henry Lopes (Sir from 1908) of Maristow.

With all of Torquay's elementary schools being Anglican, the 1902 Education Act still polarised political and religious opinion in this constituency, which both Layland-Barratt and Lopes sought to exploit in 1906 and January 1910. As 1910 approached the entwined issues of the 1909 Budget and the House of Lords enlivened many political garden parties across Torbay and ensured the heightening of antipathy between the candidates.

Influential figures such as Lord Churston, Lord Clifford, Captain Phillpotts RN and a previous local MP, Captain Richard Mallock of Cockington Court, rallied to Sir Henry Lopes' cause and rammed home through numerous meetings and large newspaper advertisements their message that the Liberal government was increasingly Socialist, deliberately stirring up civil unrest, unreasonably hostile to an effective Second Chamber and had no interest in forging a mutually supportive empire through tariff reform, and even less in keeping the navy strong.

They were joined by the alarmist propaganda issued by the Anti-Socialist League and the fiery speeches of one of its key supporters, the Reverend J. T. Jacob, vicar of Torre. Socialism, Jacob asserted, 'would destroy the monarchy, introduce anarchy, repudiate national obligations, confiscate private property, and aim a deadly blow at the religious and moral life of the people'. Their intensive electioneering failed by just eleven votes to get Lopes elected in January, but secured victory for his successor, the ultra-right wing Colonel Charles Burn, in December. Torquay joined Mid Devon and Tavistock in reverting to the Conservatives.

The major urban areas were also volatile constituencies. In 1906 Sir Edgar Vincent, a Conservative free trader, lost his Exeter seat to the Liberal Sir George Kekewich. Several decades of narrow Conservative triumphs were overturned by just eighty-five votes. Kekewich's bitterness towards the liquor trade, the 1902 Education Act and Anglicans in general served him well among the city's strong Nonconformist congregations, but amidst accusations of neglect and absenteeism he was replaced by the aristocratic Harold St Maur of Stover as Liberal candidate in 1910. However, in January the Conservative Henry Duke (later Lord Merrivale) scraped home by twenty-six votes in a contest centred on the virtues or evils of tariff reform. In December, though, he lost by three votes – until a recount,

WE WORK FOR THE WOMEN & CHILDREN

REAL FREE TRADE WILL KEEP THE BIG LOAF AND BRING MORE MONEY TO BUY IT WITH.

AND THINK OF THE BREAD WINNER ALSO.

PRINTED & PUBLISHED BY JAMES TOWNSEND & SONS, EXETER.

A free trade propaganda card circulated in Exeter by Sir Edgar Vincent, anti-tariff reform
Conservative candidate in the 1906 general election. (Devon & Exeter Institution)

and then a sensational petition that rejected some dubious Liberal papers, returned
the seat to Duke by one vote.

The same see-saw of results occurred in both Plymouth and Devonport.
For many years Plymouth had sent two Conservative MPs to Westminster, although
with only narrow majorities, but in 1906 the Liberal Imperialist Charles (later Sir)
Mallet and his Liberal colleague, T.W. Dobson, secured easy victories in the general
Liberal landslide by playing on the iniquities of the 1902 Education Act, the selfish-
ness of the House of Lords and the dangers of tariff reform.

In January 1910 Mallet and a new Liberal colleague, the ironmaster Aneurin
Williams, scraped home on the issues of social and political reform, but a strong
local reversion to Conservatism saw their defeat in December by Waldorf Astor
(later 2nd Viscount) and Arthur Shirley Benn (later Sir, and 1st Lord Glenravel).
Both Conservative candidates played shrewdly on presenting the House of Lords
as the 'people's champion' against a dictatorial House of Commons and on the
area's military and naval heritage and the employment opportunities linked to
rearmament and imperial consolidation.

In neighbouring Devonport the political pendulum had swung towards the
Conservatives in the 1880s and the Liberals from the 1890s, but the Conservatives
Sir John Jackson and Sir Charles Kinloch-Cooke retook both seats in January 1910
and held on to them in December, albeit with very narrow majorities both times.
The Liberal *Western Daily Mercury* condemned Jackson and Kinloch-Cooke as

'friends of the landlords' and aliens in a staunchly working-class constituency, while the Conservative *Western Morning News* avidly praised their dedication to the empire, a bigger navy and local dockyard expansion – and won the day.

⚜ *A Country Riven by Strikes* ⚜

By the end of 1912 Lloyd George's Budget had been enacted, the Parliament Act implemented and the Home Rule Bill ensured of a successful, if delayed, passage. The political world had been turned upside down, but peace was far from returning. The suffragettes continued with their militant campaign and Asquith remained deaf to their arguments. The tariff reformers and free traders continued to hurl insults and statistics at each other, and to claim the high moral ground regarding cheaper food and economic prosperity. The Liberal government, largely retaining the party's traditional free trade inclination, maintained the status quo.

And then there were the strikes, many of them large, long lasting and bitter. It was in the Edwardian era that the industrial trades unions managed to turn themselves from largely localised groups into huge national organisations prepared to flex their corporate muscles and establish themselves as political forces linked closely to the nascent Labour Party, and indeed helping fund it. Although the 1906 election was a Liberal landslide victory over a temporarily chaotic Conservative Party, the real victor, bearing in mind the future, was probably the Labour Party with its first twenty-nine MPs. In January 1910 Labour won forty seats, and in December forty-two.

Inspired by the legendary match girls' strike at Bryant & May's factory in 1888 and the gas workers' and dockers' strikes of 1889, union membership among the hitherto largely unorganised, unskilled and semi-skilled workers soared at the turn of the century. The attempts by employers and the courts to ban picketing (1896) and make unions liable for losses sustained by companies during strikes (1901) were temporarily successful but ensured workers' militancy festered beneath the apparent calm. Many younger workers became deeply frustrated by what they saw as the older union leaders' willingness to retain too great an affection for the Liberal Party and the Campbell-Bannerman and Asquith administrations despite their track record of social reform. Indeed, these social reforms could well have fostered the idea that they were merely the first of many that could be squeezed out of the capitalists who relied on the sweat of the working classes for their profits.

The whole of the Edwardian period witnessed uneasy and mutually suspicious relationships between employers and workers. Sudden strikes were common, and often called in defiance of the union leaders' advice. After 1910 a nation already stunned by several crises found vast numbers of trades unionists were prepared to bring commercial life to a halt unless their demands were met.

Deep in Devon, militant Labour associations among the railway workers of Newton Abbot and the clay and quarry workers along the Teign Valley met regularly to discuss contemporary political and economic issues. Despite the absence of Labour parliamentary candidates in Devon, they passed fiery resolutions condemning capitalism and promoting public ownership of the means of production that must have alarmed many readers of the local newspapers and stimulated local branches of the Anti-Socialist League into equally extreme responses. In addition, during these years the Amalgamated Society of Tailors & Tailoresses was particularly successful in unionising those workers scattered across Devon with thoughts of improving their bargaining position, conditions and wages.

In 1911 there were 872 different strikes across the country. The biggest was the miners' bitter but unsuccessful strike in South Wales over tonnage rates that lasted from September 1910 until October 1911. In June 1911 merchant seamen struck over wages. Many docks closed, many railway workers joined in and, just as in the miners' strike, police were called upon to protect men prepared to carry on working. Strikers fought pitched battles with both police and troops; hundreds on both sides were injured and two strikers killed.

Families in Devon could read all about the strikes and violence in local as well as national newspapers. 'The capital is today in the position of a blockaded city,' lamented the *South Molton Gazette* in August 1911. 'So grave is the situation, so extreme the danger to London's food, that troops are being held ready at Aldershot, Hounslow, Shorncliffe, Colchester, Dover and elsewhere; 160 rounds of ball cartridge per man have been issued.'

Other than dislocated rail connections with Paddington and Waterloo, Devon itself was little touched by strikes until 1912 when 1 million coal miners ceased work with far-reaching effect. GWR workers at Exmouth Junction sidings joined in, most GWR branch line services ceased and hundreds of coal wagons remained unloaded. Kilns at Bovey Tracey Potteries had to close down and the wages of 200 workers were under threat.

At the Trusham Granite Quarry 200 men were laid off when its coal ran out, Silverton Paper Mill closed and Messrs Willey's iron foundries in Exeter ran out of coke. Domestic coal soared in price. The Earl of Devon allowed foraging in his woods, and the Misses Carew of Haccombe House allowed the poor of Newton Abbot into Milber Wood, but added that permission would be withdrawn if any damage was done. The building trade was hard hit and workers faced a loss of wages when stocks of raw materials were used up. Exeter's soup kitchen reopened and Lord Poltimore sent £50 to the city's relief fund. Local newspapers were largely hostile, with the *South Molton Gazette* reprinting the *Daily Mail* and *Daily Chronicle*'s harrowing tales of children dying because the coal miners' strike had caused widespread unemployment when works had had to close down and relief funds had dried up.

In 1913 strikes nationwide soared to 1,459, and 1914 saw no let-up in the abrasive relationships. In May 1913 around 200 building workers in Barnstaple and Bideford went on strike, with skilled men seeking a rise from 6*d* to 7*d* an hour and unskilled from 4*d* to 5*d*. Work on new gas mains, electricity supplies and stalls for the County Show came to a halt. The strikers marched through Barnstaple with union banners advertising their cause, and later processed to a Sunday service in the parish church where the vicar diplomatically preached the need to examine both sides of the controversy carefully. After two months without a solution many striking workers drifted to other towns, but eventually a two-staged rise of ½*d* immediately and ½*d* in 1914 was agreed.

Protest marches, bands and protest songs followed the prolonged strike that summer by hundreds of Kingsteignton clay workers when Whiteways & Co. and Hexter, Humpherson & Sons sought to reduce wages by 2*d* per ton, due, they asserted, to a slump in prices. With union backing, substantial popular support and the *Mid Devon Advertiser* giving the men's grievances as much coverage as the owners' assertions, the strike spread to several other firms and then to the bargemen transporting the clay, and the men finally won their case.

Late in April 1914 the Dartmouth 'lumpers' who unloaded the colliers and also filled the bunkers of visiting steamships suddenly went on strike, demanding a rise from 2*d* to 3*d* per ton that they handled. When one ship's captain ordered his Lascar and Chinese seamen to handle the coal, the lumpers reacted violently and frightened them back to their ship.

In Barnstaple, the recently formed local branch of the National Furnishings Trades Association flexed its muscles to secure wage rises at Shapland & Petter's Raleigh Cabinet Works. In separate strikes that summer several hundred Paignton, Torquay and Exeter building workers in the General Labourers' & Gas Workers' Union downed tools demanding rises between 1*d* and 1½*d* an hour. In Paignton, angry strikers gathered outside the police court when eleven colleagues were tried for intimidation, and the prosecuting counsel had to be protected by the police each time he left the court.

In May, men at the Trusham quarries struck for higher rates of pay, and bad-tempered three-sided confrontations between the men, their union leaders and the employers persisted until after the outbreak of war. Strike breakers ran a daily gauntlet of flying stones and catcalls, and the prosecutions for violence only incited further disturbances within and outside the courts. At one meeting a striker shouted out that the managing director was 'a wavering, oily, slippery, sort of person'. The local newspapers were filled with the strikers' accusations of directors' profiteering and the owners' accusations that the strike leaders sought the company's collapse. The strident calls to defeat all capitalists and establish an egalitarian state by W. A. Bond, a self-proclaimed Socialist from Newton Abbot, received enthusiastic applause at strikers' meetings, and some strikers preferred dismissal to acceptance of any compromise, even in wartime, with the company.

◑ *Mounting Fears: The Road to War* ☚

The Edwardian era saw one international crisis after another added to the nation's domestic stresses. At various times diplomatic action seemed in danger of spilling over into military conflict against France over the control of Morocco and Egypt, and against Russia over its seemingly aggressive interests in Persia, Afghanistan and northern India.

Nevertheless, diplomacy finally triumphed and Britain found itself reaching amicable agreements with France in 1904, and then Russia in 1907. Britain secured free rein in Egypt, and France the same in Morocco; Russia bowed out of Afghanistan, but Britain agreed not to annex it and carefully cordoned spheres of influence were agreed in Persia. Both agreements fell short of full treaties of mutual support but they did ease the rivalries and tension – which was primarily what Great Britain wanted.

Unfortunately Germany, and particularly Kaiser Wilhelm II, now saw itself squashed between two potential enemies – France to the west, Russia to the east – in alliance with Great Britain. Germany was belatedly striving to establish itself as a world power, complete with an overseas empire and awesome navy. It had secured several African colonies, and from 1906 onwards built warships obviously rivalling the succession of British 'all big gun' Dreadnought battleships. The kaiser tended to present himself, and thereby his country, in consistently militaristic poses, and British newspapers frequently published extracts of his bellicose speeches to German audiences. Newspapers and popular novelists also seized hold of the profitable opportunities to publish articles and novels based upon Germany's alleged military ambitions, especially vis-à-vis Great Britain and its empire. Edwardian novels such as John Buchan's *The Thirty-Nine Steps*, Erskine Childers' *The Riddle of the Sands*, and William Le Queux's *The Invasion of 1910* portrayed Germany assiduously preparing for war with Great Britain and not hesitating to use subterfuge, spies and traitors as it did so. Many 'experts' thought the same. As early as 1908 Rear Admiral Sir John Hext gave an alarming speech in Newton Abbot highlighting the ease with which he thought Germany's huge merchant fleet could lay protective mines in the North Sea and convey 100,000 men to East Anglia. The Royal Navy would be held at bay and our tiny army crushed.

In Devon, signs of enhanced naval activity were ever present at Devonport, Dartmouth and Torbay. Reports of launchings, new technologies, mightier guns, Channel exercises and fleet reviews filled the newspapers. Large army barracks were sited in Plymouth and Exeter, and the sound of heavy gunfire often boomed across Dartmoor where an artillery training camp had been established. Units regularly unloaded quantities of equipment, horses, hay, limbers and guns at Okehampton Station and then trotted through the town and onto the moors. Other fields and commons across Devon hosted the annual manoeuvres of the volunteer militia that had been formed originally to quell local riots but more recently had fought in the Boer War. In May 1902, for example, nearly 400 men of the yeomanry camped outside Kingsteignton, complete with stables, canteen, mess tents, bandstand and servants' quarters. Each evening the band entertained visitors, and after a week of training a military tattoo was put on for the people of Newton Abbot.

In 1907 Richard Haldane, Secretary of State for War, reformed the nation's disparate volunteer forces – including the Royal North Devon Imperial Yeomanry and the Royal 1st Devon Imperial Yeomanry – into a national territorial army (TA) that would be the country's second line of home defence. The regular army would be the first line, but Haldane anticipated that much of its strength would be spread around the garrisons of the empire. The TA stayed county-based, and the two Devon forces stayed much the same, although the word 'imperial' was removed from their titles as it was thought no longer relevant. Each force had four squadrons, and each squadron between four and eight local detachments. There were additional transport and artillery units.

In May 1908 Colonel Lord Clifford addressed the territorial detachment based at Bovey Tracey. He praised the volunteers' standard of shooting and enthusiasm, but deeply regretted it did not possess a full complement of officers and men. Bovey Tracey, and also Moretonhampstead and Chagford, should be ashamed of

A Royal Horse Artillery detachment passes through Okehampton.
(Museum of Dartmoor Life, Okehampton)

themselves, he said, if they failed to rally in defence of their country. Articles and letters in local newspapers suggest that the problem lay far more in recruiting enough ordinary troopers willing to give their time and undergo training than in finding officers to wear fine uniforms and give orders. In 1911 most companies were still under strength, and the overall establishment was 400 short of the 3,570 allocated to Devon. In November 1912 Commander Curtis RN, a guest speaker at an Ilfracombe detachment dinner, expressed his disgust at the nation's idleness 'while other nations were armed to the teeth, and were ready to attack us'.

Greater efforts were made to inspire local interest. New drill halls and rifle ranges spread across the county, and in Newton Abbot, Tiverton and Bampton, for example, their openings were a cause of great celebration along with fulsome praise for the major donors. District detachments paraded regularly, frequent shooting competitions were held and the mock battles on the annual training camps drew hordes of visitors. Bazaars raised funds, supporters gave prizes and cups for the competitions and newspapers listed the proud winners. Regular church parades ensured that the volunteers were reassured by sermons equating the defence of Great Britain with that of Christianity itself.

Towards the end of King Edward's reign many people thought invasion by Germany was a distinct possibility. In February 1909, Captain Kindersley, a Boer War veteran, addressed the Boys' Club in Seaton and urged the extension of local rifle clubs to ensure that the nation stood a chance of repelling invasion 'if the channel fleet were weakened, or evaded'. The vicar amended the Collect the following Sunday to include the plea, 'stretch forth the right hand of Thy Majesty to be our defence against all our enemies'.

That July, Lieutenant Knox of the Navy League visited Seaton during a West Country lecture tour and fervently promoted peace 'in the only way which is likely to be successful, namely – by our being fully prepared for war'. The meeting was followed by a collection for a town Union Jack. With War Office permission, in 1911 the town created a rifle range, much to the vicar's delight.

In 1908 and 1909 the nation was caught up in a celebrated 'Navy Scare', during which Conservatives and Liberals hurled different statistics at each other regarding the current and estimated future strength of foreign navies, especially Germany's, and the extent to which Great Britain should respond to maintain its superiority. After huge controversies over actual needs, likely costs and possible panic mongering, eight new battleships were ordered, double the number the Liberal government had anticipated. Most Conservatives rejoiced, most Liberals felt uncomfortably compromised – as the political speeches across Devon confirmed. And Lloyd George, the Chancellor of the Exchequer, was forced to raise further taxes to include rearmament alongside his welfare reforms.

Women rallied round too. In 1907 Countess Fortescue established the Devon Branch of the British Red Cross in response to a national appeal by Queen

Alexandra that a county-based force of trained nurses and other hospital workers should be available to support the new TA. The Devon Voluntary Aid Detachment grew out of this appeal. Numerous local detachments were rapidly recruited and intensively trained across the county under its director J. S. C. Davis, an ex-Indian Civil Service officer, and his team of district assistants, supported by Lady Fortescue and influential divisional vice presidents such as Lady Churston, Lady Clinton, Lady Audrey Buller, Mrs Francis Mildmay and Mrs Ian Heathcoat-Amory. Gifts of equipment were readily forthcoming, school managers offered training rooms and owners of large houses promised their conversion to emergency hospitals should the need arise.

By early 1914 the county had sufficient equipment and trained personnel, both men and women, to mount a large-scale mock invasion exercise in east Devon and west Dorset. It involved the 'on the spot' assessment of 1,300 casualties, mostly Boy Scouts, and then their carriage by train, automobile and wagons to various temporary hospitals in Honiton, Ottery St Mary, Budleigh Salterton, Exmouth, Exeter and Topsham. Numerous smaller exercises, together with regular inspections, ensured that district groups remained highly trained. The newspapers praised the efficiency of the events, but remained slightly disdainful, no doubt thinking they were unnecessary and alarmist.

Time, though, was running out. On 24 July 1914, Torquay's Women's Liberal Association assembled for a garden party as guests of Sir Francis and Lady Layland-Barratt. They expected to discuss a host of pressing domestic issues, but the president noted 'the magnificent array of warships in the bay' and remembered that a Balkan crisis had now been added to 'the danger of civil war at home'. They then turned their attention to attacking the Conservatives and to confirming their trust in Asquith and the implementation of Irish Home Rule. On 31 July, Colonel Burn told Torquay's Primrose League that if any war were to break out it would be in Ireland, and soon.

Meanwhile, that week the LSWR advertised its bank holiday excursions, Heavitree & District Cottage Garden Society enticed visitors to its Annual Bank Holiday Show with a flying display by Marcus Manton 'The Boy Aviator', and 3,371 men from the Devon & Cornwall Territorial battalions set up camp on Woodbury Common and began their annual manoeuvres. It seemed like just another Edwardian summer.

8

CONCLUSION
1914 — Not Quite the End of an Era

❧ *The Sudden Summer Change* ❧

When the rumours of war with Germany became a reality, they did so very quickly. Indeed, in late June 1914 the assassination of Archduke Franz Ferdinand, heir to the Austro-Hungarian emperor, in an obscure Bosnian town called Sarajevo merited a mention in some Devon newspapers but was soon forgotten amidst the hurly-burly of British political controversies and the minutiae of local summer events.

But the spark had lit the tinderbox of wider European rivalries as well as merely Balkan jealousies. Nevertheless, until almost the last minute it seemed Great Britain might avoid being sucked into the maelstrom. Austria–Hungary blamed Serbian anarchists for the killing and deliberately sent Serbia an ultimatum full of conditions too humiliating to accept. Russia had no intention of letting Austria–Hungary increase its hold on the Balkans and promised Serbia support. Germany promised Austria–Hungary support and France was bound in alliance to Russia.

Everyone began mobilisation. Germany feared a war on two fronts, and as it knew the Russian Army took many weeks to mobilise it planned to rush its forces through Belgium to knock France out of the war before turning east to confront Russia. Great Britain had a treaty obligation to support Belgium, and certainly had no wish for Germany to control the other side of the English Channel. All this happened within a month of Franz Ferdinand's death.

Germany invaded Belgium on 4 August, ignoring Great Britain's ultimatum to withdraw, and we were at war – the day after a bank holiday weekend during which Devon was divided bizarrely between those enjoying themselves at the usual fetes, shows and regattas or lazing on beaches, and those who were busy responding to the call for naval reservists and Territorials to report to their ports and barracks.

Soon towns teemed with thousands of horses and tons of hay being sold to the army, and thousands of volunteers departing for training camps surrounded by cheering crowds and anxious families. Indeed, for the next four years and more Devon's extensive railway system saw hundreds of lengthy troop trains take men out of the county and hundreds more bring back casualties to the numerous hospitals and convalescent homes across the county. The military and naval hospitals in Plymouth quickly filled to overflowing. Torquay Town Hall, Exeter's Eye Hospital, Episcopal Girls' School, new Children's Home and other properties were requisitioned as emergency hospitals to receive casualties from the front, and over the next couple of years more than thirty grand houses were handed over, entirely or in part, by their owners for conversion into military convalescent homes. Across the county, the well-rehearsed nurses, auxiliaries, drivers and support staff in the Voluntary Aid Detachments sprang into effective action, well led by their district committees and well managed by their overall director, the recently commissioned Major John S. C. Davis.

The County Rallies Around

A plethora of charitable organisations, usually led by distinguished local female figures, avidly collected money together with a vast array of equipment, bedding and provisions for the hospitals, and ensured the recovering men had plenty of seaside and theatre outings, sports days and teas, and well-equipped recreation rooms. Nothing was too good for the heroes of the hour. In a unique appointment, the army placed Miss Georgiana Buller, the capable daughter of Sir Redvers, in charge of all the war hospitals in Exeter, suddenly and controversially removing them from Major Davis' control.

One celebrated committee, the Mayoress of Exeter's Depot, sent thousands of parcels of clothes, groceries, cigarettes and tobacco to local men serving in the navy and the Devonshire Regiment, whose battalions were scattered across the Western Front, the Middle East, India and Italy. The depot also handed out tens of thousands of packs of sandwiches, fruit, cake and canteens of tea to the regular troop trains stopping at Exeter Queen Street and St David's stations. Yet another Exeter-based committee received, clothed and found homes across Devon, and later Cornwall too, for several thousand refugees fleeing from the cities and villages of Belgium devastated by the sweeping German advance towards Paris.

Devon newspapers also enjoyed publishing patronising articles about the young women who took over men's jobs on the trams, at railway stations, in warehouses and workshops, and the wives and mothers who coped singlehanded with their absent husbands' small businesses as well as their growing families. Numerous families allowed the letters they received from men on active service to be published.

Contrary to common assumptions, most servicemen poured out their feelings in letters, and for better or for worse and notwithstanding the censorship, their families read a lot of harrowing descriptions of life and death around the front lines.

Getting the Men into Uniform

There were undoubtedly many heroes from the battlefield, and patriotism was wide-spread, but it was not universal. As the initial rush of men to enlist faded, loud and colourful rallies in the towns and equally raucous recruitment marches through the villages sought to incite greater patriotism in the county's young men, and also in their employers and womenfolk who were frequently accused of holding them back.

As a very active lord lieutenant, Lord Fortescue felt no compunction about publicly naming and shaming parishes whose enlistment figures were low. Many Church of England clergymen across Devon enthusiastically preached the justice of the British cause and urged men to enlist safe in the knowledge that God was on 'our' side. The Right Reverend Robert Trefusis, Bishop of Crediton, publicly damned Germany as the Anti-Christ from the pulpit of Exeter Cathedral. For all the efforts, though, it needed conscription, reluctantly introduced early in 1916, to oblige many men to leave their families, farms and businesses.

Henceforth, tribunals across the county were kept busy with hundreds of applications for exemption from military service. On the whole those express-ing conscientious objections to fighting received scant sympathy, unless they

A brake takes Witheridge Volunteers off to war, 1914. (Beaford Arts)

could prove long-term devotion to the Quakers or Plymouth Brethren, or they were running key businesses or supporting large families unaided largely because others in the business or family had enlisted. It was a tense and troubled time for all concerned. Many people across Devon were incensed when 800 conscientious objectors who refused to have anything to do with the war effort, even as non-combatant labourers or farm workers, were housed in Dartmoor Prison but allowed 'tickets of leave' to travel freely to nearby towns. Confrontations and protests were frequent.

Devon's Casualties Across the World

The records of the Devonshire Regiment, and the letters from local men who served in other regiments, reveal the multiplicity of experiences they endured – in northern India guarding the volatile frontier with Afghanistan; in Egypt watching and subjugating troublesome nationalist tribes; in Mesopotamia fighting the Turks and enduring fearsome prison camps after the defeat at Kut; in Gallipoli wrestling with disease and exposure, as well as incompetent leadership and stubborn Turkish defence; in Italy strengthening Italian resolve against Austria–Hungary and on the Western Front striving to survive trench life and the intermittent but terrifying bombardments and frontal attacks.

With its long coastline facing the Bristol and English channels and its numerous civil and naval ports, Devon families experienced all the dangers of the war at sea. Many Devon sailors died on the armoured cruisers HMS *Monmouth*, largely crewed by Devonport men, and HMS *Good Hope*, sunk at the Battle of Coronel in November 1914, and many more on the fourteen British battleships, cruisers and destroyers sunk at the Battle of Jutland in June 1916. Twenty-six men were from Exeter alone. Not surprisingly, employment at Devonport Dockyard soared to nearly 18,000 with numerous repairs, maintenance and refitting tasks and five new submarines and the light cruiser HMS *Cleopatra* under construction.

Trawlers from Brixham and Plymouth and paddle steamers from Ilfracombe, along with their crews, were taken into the navy to serve in many dangerous waters, including the North Sea and off Gallipoli, as minesweepers and guard ships. German submarines prowled around the coast and many merchantmen, fishing vessels and even hospital ships were sunk off Devon by torpedoes, gunfire or mines. In November 1916, for example, a U-boat surfaced amidst a fleet of helpless Brixham trawlers off Portland and sunk seven of them. However, the following year four Brixham skippers and bosuns gained the Distinguished Service Cross for their heroism on board small ships – two on the schooner HMS *Prize* (a Q-ship with hidden guns) and two on the armed trawler *Asama* – that, in different engagements, fought surfaced U-boats to a bloody standstill.

Careful but tentative calculations by Lord Fortescue suggest that 11,600 Devon men, together with several women, died on active service in all branches of the armed forces out of the 63,700 who served. Of these, about 8,000 were regulars, 36,700 volunteers and 19,000 conscripts. Many who survived had been badly wounded in body or mind, or both. In 1917 and 1918 part of the new Seale-Hayne College building was used for the pioneering treatment of 'shell-shocked' servicemen.

⟡ *Farmers at War* ⟡

Devon's farmers had a particularly bad press throughout the war. First, they were accused of stopping their sons and skilled workers enlisting to avoid the cost of alternative labour, then they were strongly suspected of profiteering as the price of produce rose due to the demands of the armed forces and the dislocation of overseas supplies. They were denigrated for refusing to replace enlisted workers with trained female volunteers and preferring cheap child labour, and finally roundly castigated by Lord Fortescue for complaining about the draconian order to change back from pastoral to arable farming to feed the hard-pressed nation.

The farmers' complaints went largely unheeded. From 1916 onwards conscription was enforced and exemption tribunals saw little need to favour rural occupations over urban ones in the never-ending battle to find recruits. Even Fortescue had to admit privately that, by mid-1918, farmers had been very heavily squeezed by both the high production targets and the loss of skilled men, including the vital hayrick thatchers, rabbit catchers, millers, blacksmiths and wheelwrights.

During 1917 and 1918, as army priorities and U-boat sinkings threatened civilian shortages, Devon farmers were bludgeoned into converting over 100,000 acres of pasture into high-quality fields of wheat. Indeed, the order was to return to the ratios prevailing in 1872, and fines, confiscation and imprisonment were meted out to the minority failing to comply. Devon's farmers were poorly placed to face the end of the war, the recovery of imports and the end of protected prices.

⟡ *Changing Attitudes Towards Children* ⟡

For children, the war was a turning point in public attitudes towards them. In 1914 the fee-paying public schools that catered for students until the age of 18 saw many of their charges go off to war, most with commissions should they wish them, with rousing cheers, hopes of glory, expectations of victory and pious expressions of their duty to God, the king and the empire.

The ordinary elementary schools were noticed only inasmuch as several were requisitioned by the army as hospitals or barracks, notably in Plymouth and Exeter, and all of them perceived as places where public expenditure on maintenance and supplies could be significantly reduced. Most damaging of all was the relaxation of the hard-won regulations governing school attendance by the county council with the enthusiastic support of the Devon Farmers' Union and many short-staffed urban employers.

The war had provided the perfect opportunity for all those who thought elementary education was too expensive, too lengthy, too academic and too elevating for those whose destinies lay, or ought to lie, in becoming dutiful and God-fearing servants, labourers and artisans – and perhaps the lowest ranks in the army and navy. Head teachers' logbooks record the steadily declining attendances, especially when crops were being planted and harvested and on market days.

From around 1916 a sea change in attitudes occurred as the nation mourned its mounting casualties and feared for the future of the nation and its empire. Those who had advocated more and better schooling for working-class children now found themselves listened to, and reported, sympathetically. The reasons were complex and not always altruistic. Some claimed that more and better schooling would be a just reward for the people's sacrifices during the war, while others argued that the nation's post-war security and prosperity, and likelihood of future wars, required the next generations to be as healthy, skilled and numerous as possible.

There was a belated public recognition that the vast accumulation of evidence regarding the appallingly high mortality rate among children in their first year of life had been shamefully ignored. Working-class mothers, who had been repeatedly castigated by middle-class commentators and medical practitioners such as Dr Adkins in Devon, were now seen in a new light, not least because they were essential to the war effort and the future of the empire.

In 1916, Scott's Emulsion – advertised as 'Nature's Body-Building Food' – took full and terrifying advantage of the moment and issued a series of strident advertisements in local as well as national newspapers stating that during the first fifteen months of the war more British babies and infants had died 'of weakness and disease' than British soldiers on the battlefields. In confirmation, the National Society for the Prevention of Cruelty to Children calculated that in the first thirteen months of war 109,725 British servicemen had been killed but 140,370 babies had died. The *Western Evening Herald* joined the campaign, stating that 553 of the 5,037 babies born in Plymouth in 1914 had died and asserting that if the mothers had been given expert care and advice most of the deaths could have been avoided.

The Extension of Maternity Care

During 1916 Earl and Countess Fortescue forced the pace with a memorandum to Devon County Council's Education Committee stating that 161 of the 346 practising midwives were untrained, 110,000 people in 200 parishes had no nurse and Devon had the highest puerperal mortality rate below the Wash and the Severn.

The Fortescues used their social influence and prime positions in county organisations to forge agreements between the county council's Public Health and Education committees and between them and the voluntary Devon Nursing Association, whereby the association provided a team of skilled health visitors who would work within an overall scheme built on the successful partnership already existing for inspecting school children.

The county council agreed to pay the health visitors to offer pre-natal and post-natal support, give childcare lessons and act as school nurses and pay for trained midwives, doctors and hospital care whenever the health visitors decided they were needed. It would ensure all parishes had easy access to trained midwives. All district and borough councils opting to join the scheme would provide the maternity and infant welfare clinics, and linked charities would be asked to help with the administration. The 1914 government grant, hitherto largely ignored, was now invoked to cover half the costs.

The mothers of Plymouth benefitted from vigorous support for the reforms by Mrs Astor, the local MP's high-profile wife, who offered a year's salary for a trained nurse if a baby clinic could be opened. In July 1916 the borough council voted for a scheme much like the county one. The first infant welfare clinic opened in Stonehouse in April 1917, and three more followed. Charitable efforts also intensified with the Astors, Sir John Jackson MP and his wife, and Lady Bethell and Lady Pole-Carew contributing to the establishment of three nurseries. Three voluntary-funded hostels were opened for siblings to stay in, if necessary, while their mothers had babies.

By the end of the war most districts had joined the county scheme, and the doctors and distinguished guests who spoke at the popular 'Baby Weeks' readily admitted that the war had forced the nation to recognise both the worth and needs of mothers and their babies, but agreed that it should have happened many decades earlier. Indeed, said a speaker in Torquay, 'if we had done so we could have a million more men to put in arms'. The impact of war on reform could not have been clearer.

The 1918 Education Act: Hopes Not Quite Fulfilled

Children benefitted from the 1918 Education Act. It went much further than most politicians had agreed just before the war, but not far enough to breach the social, financial and curriculum divide between the elementary and secondary schools. Soon after David Lloyd George became prime minister in December 1916 he seized upon educational reform as a major factor in improving working-class morale at a time when military victory seemed remote, and defeat a nightmare possibility.

When Herbert Fisher, the genuinely reforming president of the Board of Education, introduced his bill in August 1917 he highlighted the many pre-war weaknesses that merited attention and also the impetus the war had given to creating a more equitable society. He emphasised, too, that the extended franchise, including the imminent possibility of female suffrage, meant that the 'workers of the country are entitled to be considered primarily as citizens and as fit subjects for any form of education from which they are capable of profiteering [*sic*]'.

The ensuing act was significant but fell far short of these aspirations. The 1902 Act's 2*d* rate limit, enabling counties to promote secondary and higher education, was removed, a universal minimum leaving age of 14 was imposed with no exceptions permitted, and compulsory day continuation classes for those between 14 and 18 were to be introduced. The out-of-school employment of children was further restricted to ensure no one worked before 6 a.m. or after 8 p.m. on school days, and the provision and subsidising of medical treatment was made mandatory at last. Other clauses enforced the identification of physically and mentally handicapped pupils and the provision of special facilities for them, and encouraged education authorities to promote physical education, handicraft and domestic science.

However, Fisher had no desire to fan the flames of religious controversy, especially in wartime, and the dual system of voluntary and council schools remained inviolate. There was no move to make secondary schooling free and Fisher himself merely trusted that local authorities would build enough secondary schools and offer sufficient free places to suit the needs of their areas. The two key problems from pre-war days remained unresolved.

The Briefest Golden Dawn

After a brief pause in 1914, holidaymakers and day trippers had returned to Devon's resorts during the war, and as most towns also had troops in transit or undergoing training regularly billeted in them, the guesthouses, hotels and shops continued to do a steady trade. The seaside and moors became even more popular when peace returned, but those towards the upper end of the social scale preferred Continental chic.

Between 1919 and 1921 the railways returned from government control to private companies, although the lack of wartime maintenance had rendered timetables untrustworthy. The surviving Devon trawlers and paddle steamers underwent repairs or replacement, and hundreds of factories readapted to peacetime production with government grants. Willingly or reluctantly, women workers saw their jobs taken back by returning men, but in 1918 they had been granted the vote – if they were over the age of 30 – and their massive contributions to the war effort meant that more jobs were beginning to open up to women, if only they could find them. The wartime simplification of clothing and women's experience of working life, and the heady effect of American films and popular culture, meant that greater social freedoms were here to stay, whatever critics might say.

And just to cap everything, in 1919 a Housing and Town Planning Act was passed with the aim of fulfilling Lloyd George's commitment to build 600,000 State-subsidised 'Homes fit for Heroes', complete with baths and gardens and at affordable rents. With full employment continuing, factory order books bursting, everyone returning home and welfare reforms under way, the post-war future seemed too good to be true.

Devon in the 1920s

It was – production of raw materials and manufactured goods soared to make up immediate wartime deficits, but old markets had declined or disappeared. Great Britain's industries soon found that there was too much coal, too many ships and a surfeit of manufactured goods in the world. Prices crashed, products were stock-piled, factories went on short time or closed, unemployment soared in Britain's industrial cities and coal fields, and civil disturbances spread across the industrial heartlands of the Midlands, the North, Wales and Scotland.

Across Devon, however, the absence of heavy industry outside Devonport Dockyard and a few moderately sized foundries in Plymouth and Exeter meant that unemployment remained relatively low, although no less miserable for the hundreds without work in a region remaining comparatively buoyant economically. There were intermittent protests and dockers' strikes in Plymouth and the railway centres of Exeter and Newton Abbot in the early 1920s and during the General Strike of May 1926 but, although raucous and determined, their small scale and brief duration barely ruffled the surface of local life.

Throughout the 1920s the county's newspapers were full of alarming reports, leaders and correspondence on the massive discontent, strikes and violence else-where. A bitter irony lay in their transformation of the wartime noble Christian warrior risking his life to protect his country into a determined troublemaker, prob-ably with revolutionary Bolshevik leanings, bent upon wrecking the country. There is precious little evidence to suggest the war had unified society. Alongside the deep and bitter suffering, the war seemed to have offered the promise that the pre-war efforts at social reform would find their wider fulfillment once peace returned, but it was the return of peace that soon dashed so many people's hopes of better times.

Devon suffered in common with everywhere else when a frightened government reneged on aspects of both the Education and Housing Acts. In 1921, the national housing subsidy was drastically reduced to just 170,000 homes. Plymouth, though, was fortunate that around 800 council houses were built by 1924, alongside other new estates created by the GWR, the Admiralty and also the Astors.

The school-leavers' continuation classes that had reached the statute book after such agitation before and during the war were placed on indefinite hold and never funded nationally. Costly thoughts of raising the leaving age to 15, as hoped by Herbert Fisher, were also abandoned. Significantly, the government did not restrict the School Medical Service or hold back those local authorities that sought to promote rural and physical education, handicraft and domestic science. These subjects not only helped ensure the nation was provided with a new generation of skilled and healthy workers but also meant the essentially practical and utilitarian elementary school curriculum increasingly diverged from that of the secondary schools.

Devon's workhouses remained open to the poor and distressed, but they were more archaic reminders of past attitudes and horrors than recipients of the present generation who fell on hard times. Tramps and some desperate people without means of support still turned up at their doors but the elderly, sick and mentally ill were cared for in the workhouses' now generally separate infirmaries and wards. The end, though, was in sight. An increasing number of people had recourse to friendly society funds and to modest State pensions. A new wide-ranging Unemployment Insurance Act in 1920 provided payments of 15/- a week for fifteen weeks a year if work proved impossible to find. It was not much, but more than had ever been offered before. In 1929, the boards of guardians were finally abolished and relief became the responsibility of public assistance committees set up by local authorities, such as Devon County Council. But popular memories were long, and although the workhouses were diplomatically renamed when they became hospitals, the monumental structures retained their odious reputations.

If families had regular employment in the 1920s and 1930s, as did the vast majority in Devon, the slight but significant post-war decline in prices after their peak in 1918, combined with the steady rise in wages since 1914, meant that most working-class people felt better off than they had been several years earlier. The shops were filling with goods from abroad as well as from home, cinemas were proliferating and replete with glamorous American film stars, eating out in many cafes and restaurants remained cheap and travel by train, motor bus and motor cycle was within more and more people's reach.

The Countryside Changes Again

The Devon countryside was set to change again from its enforced wartime practices. Farmers were freed from wartime controls, but also from their military contracts and, from 1921, their protected minimum prices for wheat, oats and potatoes disappeared. Farm labourers welcomed a 1920 Act that finally set their wage levels, but amidst the growing gloom this was repealed a year later. Across the county farmers reverted to livestock and dairy production alongside the existing acres of fruit and market gardens, but profits were hard to come by as international competition stiffened during the 1920s. Acts of Parliament in 1923, to reduce the burden of rates, and in 1928, to ease the procurement of capital recognised the hardship, helped a little, but could not restore rural confidence, let alone prosperity.

For a very brief period the rural economy, like the urban one, was buoyant. Land prices held up, and many landowners who were likely to be hard hit by the massive death duty scales introduced in 1917 decided to sell large tracts of their land. As we have seen, in 1921 the 4th Lord Poltimore took the final step of putting Poltimore House and the last portion of its surrounding estate up for sale. The farms were readily purchased, most by their tenants, but the house and its adjacent gardens found no buyers. It would have required not only a family whose wealth came from sources other than the land but also one that wanted a country house at a time when lavish country house gatherings, while not abandoned, had certainly passed their impressive best. The kudos of a country estate for the nouveaux riche was rapidly diminishing. A private school eventually rented Poltimore House thereby allowing it, for at least a while, to continue to impress visitors.

Elsewhere, although many outlying fields and farms were sold after the war, especially to property developers, Earl Fortescue, the Earl of Devon, the Earl of Morley and Lord Clifford held on to much of their Castle Hill, Powderham, Saltram and Ugbrooke estates. Lord Clinton managed to keep his still vast southerly lands, Miss Chichester continued to keep the hunt off her extensive Arlington estate, the Aclands kept Killerton and its many farms, and the Heathcoat-Amorys kept Knightshayes. All the estates, though, were fast becoming hardnosed businesses, with their survival depending on high yields or a diversity of income, or both, and the earlier age of close involvement in local affairs and maintaining a generally benign paternalism was fading away.

Time continued to take its toll. Today, a century later, many of Devon's great houses, like Marley, are rubble underneath housing estates; weed-strewn ruins like Stevenstone; or deserted and vandalised shells like Poltimore. Others have been converted to hotels, like Bovey Castle, Peek House, Court Hall, Stoodleigh Court and the surviving wing of Haldon House, or apartments, like Flete, or tourist attractions frozen in a semblance of their historic grandeur, like Arlington, Castle Drogo, Killerton, Knightshayes and Saltram.

BIBLIOGRAPHY

Newspapers

Crediton Chronicle

Devon & Exeter Gazette

Devon & Somerset Weekly News

Devon Weekly Times

East & South Devon Advertiser

Hartland Chronicle

Ilfracombe Chronicle

Ilfracombe Gazette

Mid Devon Advertiser

Mid Devon & Newton Times

North Devon Journal

Okehampton Gazette & Advertiser

Paignton Observer & Echo

South Molton Gazette

Tiverton Gazette

Torquay Times & South Devon Advertiser

Totnes Times & Devon News

Trewman's Exeter Flying Post

Western Evening Herald

Western Express & Torrington Chronicle

Devon Heritage Centre, Sowton, Exeter

Census tables and statistics for Devon: 1891, 1901, 1911.

Devon County Council: Education Committee Minutes, 1904–14, 150/4/1/1-11.

Devon County Council Minutes, 1901–14, 148/4-5.

Devon & Exeter Central Schools (Combe Street & Rack Street) Association Annual Reports, 68/3/3/1.

'Diary of a North Devon Holidaymaker', 31 July–15 August 1907, 3252Z/Z1.

Digby Hospital Visitors' Book, 1900–07, 3769A/HZ2/1.

Digby Hospital Visitors' Book, 1907–20, 4034A/UH/1/51/2.

Exeter, Maynard Girls' High School: file of newspaper cuttings, 68/5/1/2-4.

Exeter, Maynard Girls' High School: school magazines, 68/5/2/1-5.

Fortescue, Hugh 4th Earl, 'A Chronicle of Castle Hill 1454–1918' – A privately printed history and memoirs (1929).

'Particulars of the Membland Hall Estate' – 1915 sale catalogue.

Ruth Whitaker's Memoirs, 2667M/F1.

Sellman, R. R., 'Notes on Some Devon Rural Schools' – two typed volumes (A–K and L–Z) on the history of individual schools (1982).

School Logbooks (All Schools Elementary in Status)

Ashcombe C of E, 624C/EFL1.

Aveton Gifford C of E, 2438C/EAL2.

Beer C of E, 2269C/EFL1 & 2.

Bicton C of E, 628C/EFL1.

Brixham, C of E Boys', 3651C/EFL4.
Brixham, Furzeham Hill Board/Council Girls', 3652Cadd/EAL4.
Broadclyst, Westwood C of E, 456C/EFL1.
Burlescombe C of E, 2767C/EFL1/1.
Cadbury C of E, 647C/EFL1.
Cheriton Bishop Board/Council, 1933C/EAL1.
Clyst St Mary C of E, 2252C/EFL1.
Crediton, Haywards C of E Boys', 1510C/EFL8.
Crediton, Haywards C of E Girls', 1510C/EFL2.
Crediton, Hookway Board/Council, 659C/EAL2.
Culmstock Board/Council, 2679C/EAL1.
Exeter, Cowick Street Board/Council, 76/5/1/1.
Exeter, Episcopal C of E Boys', 72/15/1/1 & 2.
Exeter, Rack Street Central Boys', 68/3/1/5 & 7.
Exeter, St Thomas's Board/Council, 68/4/2/4.
Exeter, Heavitree C of E, 76/7/1/3.
Loddiswell C of E School, 1934C/EAL 1 & 2.
Loddiswell British/Council School, 1934C/EAL 4.
Moretonhampstead, Pound Lane Board/Council Boys', 704C/EAL1.
Moretonhampstead, Greenhill Board/Council Girls', 2300C/EFL1.
Okehampton, Board/Council Girls', 2326C/EFL2.
Paignton, Grosvenor Boys', 2731C/ESL1 & 2.
Pinhoe C of E, 76/17/1/1 & 2.
Poltimore Board/Council, 2187C/EFL1.
Sheepstor C of E, 733C/EFL2.
Shillingford & Petton Board/Council, 3476C/EAL2.
Stoodleigh Manor C of E, 2713C/EFL1.
Tavistock, C of E Boys', 792C/EFL6.
Tavistock, C of E Girls', 792C/EFL4.
Tiverton, Heathcoat British/Council Boys', 3029C/EAL1 & 2.
Torquay, St Saviour & All Saints C of E Boys', 3675C/EFL5.
Torquay, St Saviour & All Saints C of E Girls', 3657C/EFL8.
Torquay, Cockington, Shiphay Collaton C of E, 655C/EFL2.
Totnes, Grove Board/Council Boys', 2440C/EAL7.
Totnes, Grove Board/Council Girls', 2440C/EAL4.

North Devon Record Office, Barnstaple

School Logbooks (All Elementary in Status)
Barnstaple, Blue Coat, 1805C (add2)/EFL2.
Barnstaple, Holy Trinity C of E Boys', 1903C/EEL35 & 36.
Bishop's Tawton Board/Council, 2310C/EFL1.
Bradworthy Board/Council, 2327C/EFL3.
Ilfracombe, St Philip & St James C of E Boys', 682C/EFL4 & 5.
Landkey C of E, 2317C/EFL3 & 4.
Little Torrington C of E, 393C/EFL1 & 2.
North Molton, Heasley Mill Board/Council, 710C/EAL2.
Roseash Board/Council, 723C/EAL2.

Axe Valley Museum, Seaton

Axe Valley Heritage Association Newsletter, May 2014 ('Recollections of a Victorian Holiday' by
    Kenneth Harman-Young).
Seaton Parish Magazines 1900–14.

Buckfastleigh Museum

Buckfastleigh Board/Council School logbook.
Records of the Hamlyn family and factories.

Devon & Exeter Institution

Directories, brochures, surveys, maps and privately printed histories of Devon towns and villages.
'Stones Scrapbooks' (Volumes 1–36) of Exeter events and personalities.

Ilfracombe Museum

Lily Phillips Diary, 'A Holiday Spent in Ilfracombe, June 10–24 1910', ILFCM 17661 Box A75(i).
Papers on and illustrations of Victorian/Edwardian Ilfracombe, including Oxford Park
    Gardens, Empire Day and the waterworks.

Museum of Dartmoor Life, Okehampton

Scrapbooks with Edwardian newspaper cuttings and illustrations on events in and
    around Okehampton.

Poltimore Estate Research Society

Papers and research findings on the Poltimore family and estate.

Plymouth & West Devon Record Office

The diaries of Miss Edrica de la Pole, 1306/1-22.

School Logbooks (All Elementary in Status)
East Stonehouse, St George's C of E, 2314/3.
Lee Moor Board/Council, 1016/3 & 4.
Tracy Street Board/Council, 1502/2.
Laira Green Board/Council, 1513/3& 4.
Lydford Board/Council, 2053/1 & 2.
Newton Ferrers C of E, 2063/1 & 2.
Plymouth, Salisbury Road Board/Council Girls', 2329/1.
St Joseph's RC Boys', 2069/2 & 3.

Seale-Hayne College Library & Archive, Newton Abbot

Books of newspaper cuttings recording the foundation and development of Seale-Hayne
    College of Agriculture.

Tiverton Museum

Archaeological evaluation and historic building report on Belmont Hospital
    (formerly Tiverton Union Workhouse) prepared for Devonshire Homes Ltd, 2010.
Files on Knightshayes and Heathcoat Lace Factory, including William Huxtable's
    factory logbook.

Torquay Library

1908 and 1913 *Annual Reports on the Medical Inspection of Schoolchildren* published by Torquay
    Education Authority.

Articles & Reports

Brayshay, M., 'Government Assisted Emigration from Plymouth in the Nineteenth Century' in *The Devonshire Association Reports & Transactions*, Volume 112: 185–213 (1980).

British Medical Journal, 'Reports on the Nursing & Administration of Provincial Workhouses & Infirmaries': Report XV – Plymouth (8/8/1894); XXXIV – Okehampton (19/1/1895); XXXV – Exeter (26/1/1895); XXXVII – Totnes (9/2/1895); XXXIX – St Thomas (23/2/1895); XLIII – Honiton (14/4/1895).

Finch, D., 'Devon Farm Labourers in the Victorian Period: the Impact of Economic Change' in *The Devonshire Association Reports & Transactions*, Volume 119: 85–100 (1987).

Fulford Williams, H. F., 'Memories of a Devon Childhood' in *The Devonshire Association Reports & Transactions*, Volume 92: 302–310 (1960).

Fussell, G. E., 'Four Centuries of Farming Systems in Devon 1500–1900' in *The Devonshire Association Reports & Transactions*, Volume 83: 179–204 (1951).

Irvine, E. D., 'A Century of Voluntary Service: The Exeter Diocesan Association for the Care of Girls (St Olave's Trust)' in *The Devonshire Association Reports & Transactions*, Volume 113: 133–145 (1981).

Jackson, A. J. H., 'Managing Decline: The Economy of the Powderham Estate in Devon, 1870–1939' in *The Devonshire Association Reports & Transactions*, Volume 128: 197–215 (1996).

Luscombe, W. L. 'Electricity in Plymouth: Its Origins and Development' in *The Devonshire Association Reports & Transactions*, Volume 131: 221–252 (1999).

Luscombe, W. L., 'The Devonport Royal Dockyard School: Apprentice Education, 1844–1971' in *The Devonshire Association Reports & Transactions*, Volume 137: 245–270 (2005).

McLain, R. D., 'Aristocratic Leadership in the Advancement of Secondary Education during the Mid-Victorian Period: the Earl of Devon, Earl Fortescue and Sir Stafford Northcote' in *The Devonshire Association Reports & Transactions*, Volume 133: 175–190 (2001).

Martin, E. W., 'Rural Society in Devon in the Twentieth Century: The Fate of the Rural Tradition' in *The Devonshire Association Reports & Transactions*, Volume 132: 233–248 (2000).

Porter, J., 'Peter Kropotkin on Devon Agriculture' in *The Devon Historian*, Volume 17: 25–26 (1978).

Porter, J. H., 'The Incidence of Industrial Conflict in Devon, 1860–1900' in *The Devonshire Association Reports & Transactions*, Volume 116: 63–75 (1984).

Sadler, M. E., *Report on Secondary and Higher Education in Devon* (no publisher cited, 1905).

Satterly, J., 'Memories of Ashburton in Late Victorian Days' in *The Devonshire Association Reports & Transactions*, Volume 84: 20–51 (1952).

Shorter, A. H., 'The Historical Geography of the Paper-Making Industry in Devon, 1684–1950' in *The Devonshire Association Reports & Transactions*, Volume 82: 205–216 (1950).

Slee, A. H., 'Some Dead Industries of North Devon' in *The Devonshire Association Reports & Transactions*, Volume 70: 213–221 (1938).

Wallace, J., 'The Devon House of Mercy at Bovey Tracey' in *The Devonshire Association Reports & Transactions*, Volume 133: 191–216 (2001).

Books

Abraham, A. G., *Old Newton St Cyres: Memories of Boyhood in a Devonshire Village* (Arthur H. Stockwell Ltd, 1972).

Acland, A., *A Devon Family: The Story of the Aclands* (Phillimore, 1981).

Aggett, W. J. P., *The Bloody Eleventh: History of the Devonshire Regiment Volume II 1815–1914* (The Devonshire & Dorset Regiment, 1994).

Allan, S. M., *Devon Mental Hospital (Exminster) 1845–1945: Centenary Souvenir* (no publisher or date, but probably the DMH and *c.* 1945–46).

Anon., *A Handbook for Travellers in Devonshire* (John Murray, 1879).

Anon., *A Handbook of the Forty-Second Annual Co-operative Congress 1910: Plymouth* (Manchester Co-operative Wholesale Society Ltd, 1910).

Anon., *All in School: One Hundred Years of Education in Devon* (Devon County Council, 1970).

Anon., *Devonshire: Historical, Descriptive, Biographical* (W. Mate & Co., 1907).

Anon., *Digby-Wonford Hospital, Exeter* (Digby-Wonford Hospital Executive Committee, 1959).

Anon., *Mate's Illustrated Devonshire* (W. Mate & Co., 1906).

Anon., *Royal West of England Residential School for the Deaf: Historical Survey 1826–1976* (Heavitree Publishing Company, 1976).

Ashworth, W., *An Economic History of England: 1870–1939* (Methuen & Co., 1960).

Barlow, F. (ed.), *Exeter and its Region* (University of Exeter Press, 1969).

Booker, F., *The Great Western Railway: A New History* (David & Charles, 2nd edition, 1985).

Bovett, R., *Historical Notes on Devon Schools* (Devon County Council, 1989).

Bradbeer, D. M., *Joyful Schooldays: A Digest of the History of Exeter Grammar Schools* (Exeter: Sydney Lee Ltd, 1973).

Burns, K. V., *Devonport Built Warships since 1860* (Maritime Books, 1981).

Burns, K. V., *The Devonport Dockyard Story* (Maritime Books, 1984).

Cannadine, D., *The Decline and Fall of the British Aristocracy* (Yale University Press, 1990).

Carter, P., *Newton Abbot* (Mint Press, 2004).

Chadwick, O., *The Victorian Church: Part Two, 1860–1901* (SCM Press, 1987).

Cherry, B. & Pevsner, N., *The Buildings of England: Devon* (Penguin, 1991).

Cluett, D., *A Village Childhood: Memories of Living in Rural Devon before the Age of the Motor Car* (Sampford Peverell Society, 2007).

Collins, E. J. T. (ed.), *The Agrarian History of England & Wales: Volume VII: 1850–1914* (Cambridge University Press, 2001).

Constantine, S., Kirby, M. W., & Rose, M. B., (eds.), *The First World War in British History* (Edward Arnold, 1995).

Coulson, J., *A History of Bystock and Marley, Devonshire* (Exmouth Local History Group, 2013).

Currie, J. R. & Long, W. H., *An Agricultural Survey in South Devon* (Seale-Hayne College & Dartington Hall, 1929).

Delderfield, E., *Exmouth Yesterdays* (Exmouth: ERD Publications, 1952).

Dickinson, M. G., *A Living from the Sea: Devon's Fishing Industry and its Fishermen* (Devon Books, 1987).

Duffy, M., Fisher, S., Greenhill, B., Starkey, D. J., & Youngs, J., (eds.), *The New Maritime History of Devon*, Volume II – 'From the Late Eighteenth Century to the Present Day' (University of Exeter & Conway Martin Press, 1994).

Dyer, J. R., *The Jubilee History of the Buckfastleigh Co-operative Society Ltd, 1869–1919* (Plymouth Printers, 1919).

Edwards, R. A., *Devon's Non-Metal Mines* (Halsgrove, 2011).

Ellis, A. C., *An Historical Survey of Torquay* (Torquay Directory, 1930).

Englander, D., *Poverty and Poor Law Reform in Nineteenth Century Britain, 1834–194* (Longman, 1998).

Ernle, Lord, *English Farming Past and Present* (Heinemann, 1912).

Flanders, J., *Consuming Passions: Leisure and Pleasure in Victorian Britain* (Harper Perennial, 2006).

Fraser, R., *General View of the County of Devon with Observations on its Means of Improvement* (C. Macrae, 1745, reprinted by Porcupine, Barnstaple, 1970).

Freeman, R., *Dartmouth and its Neighbours: A History of the Port and its People* (Richard Webb, 1990).

Gardiner, W. F., *Barnstaple: 1837–1897* (Barnstaple: Ralph Allan, 1897).

Gill, C. (ed.), *Dartmoor: A New Study* (David & Charles, 1970).

Gill, C., *Plymouth: A New History* (Devon Books, 1993).

Gregory, A. T., *Recollections of a Country Editor* (Tiverton Gazette, 1932).

Hamilton Jenkin, A. K., *Mines of Devon: Volume I: The Southern Area* (David & Charles, 1974).

Harris, H., *Devon's Century of Change* (Peninsula Press, 1998).

Harris, J., *Private Lives: Public Spirit: Britain 1870–1914* (Penguin, 1993).

Hattersley, Roy., *The Edwardians* (Abacus, 2004).

Hawkins, M., *LSWR West Country Lines: Then and Now* (Grange Books/Hawk Editions, 1999).

Hemming, J., *The House that Richard Built: Six Centuries at Poltimore House* (Poltimore House Press, 2013).

Hopkins, E., *Childhood Transformed: Working-Class Children in Nineteenth-Century England* (Manchester University Press, 1994).

Hoppen, K. T., *The Mid-Victorian Generation 1846–1886* (Oxford University Press, 1998).

Hoskins, W. G., *A New Survey of England: Devon* (Collins, 1954).

Hughes, B. D., *Strong's Industries of North Devon 1889* (David & Charles Reprints, 1971).

Hurt, J., *Elementary Schooling and the Working Classes 1860–1918* (Routledge & Keegan Paul, 1979).

Jennings, A., *Edwardian Gardens* (English Heritage and the Museum of Garden History, 2005).

Jones, A., *Victorian North Devon* (Andrew Jones, 2010).

Jones, D. K., *The Making of the Education System 1851–1881* (Routledge & Kegan Paul, 1977).

Judd, D. & Surridge, K., *The Boer War: A History* (IB Tauris, 2013).

Kelly's Directories – Devonshire.

Lamplugh, L., *A History of Ilfracombe* (Phillimore, 1984).

Lauder, R. A., *Vanished Houses of North Devon* (R. A. Lauder, 1981).

Lauder, R. A., *Vanished Houses of South Devon* (Bideford: North Devon Books, 1997).

Le Messurier, B. (ed.), *Crossing's Dartmoor Worker* (David & Charles, 1966).

Le Messurier, B. (ed.), *Crossing's Hundred Years on Dartmoor* (David & Charles, 1967).

Lethbridge, H. J., *Torquay and Paignton: The Making of a Modern Resort* (Phillimore, 2003).

Lowndes, G. A. N., *The Silent Social Revolution* (Oxford University Press, 1969).

Maclure, J. S., *Educational Documents: England and Wales: 1816 to the Present Day* (Methuen, 1973 edition).

Maggs, C., *Branch Lines of Devon: Exeter and South, Central and East Devon* (Alan Sutton, 1995).

Massie, R. K., *Dreadnought: Britain, Germany, and the Coming of the Great War* (Vintage, 2007).

Murray's 1859 Handbook for Devon and Cornwall (David & Charles Reprints, 1971).

Newton, R., *Victorian Exeter 1837–1914* (Leicester University Press, 1968).

Nicholas, J. & Reeve, G., *The North Devon Line: The Southern Railway Route between Exeter and Ilfracombe* (Irwell Press, 2010).

Nicholas, J. & Reeve, G., *The Okehampton Line: The Southern Railway Route between Exeter, Tavistock and Plymouth* (Irwell Press, 2001).

Orme, N., *Unity and Variety: A History of the Church in Devon and Cornwall* (University of Exeter Press, 1991).

Orwin, C. S. & Whethem, E. H., *History of British Agriculture 1846–1914* (David & Charles, 1971 edition).

Paige, R. T., *The Tamar Valley and its People: The Years of Change 1840–1940* (Dartington Amenity Research Trust, 1984).

Parker, D., *The People of Devon in the First World War* (The History Press, 2013).

Parsons, G. (ed.), *Religion in Victorian Britain: Volume I: Traditions* (Manchester University Press, 1988).

Penwill, F. R., *Paignton in Six Reigns* (Paignton UDC, 1953).

Perren, R., *Agriculture in Depression 1870–1940* (Cambridge University Press, 1995).

Perry, P. J., *British Farming in the Great Depression 1870–1914* (David & Charles, 1974).

Pollard, W., *A Book of the South West printed for the 75th Annual Meeting of the BMA held in Exeter* (William Pollard, 1907).

Pollard, W., *Guide to Exeter* (William Pollard, 1894).

Ponting, K. G., *The Woollen Industry of South-West England* (Adams & Dart, 1971).

Powell, G., *Buller: A Scapegoat. A Life of General Sir Redvers Buller VC* (Leo Cooper, 1994).

Pring, G., *Records of the Culmstock Otterhounds* (Quay Printing Works, Exeter, 1958).

Pugh, M., *The Pankhursts* (Vintage, 2008).

Pugh, M., *Women's Suffrage in Britain 1867–1928* (The Historical Association, 1980).

Pugsley, S. (ed.), *Devon Gardens: An Historical Survey* (Alan Sutton, 1994).

Radford, J. P. & Tipper, A., *Starcross: Out of the Mainstream* (The G. Allan Roehr Institute, 1988).

Rowland, A. B., *The Royal Western Counties Hospital* (privately published, 1985).

Russell, P., *A History of Torquay and the Famous Anchorage of Torbay* (Torquay Natural History Society, 1960).

Russell, P. M. G., *A History of Exeter Hospitals 1170–1948* (James Townshend, 1976).

Sadler, M. E., *Report on Secondary and Higher Education in Exeter* (no publisher cited, 1905).

Sampson, M., *A History of Tiverton* (Tiverton War Memorial Trust, 2004).

Sampson, M., *A History of Blundell's School* (Blundell's School, 2011).

Saville, J., *Rural Depopulation in England and Wales 1851–1951* (Dartington Hall/Routledge & Kegan Hall, 1957).

Sellman, R. R., *Devon Village Schools in the Nineteenth Century* (David & Charles, 1967).

Shaw, A. M., *When You Were There: Edgehill College 1884–1984* (privately printed, 1984).

Slade, W. J., *Out of Appledore* (Conway Maritime Press, 1980 reprint).

Slee, A. H., *Victorian Days in a Devon Village* (Braunton: AH Slee, 1966).

Snell, F. J., *North Devon* (A & C Black, 1906).

Stanes, R., *Old Farming Days: Life on the Land in Devon & Cornwall* (Halsgrove, 2005).

Stevenson, D., *1914–1918: The History of the First World War* (Penguin, 2004).

Tapley-Soper, H. (ed.), *Devonshire Past & Present: Historical, Pictorial and Descriptive Guide* (Derby: Bemrose & Sons, 1913)

Thirsk, J. (ed.), *The Agrarian History of England & Wales*, Volume VII, '1850–1914', Part I (Cambridge University Press, 2000).

Thomas, D. S., *West Country Railway History* (David & Charles, 1974).

Thompson, F. M. L., *The Rise of Respectable Society: A Social History of Victorian Britain 1830–1900* (Fontana, 1988).

Tozer, E. J., *The South Devon Hunt* (no publisher given, 1916).

Travis, J. F., *The Rise of Devon Seaside Resorts 1750–1900* (University of Exeter Press, 1993).

Trump, H. J., *West-country Harbour: The Port of Teignmouth* (Brunswick Press, 1976).

Van der Kiste, J., *Plymouth* (The History Press, 2009).

Wall, R., *Bristol Channel Pleasure Steamers* (David & Charles, 1973).

Walling, R. A. J., *The Story of Plymouth* (Westaway Books, 1950).

Wilson, L., *Ilfracombe's Yesterdays* (A & P Oldale, 1976).

White, W., *History, Gazetteer and Directory of the County of Devon* (Simpkin, Marshall & Co., 1890).

Woodcock, G., *Tavistock's Yesteryears* – Nos 2 (1986), 4 (1988), 5 (1989), 8 (1992), 9 (1993), 10 (1994), 14 (2005) (Callington: Penwell Ltd).

Yallop, H. J., *The History of the Honiton Lace Industry* (University of Exeter Press, 1992).

Websites

www.brucehunt.co.uk/Training%20Ship%20Mount%20Edgcumbe.html
 [Training Ship *Mount Edgcumbe*].

www.dartmoor-ranges.co.uk/militaryuse_3_brief_history.html [military activity on Dartmoor].

www.exetermemories.co.uk [streets and shops, annual Cart Horse Parade].

www.plymouthdata.info/Workhouses/html [Plymouth workhouses].

www.workhouses.org.uk [Devon Union workhouses].

www.nfa.dept.shef.ac.uk/history/charter/barn.html [Barnstaple Fair]

www.visitlyntonandlynmouth.com/about/hollerday-house [Hollerday House].

www.MeasuringWorth.com/ukearncpi [comparative money values].

INDEX